Microsoft 365 Identity and Services Exam Guide MS-100

Expert tips and techniques to pass the MS-100 exam on the first attempt

Aaron Guilmette

BIRMINGHAM—MUMBAI

Microsoft 365 Identity and Services Exam Guide MS-100

Group Product Manager: Pavan Ramchandani
Publishing Product Manager: Prachi Sawant
Senior Editor: Athikho Sapuni Rishana
Technical Editor: Nithik Cheruvakodan
Copy Editor: Safis Editing
Project Coordinator: Ashwin Dinesh Kharwa
Proofreader: Safis Editing
Indexer: Tejal Daruwale Soni
Production Designer: Arunkumar Govinda Bhat
Marketing Coordinator: Marylou De Mello

First published: June 2023

Production reference: 1070623

Published by Packt Publishing Ltd.
Livery Place
35 Livery Street
Birmingham
B3 2PB, UK.

ISBN 978-1-83898-794-7

www.packtpub.com

To all the exam takers – I hope you didn't save studying until the last minute.

Contributors

About the author

Aaron Guilmette is a senior architect at Planet Technologies, helping customers make the most of their Microsoft 365 investments. Prior to that, Aaron was a senior program manager for customer experience at Microsoft, working with customers to overcome inferior technology and old ways of doing things. When he's not writing or studying for his next exam, he's probably eating a taco.

I want to thank my long-suffering girlfriend, Christine, who has tolerated me through nine books now. And I also want to thank my kids for helping me get this finished. Without them, it would have been done much earlier.

About the reviewer

Paweł Serwan is an architect and consultant with 14 years of IT experience. Most of his career has been focused on identity and access management, end user computing, and Microsoft 365 topics. He currently works as a senior principal architect at Predica, a SoftwareOne company, where he primarily focuses on the Microsoft 365 platform, including identity, security, compliance, and endpoint management projects. He provides guidance and assistance to customers implementing the Microsoft 365 platform in their organizations.

Paweł speaks at user groups and conferences both in person and virtually throughout the year, and he runs a blog (ITConstructors) with his friends. He is a local leader of the Microsoft 365 User Group in Poland.

Table of Contents

Part 2: Planning and Managing User Identity and Roles

3

Planning Identity Synchronization   61

4

Implementing and Managing Identity Synchronization with Azure AD   81

5

Planning and Managing Azure AD Identities   113

6

Planning and Managing Roles in Microsoft 365   153

Part 3: Managing Access and Authentication

7

Planning and Implementing Authentication   173

8

Planning and Implementing Secure Access   209

9

Planning and Implementing Application Access   245

Part 4: Planning Microsoft 365 Workloads and Applications

10

11

12

Planning and Implementing Microsoft SharePoint Online, OneDrive, and Microsoft Teams   335

Part 5: Preparation

13

Practice Exam 1   381

14

Practice Exam 2   403

Preface

Microsoft 365 is the premier collaboration and business productivity platform on the market today. It is made of up dozens of integrated **Software-as-a-Service (SaaS)** applications and services, including Exchange Online, SharePoint Online, and Microsoft Teams. Microsoft also offers a full range of cloud data center and development products, all built on the Azure platform.

Together, the Microsoft 365 and Azure platforms are used by millions of users and businesses every day to enhance communications, build relationships, connect communities, and create new products.

This book is designed to help you understand key Microsoft 365 concepts and how those concepts are represented in the MS-100 exam.

This book will focus on the following key areas:

- Microsoft 365 tenant architecture and design
- Identity and access management
- Microsoft 365 apps
- Identity synchronization technologies
- Deploying core services such as Exchange Online and Microsoft Teams

The MS-100 exam focuses on the basic concepts and interdependencies between these services. This book will help you understand the basics of identity and authentication in **Azure Active Directory (Azure AD)**, as well as ways to secure the identity platform using tools such as multi-factor authentication and Conditional Access.

By the end of this book, you'll not only be equipped to pass the MS-100 exam but also to confidently articulate the features and capabilities of the Microsoft 365 platform.

Who this book is for

This book is targeted at Microsoft 365 service administrators and cloud technologists who want to prove their knowledge by passing the MS-100 certification exam. The qualified exam candidate should be able to demonstrate foundational knowledge of the Microsoft 365 suite, Azure AD identity, and onboarding core services such as Exchange Online and Microsoft Teams. Mastering the concepts tested in this exam provides a solid stepping stone to other more advanced Microsoft certifications. You can learn more about this exam at `https://learn.microsoft.com/en-us/certifications/exams/ms-100`.

What this book covers

Chapter 1, Planning and Implementing a Microsoft 365 Tenant, begins by explaining the foundational concepts and structure of a Microsoft 365 tenant.

Chapter 2, Monitoring Microsoft 365 Tenant Health, explores the tools and capabilities around managing and monitoring a Microsoft 365 tenant.

Chapter 3, Planning Identity Synchronization, explains how to plan identity and authentication schemes for Azure AD.

Chapter 4, Implementing and Managing Identity Synchronization with Azure AD, walks through deploying both Azure AD Connect and Azure AD Connect cloud sync, as well as advanced features such as object filters and troubleshooting synchronization issues.

Chapter 5, Planning and Managing Azure AD Identities, shows you how to manage both cloud and synchronized identity using PowerShell and the Microsoft 365 admin center.

Chapter 6, Planning and Managing Roles in Microsoft 365, introduces the concept of role-based access control in Microsoft 365 and Azure AD.

Chapter 7, Planning and Implementing Authentication, dives deeper into identity and authentication topics, including Azure AD password protection, password-less authentication methods, and self-service password reset.

Chapter 8, Planning and Implementing Secure Access, discusses Azure AD Premium features such as entitlement management, Azure AD Identity Protection, and Azure AD Identity Governance.

Chapter 9, Planning and Implementing Application Access, explores features such as enterprise application registration and Azure AD Application Proxy.

Chapter 10, Planning and Implementing Microsoft 365 Apps Deployment, introduces management, deployment capabilities, and processes around the Microsoft 365 Apps suite.

Chapter 11, Planning and Implementing Exchange Online Deployments, provides an overview of deploying Exchange Online and Exchange Online hybrid scenarios.

Chapter 12, Planning and Implementing Microsoft SharePoint Online, OneDrive, and Microsoft Teams, discusses onboarding for SharePoint Online, OneDrive for Business, and Microsoft Teams features.

Chapter 13, Practice Exam 1, is a complete set of exam preparation questions designed to test your knowledge.

Chapter 14, Practice Exam 2, is another complete set of exam preparation questions designed to test your knowledge.

To get the most out of this book

The Microsoft 365 platform is best experienced with either a laptop or desktop computer running a modern operating system, such as Windows 10 or macOS X 10.12 or later. Additionally, modern browsers such as Microsoft Edge or a current version of Chrome, Safari, or Firefox are necessary for the Microsoft 365 portal user interface to render properly. Older versions of Microsoft Internet Explorer will not work correctly.

A Microsoft 365 tenant will also be required to follow along with some of the configuration examples. You can sign up for a trial tenant (no credit card required) at `https://www.microsoft.com/en-us/microsoft-365/business/compare-more-office-365-for-business-plans`. Some configuration options will require an Azure AD Premium subscription, which you can obtain as part of a Microsoft 365 trial, or by activating an Azure AD Premium trial within the Azure portal (`https://portal.azure.com`) once you have obtained a trial Microsoft 365 tenant.

Some examples may require various tools, such as the SharePoint Online Management Shell (`https://www.microsoft.com/en-us/download/details.aspx?id=35588`), the Microsoft Teams module (`https://www.powershellgallery.com/packages/MicrosoftTeams/`), or the Office Deployment Tool (`https://www.microsoft.com/en-us/download/details.aspx?id=49117`). Some features or products, such as Azure AD Connect or the Exchange Hybrid Configuration wizard, will require Windows-based servers to deploy. You can obtain a free trial of Azure products, including Azure virtual machines, at `https://portal.azure.com`.

Download the color images

We also provide a PDF file that has color images of the screenshots and diagrams used in this book. You can download it here: `https://packt.link/rEtBu`

Conventions used

There are a number of text conventions used throughout this book.

`Code in text`: Indicates code words in text, database table names, folder names, filenames, file extensions, pathnames, dummy URLs, user input, and Twitter handles. Here is an example: "The `ImmutableID` value in Azure AD as a base64 conversion of an object's on-premises Active Directory object GUID."

Any command line input and output is written as follows:

```
Get-Msoluser -MaxResults 10 -Department "Project Management" | Select
DisplayName,UserPrincipalName,Department
```

Bold: Indicates a new term, an important word, or words that you see on screen. For instance, words in menus or dialog boxes appear in **bold**. Here is an example: "To export a list of audit log entries, an administrator can open the audited data and click on **Export results**."

Tips or important notes
Appear like this.

Get in touch

Feedback from our readers is always welcome.

General feedback: If you have questions about any aspect of this book, email us at `customercare@packtpub.com` and mention the book title in the subject of your message.

Errata: Although we have taken every care to ensure the accuracy of our content, mistakes do happen. If you have found a mistake in this book, we would be grateful if you would report this to us. Please visit `www.packtpub.com/support/errata` and fill in the form.

Piracy: If you come across any illegal copies of our works in any form on the internet, we would be grateful if you would provide us with the location address or website name. Please contact us at `copyright@packt.com` with a link to the material.

If you are interested in becoming an author: If there is a topic that you have expertise in and you are interested in either writing or contributing to a book, please visit `authors.packtpub.com`.

Share Your Thoughts

Once you've read *Microsoft 365 Identity and Services Exam Guide MS-100*, we'd love to hear your thoughts! Scan the QR code below to go straight to the Amazon review page for this book and share your feedback.

`https://packt.link/r/1838987940`

Your review is important to us and the tech community and will help us make sure we're delivering excellent quality content.

Download a free PDF copy of this book

Thanks for purchasing this book!

Do you like to read on the go but are unable to carry your print books everywhere? Is your eBook purchase not compatible with the device of your choice?

Don't worry, now with every Packt book you get a DRM-free PDF version of that book at no cost.

Read anywhere, any place, on any device. Search, copy, and paste code from your favorite technical books directly into your application.

The perks don't stop there, you can get exclusive access to discounts, newsletters, and great free content in your inbox daily

Follow these simple steps to get the benefits:

1. Scan the QR code or visit the link below

https://packt.link/free-ebook/9781838987947

2. Submit your proof of purchase

3. That's it! We'll send your free PDF and other benefits to your email directly

Part 1: Planning and Implementing a Microsoft 365 Tenant

In this part, you will become familiar with the tasks associated with navigating and administering a Microsoft 365 tenant, including provisioning the tenant, customizing domains, and managing service issues.

This part has the following chapters:

- *Chapter 1, Planning and Implementing a Microsoft 365 Tenant*
- *Chapter 2, Monitoring Microsoft 365 Tenant Health*

1
Planning and Implementing a Microsoft 365 Tenant

The Microsoft 365 tenant is the security and content boundary for your organization. While deploying a tenant is—on the face of it—a simple task of entering contact and payment details, there are many considerations that go into designing and implementing a tenant that will be used to securely provide access to an organization's data.

In this chapter, we'll look at the core components of planning for your Microsoft 365 experience, as it pertains to the MS-100 exam. The objectives and skills we'll cover in this chapter include the following:

- Planning a tenant
- Creating a tenant
- Implementing and managing domains
- Configuring organizational settings

By the end of this chapter, you should be able to articulate the core concepts around planning and implementing a Microsoft 365 tenant successfully. Let's begin!

Planning a tenant

There are a number of early planning stages for a Microsoft 365 tenant, but the one you're presented with first will be which kind of subscription and tenant you acquire. Tenants and subscriptions are available for different sizes of organizations as well as different industry verticals. Depending on what options you choose, you may not be able to easily change plans without performing a migration (for example, when moving between Microsoft 365 Commercial and Microsoft 365 GCC).

Selecting a tenant type

Microsoft has made a variety of packages available, targeting different types of organizations, as shown in *Figure 1.1*:

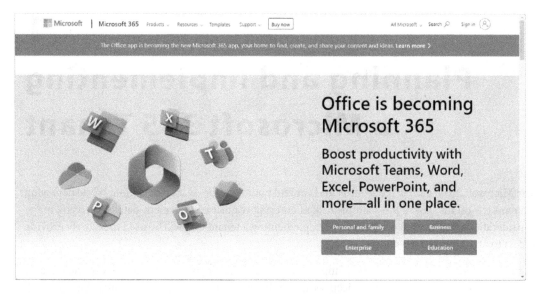

Figure 1.1 – Types of tenants

The following table list the types of tenants available:

Tenant and subscription type	Target customer
Microsoft 365 Personal	A single person or home user
Microsoft 365 Family	A single person, up to 6 users
Microsoft 365 Business	Up to 300 users
Microsoft 365 Enterprise	Unlimited users
Microsoft 365 for US Government	Unlimited users
Microsoft 365 for Education	Unlimited users

Table 1.1 – Tenant types and target customers

For the purposes of the MS-100 exam, we'll focus on the Microsoft 365 Enterprise service plans.

Tenant type deep dive

The MS-100 exam focuses on the feature set and product or service bundles available in Microsoft 365 Enterprise plans, though the technologies available are largely the same across all plans. Microsoft 365 for US Government is available only for local, state, and federal government customers (and their partners or suppliers) and has a subset of the currently commercially available features, trailing by anywhere from 6 months to 2 years, depending on the certification level of the environment. Microsoft 365 for Education has the same feature set as the commercial enterprise set, with a few added features targeted to educational institutions. Microsoft 365 for Education is only available to schools and universities.

Selecting a managed domain

After choosing what type of subscription and tenant you'll acquire, one of the next steps you'll be faced with is naming your tenant. When you sign up for a Microsoft 365 subscription, you are prompted to choose a name in the Microsoft onmicrosoft.com managed namespace. The name you select will need to be unique across all other Microsoft 365 customers.

Tenant name considerations

The tenant name (or managed domain name) cannot be changed after it has been selected. As such, it's important to select one that is appropriate for your organization. The tenant name is visible in a handful of locations, so be sure to select a name that doesn't reveal any private information and looks professionally appropriate for the type of organization you're representing.

Creating a tenant

The act of creating a tenant is a relatively simple affair, requiring you to fill out a basic contact form and choose a tenant name. Microsoft periodically changes what plans are available for new trial subscriptions. As of this writing, Office 365 E3 is available for a trial subscription. Currently available public trial subscriptions require the addition of payment information, which will cause a trial to roll over to a fully-paid subscription after the trial period ends. See *Figure 1.2*:

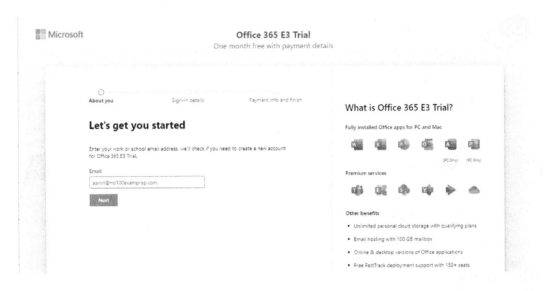

Figure 1.2 – Starting a trial subscription

The signup process may prompt for a phone number to be used during verification (either a text/SMS or call) to help ensure that you're a valid potential customer and not an automated system.

After verifying your status as a human, you'll be prompted to select your managed domain, as shown in *Figure 1.3*:

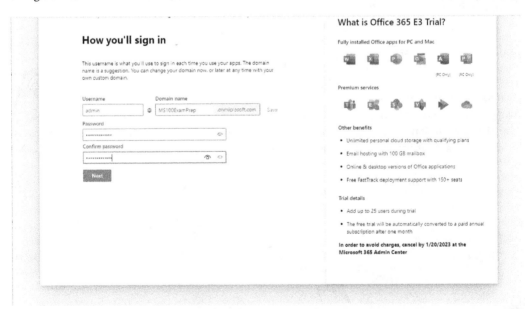

Figure 1.3 – Choosing a managed domain

In the **Domain name** field, you'll be prompted to enter a domain name. If the domain name value you select is already taken, you'll receive an error and be prompted to select a new name.

After you've finished, you can enter payment information for a trial subscription. Note the end date of the trial; if you fail to cancel by that time, you'll be automatically billed for the number of licenses you have configured during your trial!

Implementing and managing domains

The managed domain is part of the Microsoft 365 tenant for its entire lifecycle. While it is a fully-functioning domain name space (complete with its own managed publicly available domain name system), most organizations will want to use their organization's domain names—especially when it comes to sending and receiving email or communicating via Microsoft Teams.

Organizations can use any public domain name with Microsoft 365. Microsoft supports configuring up to 900 domains in a tenant; you can configure both top-level domains (such as `contoso.com`) and subdomains (`businessunit.contoso.com`) with your Microsoft 365 tenant.

Acquiring a domain name

Many organizations begin their Microsoft 365 journey with existing domain names. Those existing domain names can be used with Microsoft 365. In addition, you can purchase new domain names to be associated with your tenant.

Third-party registrar

Most large organizations have existing relationships with third-party domain registrars, such as Network Solutions or GoDaddy. You can use any ICANN-accredited registrar for your region to purchase domain names.

> **About ICANN**
>
> **ICANN** (short for **Internet Corporation for Assigned Names and Numbers**) is a non-profit organization tasked with providing guidance and policy around the internet's unique identifiers (domains). It was chartered in 1998. Prior to 1998, Network Solutions operated the global domain name system registry under a subcontract from the United States Defense Information Systems Agency.

You can search the list of domain registrars here: `https://www.icann.org/en/accredited-registrars`.

Microsoft

In addition to choosing a third-party registrar, organizations may also wish to use Microsoft as the registrar. Depending on your subscription, you may have direct access to purchasing domain names from within the Microsoft 365 admin center, as shown in *Figure 1.4*:

Figure 1.4 – Purchasing a domain through the Microsoft 365 admin center

When purchasing a domain through Microsoft, you can select from the following top-level domains:

- `.biz`
- `.com`
- `.info`
- `.me`
- `.mobi`
- `.net`
- `.org`
- `.tv`
- `.co.uk`
- `.org.uk`

Domain purchases will be billed separately from your Microsoft 365 subscription services. When purchasing a domain from Microsoft, you'll have limited ability to manage **Domain Name System (DNS)** records. If you require custom configuration (such as configuring an MX record to point to a non-Microsoft 365 server), you'll need to purchase a domain separately.

Configuring a domain name

Configuring a domain for your tenant is a simple procedure and requires access to your organization's public DNS service provider. Many large organizations may host DNS themselves, while other organizations choose to pay service providers (such as the domain registrar) to host the services.

In order to be compatible with Microsoft 365, a DNS service must support configuring the following types of records:

- **CNAME: Canonical Name** records are alias records for a domain, allowing a name to point to another name as a reference. For example, let's say you have a website named `www.contoso.com` that resolves to an IP address of `1.2.3.4`. Later, you want to start building websites for `na.contoso.com` and `eu.contoso.com` on the same web server. You might implement a CNAME record for `na.contoso.com` to point to `www.contoso.com`.

- **TXT:** A **Text Record** is a DNS record used to store somewhat unstructured information. **Request for Comments** (**RFC**) 1035 (`https://tools.ietf.org/html/rfc1035`) specifies that the value must be a text string and gives no specific format for the value data. Over the years, **Sender Policy Framework** (**SPF**), **DomainKeys Identified Mail** (**DKIM**), and other authentication and verification data have been published as TXT records. In addition to SPF and DKIM, the Microsoft 365 domain addition process requires the administrator to place a certain value in a TXT record to confirm ownership of the domain.

- **SRV:** A **Service Locator** record is used to specify a combination of a host in addition to a port for a particular internet protocol or service.

- **MX:** The **Mail Exchanger** record is used to identify which hosts (servers or other devices) are responsible for handling mail for a domain.

In order to use a custom domain (sometimes referred to as a vanity domain) with Microsoft 365, you'll need to add it to your tenant.

To add a custom domain, follow these steps:

1. Navigate to the Microsoft 365 admin center (`https://admin.microsoft.com`) and log in.

2. Expand **Settings** and select **Domains**.

Figure 1.5 – Domains page of the Microsoft 365 admin center

3. Click **Add domain**.

4. On the **Add a domain** page, enter the custom domain name you wish to add to your Microsoft 365 tenant. Select **Use this domain** to continue.

Figure 1.6 – Add a domain page

5. If your domain is registered at a host that supports **Domain Connect**, you can provide your credentials to the Microsoft 365 **Add domain** wizard and click **Verify**. Microsoft will automatically configure the necessary domain records and complete the entire DNS setup for you. You can also select **More options** to see all of the potential verification methods available, as shown in *Figure 1.7*:

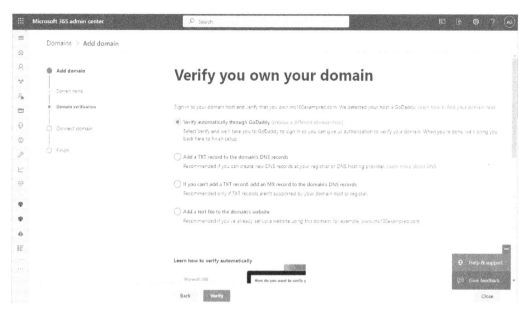

Figure 1.7 – Verify domain ownership

6. If you choose any of the additional verification options (such as **Add a TXT record to the domain's DNS records**), you'll need to manually add DNS records with your DNS service provider. Microsoft provides the value configuration parameters necessary for you to configure DNS with your own service provider. After entering the values with your service provider, you can come back to the wizard and select **Verify**, as shown in *Figure 1.8*:

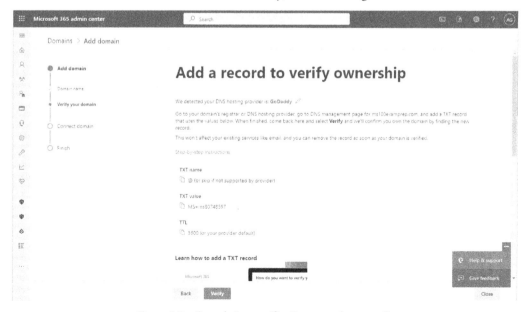

Figure 1.8 – Completing verification records manually

7. If you're using Domain Connect, enter the credentials for your registrar. When ready, click **Connect**.

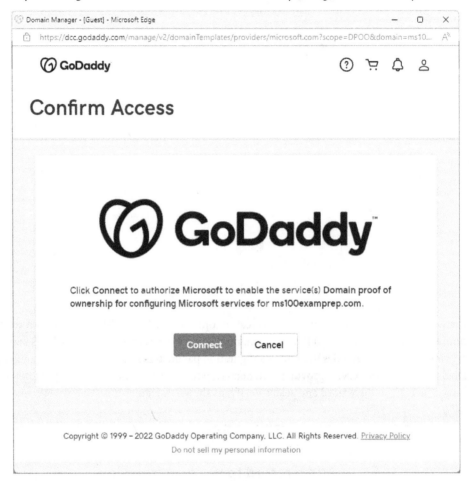

Figure 1.9 – Authorizing Domain Connect to update DNS records

8. Select **Let Microsoft Add your DNS records (recommended)** to have the Microsoft 365 wizard update your organization's DNS records at the registrar. However, if you are going to be configuring advanced scenarios such as Exchange Hybrid for mail coexistence and migration or have other complex requirements, you may want to consider managing the DNS records manually or opting out of select services. Click **Continue**.

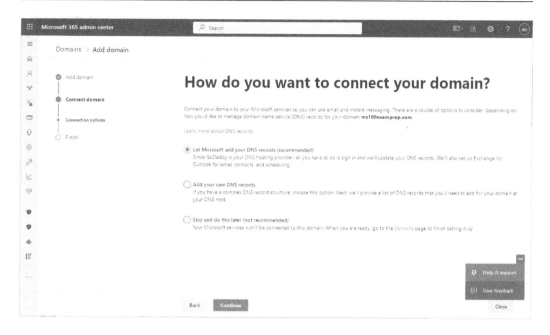

Figure 1.10 – Connecting domain to Microsoft 365

9. Choose whether to allow Microsoft to add DNS records. Expand the **Advanced options** drop-down:

A. The first checkbox, **Exchange and Exchange Online Protection**, manages DNS settings for Outlook and email delivery. If you have an existing Exchange Server deployment on-premises (or another mail service solution), you should clear this checkbox before continuing. You'll need to come back to configure DNS settings to establish hybrid connectivity correctly. The default selected option means that Microsoft will make the following updates to your organization's DNS:

i.   Your organization's MX record will be updated to point to Exchange Online Protection.

ii. The Exchange Autodiscover record will be updated to point to `autodiscover.outlook.com`.

iii. Microsoft will update your organization's SPF record with `v=spf1 include:spf.protection.outlook.com -all`.

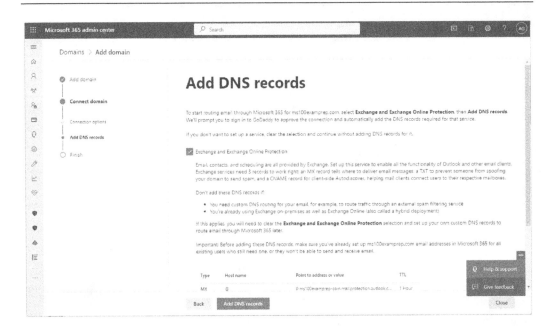

Figure 1.11 – Adding DNS records

B. The second setting, **Skype for Business**, will configure DNS settings for Skype for Business. If you have an existing Skype for Business Online deployment or you're using Skype for Business on-premises, you may need to clear this box until you verify your configuration:

i.   Microsoft will add two SRV records: `_sip._tls.@<domain>` and `_sipfederationtls._tcp@<domain>`.

ii. Microsoft will also add two CNAMEs for Lync: `sip.<domain>` to point to `sipdir.online.lync.com` and `lyncdiscover.<domain>` to point to `webdir.online.lync.com`.

C. The third checkbox, **Intune and Mobile Device Management for Microsoft 365**, configures applicable DNS settings for device registration. It is recommended to leave this enabled:

i.   Microsoft will add the following CNAME entries to support mobile device registration and management: `enterpriseenrollment.<domain>` to `enterpriseenrollment.manage.microsoft.com` and `enterpriseregistration.<domain>` to `enterpriseregistration.windows.net`.

10. Click **Add DNS records**.

11. If prompted, click **Connect** to authorize Microsoft to update your registrar's DNS settings.

12. Click **Done** to exit the wizard or **View all domains** to go back to the **Domains** page if you need to add more domains.

You can continue adding as many domains as you need (up to the tenant maximum of 900 domains).

> **Adding a domain deep dive**
>
> To review alternative steps and more information about the domain addition process, see https://learn.microsoft.com/en-us/microsoft-365/admin/setup/add-domain.

Managing DNS records manually

If you've opted to manage DNS records manually, you may need to go back to the Microsoft 365 admin center and view the settings. To do this, you can navigate to the **Domains** page in the Microsoft 365 admin center, select your domain, and then select **Manage DNS**:

Figure 1.12 – Managing DNS settings for a domain

On the **Connect domain** page, click **More options** to expand the options, and then select **Add your own DNS records**. From here, you can view the specific DNS settings necessary per service by record type. You can also download a CSV file or a zone file that can be uploaded to your own DNS server.

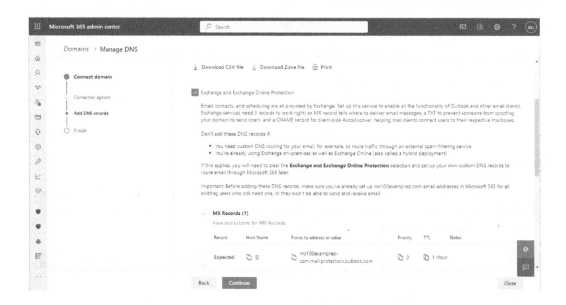

Figure 1.13 – Viewing DNS settings

The CSV output is formatted as columns, while the zone file output is formatted for use with standard DNS services and can be imported or appended to BIND or Microsoft DNS server zone files.

Configuring a default domain

After adding a domain, Microsoft 365 automatically sets that first custom domain as the default domain, which will get used when creating new users. However, if you have additional domains, you may choose to select a different domain to be used as the default domain when creating objects.

To manage which domain will be set as your primary domain, select the domain from the **Domains** page and then click **Set as default** to update the setting:

Figure 1.14 – Setting the default domain

The default domain will be selected automatically when creating cloud-based users and groups.

> **Custom domains and synchronization**
>
> When creating new cloud-based objects, you can select from any of the domains available in your tenant. However, when synchronizing from an on-premises directory, objects will be configured with the same domain configured with the on-premises object. If the corresponding domain hasn't been verified in the tenant, synchronized objects will be set to use the tenant-managed domain.

Next, we'll look at core organizational settings in a tenant.

Configuring organizational settings

Organizational settings, as the name implies, are configuration options that apply to the entire tenant. They are used to enable or disable features at the service or tenant level. In many instances, organizational settings are coarse controls that can be further refined by configuration settings inside each individual service.

To access the organizational settings, follow these steps:

1. Navigate to the Microsoft 365 admin center (`https://admin.microsoft.com`).

2. In the navigation pane, expand **Settings** and select **Org settings**.

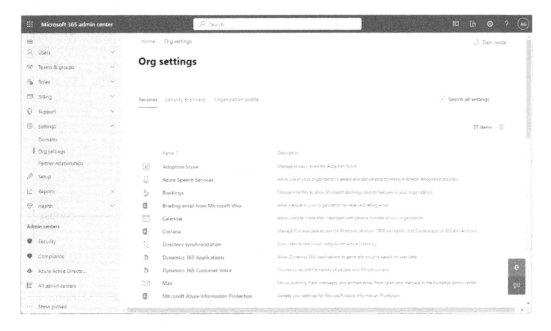

Figure 1.15 – Org settings in the Microsoft 365 admin center

The **Org settings** page has three tabs:

- **Services**
- **Security & privacy**
- **Organizational profile**

In the next section, we'll look at the settings available in each of them.

Services

The **Services** tab displays settings available for workloads, services, and features available in the Microsoft 365 tenant. The following table lists the services that have configurable options in the tenant.

Service	Description
Adoption Score	Manage privacy levels for Adoption Score as well as setting the scope for users to be included or excluded.
Azure Speech Services	Manage whether Azure Speech Services can work using content in your tenant to improve the accuracy of speech services. Disabled by default.
Bookings	Choose whether the Bookings service is available for use in the tenant. If Bookings is enabled, you also manage specific options, such as whether social sharing options are available or whether Bookings can be used by users outside the organization as well as restricting the collection of customer data.
Briefing email from Microsoft Viva	Choose whether to allow users to receive the Viva briefing email. By default, the briefing email is enabled. Users can unsubscribe themselves.
Calendar	Choose whether to enable users to share the calendar outside the organization. If sharing is enabled, choose what level of detail is supplied.
Cortana	Choose whether to allow Cortana on devices to connect to data in your Microsoft 365 tenant.
Directory synchronization	Provides a link to download the Azure AD Connect synchronization tool.

Service	Description
Dynamics 365 Applications	Choose whether to allow insights for each user, aggregated insights for other users (non-identifiable), and identifiable insights for other users.
Dynamics 365 Customer Voice	Configure email parameters for collecting survey data from Dynamics 365.
Mail	There are no org-wide settings to manage here; however, there are links to various tools in the Exchange admin center and the Microsoft Defender 365 portal for things such as transport rules and anti-malware policies.
Microsoft Azure Information Protection	There are no settings to manage for this feature; it is a link to documentation for configuring Azure Information Protection settings.
Microsoft communication to users	Choose whether to enable Microsoft-generated training and education content delivery to users.
Microsoft Edge product messaging for users	Provides information on configuring the Edge spotlight experience for end users.
Microsoft Edge site lists	Manage lists of sites and specify which browser experience (Edge or Internet Explorer) users should receive when navigating to those sites.
Microsoft Forms	Manage external sharing settings for Microsoft Forms as well capturing the names of internal organization users who fill out forms.
Microsoft Graph Data Connect	Choose to enable Microsoft Graph Data Connect for the bulk transfer of data to Azure.
Microsoft Planner	Choose whether Planner users can publish to Outlook or iCal.
Microsoft Search on the Bing homepage	Customize the Bing.com search page for organization users.
Microsoft Teams	Choose whether to enable Teams organization-wide (users who are licensed will be blocked from using Teams). Also, choose coarse control for whether guest access is allowed in Teams.
Microsoft To Do	Choose to allow internal users the ability to join and contribute to external task lists and receive push notifications.

Service	Description
Microsoft Viva Insights (formerly MyAnalytics)	Manage which Viva Insights settings users have access to. By default, all options are selected (Viva Insights web experience, Digest email, Insights Outlook add-in and inline suggestions, and Schedule send suggestions).
Microsoft 365 Groups	Configure guest access and ownership settings for Microsoft 365 Groups.
Modern authentication	Provides links to information on configuring modern authentication and viewing basic authentication sign-in reports.
Multi-factor authentication	Provides links to information on configuring and learning about multi-factor authentication.
News	Choose organization and industry settings used to display relevant news information on the Bing home page as well as settings for delivering Microsoft-generated industry news to your organization users.
Office installation options	Choose the update channel for Microsoft 365 apps.
Office on the web	Choose whether to allow users to connect to third-party cloud storage products using Office on the web products.
Office Scripts	Configure Office Scripts settings for Excel on the web.
Reports	Choose how to display users' personally identifiable information in internal reports and whether to make data available to Microsoft 365 usage analytics.
Search and intelligence usage analytics	Choose whether to allow usage analytics data to be filtered by country, occupation, department, or division.
SharePoint	Choose whether to enable external sharing.
Sway	Choose whether to allow the sharing of Sways outside the organization as well as what content sources are available (Flickr, Pickit, Wikipedia, and YouTube).
User consent to apps	Choose whether users can provide consent to OAuth 2 apps that access organization data.
User-owned apps and services	Choose whether to allow users to auto-claim licenses as well as start trials and access the Office Store.

Service	Description
Viva Learning	Choose which content provider data sources to use for Viva Learning. By default, LinkedIn Learning, Microsoft Learn, Microsoft 365 Training, and Custom Uploads are enabled. You can also manage the level of diagnostic data sent to Microsoft.
What's new in Office	Choose whether to display messages to users about new features that are available. This does not change the availability of the feature—only the display of the notification message.
Whiteboard	Choose whether to allow the Whiteboard app to be used. Additionally, manage the amount of diagnostic data collected.

Table 1.2 – Organizational service settings

While there are no deep questions about what each of the service options do, we recommend you spend time exploring the options for the services in the Microsoft 365 admin center.

Security & privacy

The **Security & privacy** tab houses settings that govern various security controls for the organization. On this page, you'll find access to the following settings:

Setting	Description
Bing data collection	Choose whether to allow Bing to collect organization query data.
Idle session timeout	Configure the idle session timeout period for Office web apps.
Password expiration policy	Choose whether to enable password expiration. Password expiration is disabled by default (and the password policy is governed by the on-premises Active Directory if password hash sync has been configured).
Privacy profile	Configure the URL for the organization's privacy policy and the organization's privacy contact. The privacy URL is displayed on the **Privacy** tab of the **Settings & Privacy** page in the user account profile and when a sharing request is sent to an external user.
Self-service password reset	Provides a link to the Azure portal to configure self-service password reset.
Sharing	Choose whether to allow users to add guests to the organization.

Table 1.3 – Security & privacy settings

These options can be used to broadly configure security and privacy settings for your organization. As with the settings on the **Services** tab, these are coarse controls. Fine-grained control is available for some of these items inside their respective admin centers.

Organization profile

Settings on the **Organization profile** tab are largely informational or used to manage certain aspects of the user experience. On this tab, you'll find the following settings:

Setting	Description
Custom app launcher tiles	Configure additional tiles to show up on the Microsoft 365 app launcher.
Custom themes	Create and apply themes to the Microsoft 365 portal for end users, including mandating the theme as well as specific organization logos and colors.
Data location	View the regional information where your tenants' data is stored.
Help desk information	Choose whether to add custom help desk support information for end users to the Office 365 help pane.
Keyboard shortcuts	View the shortcuts available for use in the Microsoft 365 admin center.
Organization information	Update your organization's name and other contact information.
Release preferences	Choose the release settings for Office 365 features (excluding Microsoft 365 apps). The available options are Standard release for everyone, Targeted release for everyone, and Targeted release for select users. The default setting is Standard release for everyone.
Support integration	Use the settings on this page to configure integration with third-party support tools such as Service Now.

Table 1.4 – Organization profile settings

Like the other **Org settings** tabs, the settings on this page will be used infrequently—typically when just setting up your tenant and customizing the experience. As with the other **Organization profile** setting areas, you should spend some time in a test environment navigating the tenant to view these settings and update them to see their effects.

Summary

In this chapter, you learned about the fundamental aspects and terminology of configuring a Microsoft 365 tenant, such as selecting a tenant and subscription type, adding domains, and configuring the basic organization settings.

In the next chapter, we will learn how to monitor the Microsoft 365 tenant's health.

Knowledge check

In this section, we'll test your knowledge of some key elements from this chapter.

Questions

1. What is the maximum number of domains that can be added to a Microsoft 365 tenant?

    A. 100

    B. 500

    C. 900

    D. 1,000

2. You are the administrator for an organization with 250 employees. Which Office 365 subscription best fits the size of the organization?

    A. Microsoft 365 Family

    B. Microsoft 365 Business

    C. Microsoft 365 Enterprise

    D. Microsoft 365 Education

3. You recently took over the administration duties for a Microsoft 365 tenant for a start-up organization. The organization purchased a domain from a third-party registrar. Can this domain be used with Microsoft 365?

    A. Yes

    B. Yes, but it must be transferred to Microsoft first

    C. No

    D. Only domains purchased through the Microsoft 365 admin center can be configured for use with Microsoft 365

4. Your organization wants to turn off Microsoft Books for all employees until the support staff has had time to read the documentation. From the available options, what should you do?

    A.   Disable all Azure AD user accounts

    B.   Disable directory synchronization

    C.   Disable bookings from **Org settings | Services**

    D.   Disable bookings from **Org settings | Security & privacy**

5. The Service Desk manager for Contoso has asked you to update the help desk information for your Microsoft 365 tenant with the internal help desk contact information. Where would you make this update?

    A.   **Org settings | Organization profile**

    B.   **Org settings | Services**

    C.   Microsoft Service Now Admin center

    D.   Microsoft 365 portal | **Account settings**

Answers

1. C: 900

2. B: Microsoft 365 Business

3. A: Yes

4. C: Disable Bookings from **Org settings | Services**

5. A: **Org settings | Organization profile**

2

Monitoring Microsoft 365 Tenant Health

As you learned in the previous chapter, the Microsoft 365 tenant is the security and content boundary for your organization. You have control over the content that goes into your tenant, as well as the security controls that you apply to it. However, you don't have control over external factors such as connectivity between platform services, errors that are introduced from the service provider's side, or errors with your environment connecting to Microsoft 365.

That's where monitoring the health of the tenant comes into play.

Like any other service that you are responsible for managing, you also need to be able to develop and execute an incident response plan.

In this chapter, we'll discuss monitoring and managing the health of a Microsoft 365 tenant. The objectives and skills we'll cover in this chapter include the following:

- Creating and managing service requests
- Creating an incident response plan
- Monitoring service health
- Monitoring application access
- Configuring and reviewing reports
- Reviewing usage metrics

By the end of this chapter, you should be able to describe day-to-day operations such as monitoring and reporting, as well as important tasks such as creating an incident response plan.

Let's begin!

Creating and managing service requests

While Microsoft is committed to ensuring the Microsoft 365 platform is as reliable as possible, service interruptions may occur.

Service requests for Microsoft 365 issues are typically raised through the Microsoft 365 admin center. You can create a support request by performing the following steps:

1. Log in to the Microsoft 365 admin center (`https://admin.microsoft.com`) and navigate to **Support | New service request**:

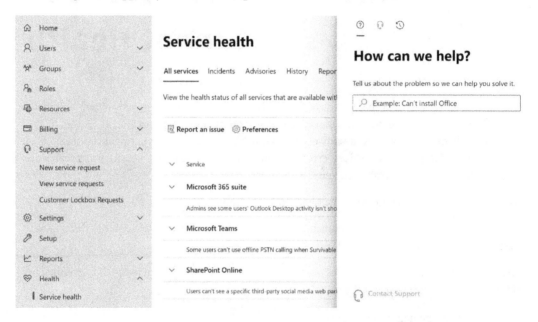

Figure 2.1 – Creating a service request in the Microsoft 365 admin center

2. In the fly-out panel, type in a question or keywords that relate to your service issue or request. If applicable, a list of potential suggested solutions will be displayed. If no suitable options are displayed, you can select **Contact Support**:

How can we help?

Tell us about the problem so we can help you solve it.

Can't Install Microsoft 365 Apps	✕

View insights

How to install Office

To install the Office client apps, ensure you have a business subscription such as Microsoft 365 Business Standard, Microsoft 365 Apps for business, or Office 365 Education.

Note

Office Home and Business is an Office for home product and not part of a business subscription. For specific instructions on Visio or Project, see Install Visio or Install Project.

Show more

Recommended articles

Troubleshoot installing Office - support.microsoft.com ⌐
Troubleshoot installing Office. The issues you encounter when trying to install Office 365, or Office 2019, 2016 or 2013 and how you fix...

Download and install or reinstall Microsoft 365 or Office ... ⌐
After signing in with your work or school account you don't see an option to install the desktop applications on the Microsoft 365...

Install Office applications - Microsoft 365 admin ... ⌐
Install Office applications: Install Office on your PC or Mac. Install other apps: Project, Visio, or Skype for Business. Set up mobile...

 Contact Support

Figure 2.2 – Microsoft 365 service ticket suggestions

3. On the **Contact support** view, you can fill out any required information, select the preferred option to be contacted, and, once ready, click **Contact me**:

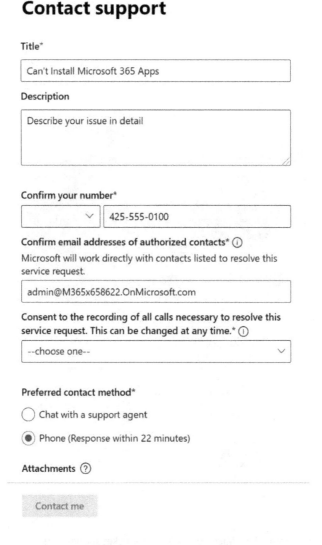

Figure 2.3 – Contacting support

4. Once a support request has been created, you can select the **Support | View service requests** option in the Microsoft 365 admin center to track the status of your service request or update it with new information:

Figure 2.4 – Service request history

After opening your support ticket, the following Microsoft support matrix details how quickly support personnel will contact you:

Severity Rating	Impact Level	Initial Response Time	Customer Expectations and Notes
A	Critical business impact Experiencing significant loss or degradation of services, requiring immediate attention	Developer: N/A Standard: < 1 hr ProDirect: < 1 hr Premier: < 1 hr Azure Rapid Response: < 15 min 24/7 access	Severity A is reserved for issues that have a critical business impact, with severe loss and degradation of services for multiple users. You must commit to 24/7 availability to work on the issue every day with the Microsoft team until resolution. Should you not be available, Microsoft may, at its discretion, decrease the issue to Severity B.

Severity Rating	Impact Level	Initial Response Time	Customer Expectations and Notes
B	Moderate business impact The organization has moderate loss or degradation of services affecting multiple users, but work can continue in a somewhat impaired manner	Developer: N/A Standard: < 4 hrs ProDirect: < 2 hrs Premier: < 2 hrs Azure Rapid Response: < 2 hrs Business hours access 4 (24/7 available)	Severity B issues have a moderate impact on your business with loss and degradation of services, but workarounds are available. If you've submitted an issue as Severity B, you have indicated that the issue demands an urgent response. If you choose 24/7 when you submit the support request, you commit to a continuous, 24/7 operation every day with the Microsoft team until resolution, similar to Severity A issues. If you open the ticket with 24/7 expectations but are not available, Microsoft may, at its discretion, lower the issue to Severity C. If you choose business hours-only support when you submit a Severity B incident, Microsoft will contact you during business hours only.
C	Minimum business impact The customer can conduct business with minor disruptions or a reduction of services	Developer: < 8 hrs Standard: < 8 hrs ProDirect: < 4 hrs Premier: < 4 hrs Azure Rapid Response: < 4 hrs Business hours access	Issues opened as Severity C indicate that the issue has a small impact on your business with a minor impediment to the service. For issues opened with Severity C, Microsoft will contact you during business hours only.

Table 2.1 – Severity and service response times

Use the preceding table to help determine how to categorize the issues you are facing.

In addition to the support options already mentioned, customers can also purchase paid service and support contracts. This service, called **Premier Support**, comes with access to a named support manager (a customer success account manager) that can act on both proactive and reactive issues.

Next, we'll look at developing a plan for managing issues and incidents.

Creating an incident response plan

If an incident occurs that affects the availability of services or features in your tenant, you need to be able to respond quickly. An incident response plan is a framework that you can prepare to help you address issues quickly.

While the details of each incident may differ, the steps you take to both prepare and work through one are the same:

1. **Validate the incident scope details and confirm that your environment is affected**. Not all incidents affect all tenants, so use the information in the Message Center (`https://admin.microsoft.com/#/MessageCenter`), as well as investigative procedures such as self-assessments and tests or synthetic transactions.

2. **Determine whether the incident is relevant to your organization**. If the incident involves a service that your organization hasn't yet deployed or doesn't interfere with business operations, it may not be relevant.

3. **Once degradation and relevancy to your environment have been confirmed, review information sources for details on the timeline of Microsoft's response**. Microsoft will post regular status updates in the Message Center. If information such as a timeline has not been established, you can open a service ticket with Microsoft to request this information.

4. **Develop a backup solution in case the service outage or degradation lasts longer than an acceptable time frame for your organization**. Depending on the type of outage, this may mean working offline to fulfill business requirements.

Business continuity planning (BCP) is important regardless of the technology platforms or services being used. Work with various business unit owners to establish communication plans and methods to continue business operations should a service interruption occur.

Monitoring service health

Service health information is available from the Microsoft 365 admin center (`https://admin.microsoft.com`). Microsoft provides health information for a variety of services and features, including the SaaS services such as Exchange Online or SharePoint Online, the health of the directory synchronization environment, as well as the Windows operating system feature issues and service health.

You can check the overall service health by navigating to the health dashboard (**Health | Dashboard**), as shown in *Figure 2.5*:

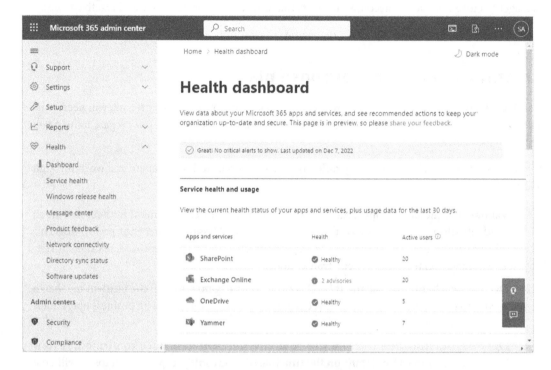

Figure 2.5 – Service health dashboard

The health dashboard contains the current health status of all Microsoft 365 services. Normally, services will appear as **Healthy**, though this status will be updated when a service experiences an issue.

The **Service health** page (**Health | Service health**) will display the most detailed and comprehensive information on any ongoing or resolved issues:

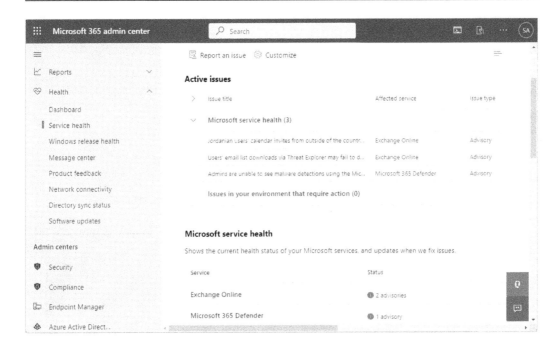

Figure 2.6 – Service health page

If a service has an advisory or incident, you can expand the issue item under **Active issues** to display relevant events, as shown in *Figure 2.7*:

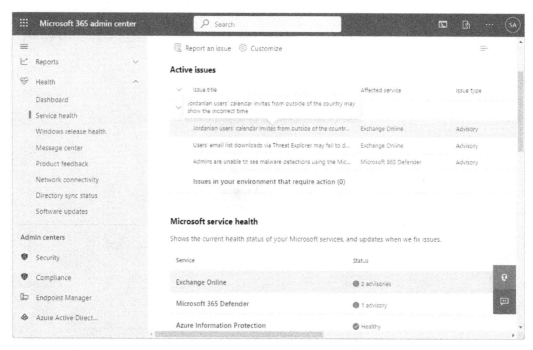

Figure 2.7 – Service health active issues

Selecting an individual item reveals expanded information about the particular issue. See *Figure 2.8* for an example:

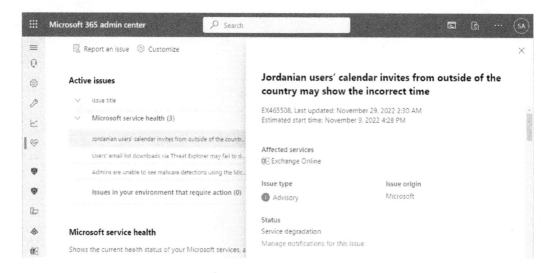

Figure 2.8 – Expanded active issue

Each service with an incident will display a status. Possible statuses include the following:

- **Normal service**: This status indicates the service is available and has no current incidents or incidents during the reporting period.

- **Extended recovery**: This status indicates that while steps have been completed to resolve the incident, it may take time for operations to return to normal. During an extended recovery period, some service operations might be delayed or take longer to complete.

- **Investigating**: This status indicates that a potential service incident is being reviewed.

- **Service restored**: This status indicates that an incident was active earlier in the day but the service was restored.

- **Service interruption**: This status indicates the service isn't functioning and that affected users are unable to access the service.

- **Additional information**: This status indicates the presence of information regarding a recent incident from the previous day.

- **Service degradation**: This status indicates that the service is slow or occasionally seems to be unresponsive for brief periods.

- **PIR published**: This status indicates that a Post-Incident Report (PIR) of the service incident has been published.

- **Restoring service**: This status indicates that the service incident is being resolved.

As an administrator, it's important to frequently check the **Service health** dashboard to be apprised of alerts or incidents. If a service issue is affecting the Microsoft 365 admin center, you can also try the Office 365 status page (`https://status.office.com`) and the Azure status page (`https://status.azure.com`).

Monitoring application access

While many cloud-based applications and services may use their own identity stores, it is becoming more common for application vendors to allow bring-you-own-identity scenarios. You might see this with websites allowing social media logins or other types of identity.

Like other identity providers, Azure AD identity can be used to authenticate users to external applications. While many of those applications are legitimate (and their use derives from a legitimate business use case), malicious websites or individuals can publish applications to steal data. As part of your operational practices, you should periodically review allowed applications in your environment and remove the authorizations for applications that look suspicious or are no longer being used.

Applications that are registered or authorized in Azure AD can be used to provide single sign-on to both SaaS cloud applications as well as internally managed applications. Depending on your organization's settings, applications may be authorized by end users, administrators, or both.

There are several things you can do to monitor application access:

- Create and manage access reviews
- Review audit logs
- Review the sign-ins report
- Send activity log data to Azure Monitor

Let's look at each of these areas briefly.

Creating and managing access reviews

The primary goal of an access review is to confirm that those who have access to an application or other resource still have access. If a user, whether internal or external, no longer requires the ability to use a resource, their access to that resource should be terminated.

> **Note**
> Access reviews are a feature of Identity Governance and require Azure AD Premium P2.

To create an access review, follow these steps:

1. Log in to the Azure portal (`https://portal.azure.com`) with a user that has one of the prerequisite role assignments (Global Administrator, User Administrator, Identity Governance Administrator, or Privileged Role Administrator) or who is an owner of the group for which the access review will be created.

2. In the search box, enter `Identity Governance` and select the **Identity Governance** item.

3. Under the **Access reviews** navigation menu item, select **Access reviews**:

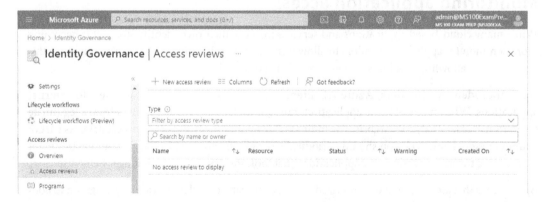

Figure 2.9 – Access reviews

4. Select **+ New access review**.

5. In the **Select Review** dropdown, select **Teams + Groups** or **Applications**:

Figure 2.10 – New access review – the Select Review dropdown

6. Depending on your selection, choose from **All Microsoft 365 groups with guest users**, **Select Teams + groups** (if you choose the **Teams + Groups** option), or one or more registered applications (if you choose the **Applications** option). If you select **Teams + Groups**, you may have additional selections regarding specific groups to include or exclude or specific scopes of users to include or exclude.

7. Click **Next**.

8. Under **Specify reviewers**, select the individuals who will be responsible for auditing the group. You may be asked to provide **Fallback reviewers** (if the ones you initially select cease to exist in the future), depending on the options you select.

9. Depending on your settings, you may see an option to perform a multi-stage review. Multi-stage reviews allow you to add up to three stages of reviewers to audit the membership of a group.

10. Under **Specify recurrence of review**, set a **Duration (in days) period**, a **Review recurrence** option (one-time, weekly, monthly, quarterly, semi-annually, or annually), and start and end date parameters. Click **Next**.

11. Under **Upon completion settings**, choose whether to **Auto apply results to a resource** and what to do **If reviewers don't respond**:

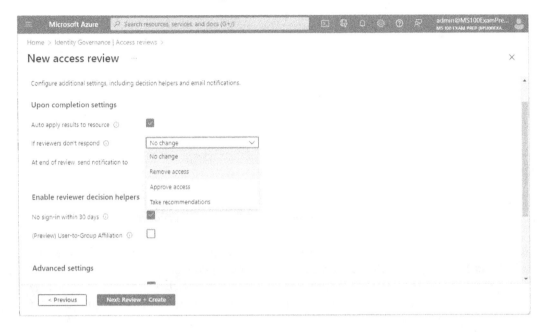

Figure 2.11 – Access review additional settings

12. You can also choose to **Enable reviewer decision helpers**, which are like tooltips that provide additional information on the selected actions during the access review.

13. Under **Advanced settings**, you can choose additional options such as **Justification required**, enable **Email notifications** and **Reminders to complete access reviews**, and use a text box to specify **Additional context for reviewer email**, which can be used to further explain the access review process to the individuals you've selected.

14. Click **Next**.

15. Enter a name for the access review, review the configured options, and then click **Create** to create your access review.

After an access review has been created, Azure AD will evaluate whether it needs to run. If the workflow determines it is time for the access review to run, it will do so.

You can view the status of an access review by clicking on it on the **Identity governance | Access reviews** page.

Users who have been selected to be reviewers will receive an email notification with a link to the access review page. You can also view the access review by selecting **Results** under the **Manage** menu item. From there, you'll be able to view the recommended actions and the audit information for review:

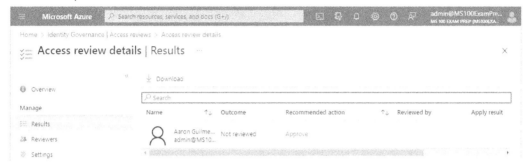

Figure 2.12 – Access review results

Next, we'll look at some of the logging and reporting data available for applications.

Reviewing audit logs

Application audit logs are useful for reviewing actions that have occurred in your tenant. You can view these audit logs from the **Enterprise applications** page in the Azure portal, as shown in *Figure 2.13*:

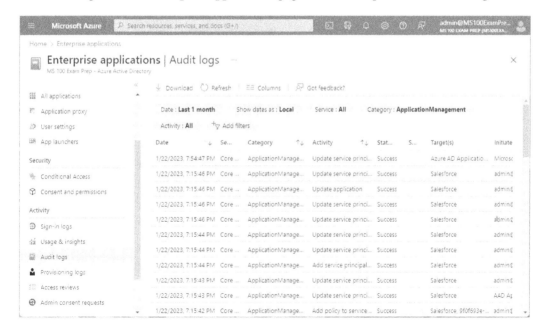

Figure 2.13 – Enterprise application audit logs

These audit logs show data regarding the service principal, applications, and type of action performed. You can select an individual audit item to view additional details. You can also perform filtering on several fields such as **Status (Success** or **Failure)**, **Initiated by (actor)** (user or security principal that executed the action), **User agent** (device type or browser where the action was submitted), and **Target** (application or service that was affected).

You can also select an individual application (**Enterprise applications | All applications**) and view all of the audit logs that pertain specifically to that application.

Reviewing the sign-ins report

The sign-ins report shows data related specifically to sign-ins. Like the audit log data, you can view it across all applications (from the **Enterprise applications | Audit logs** page) or just for an individual application, as shown in *Figure 2.14*:

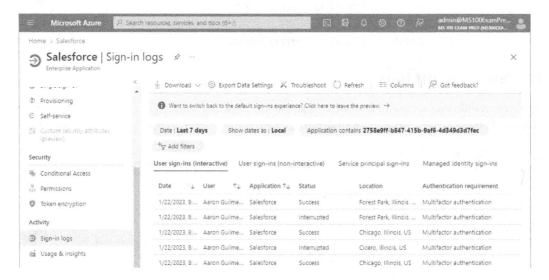

Figure 2.14 – Application sign-in logs

The application sign-in logs are useful for identifying potentially anomalous or malicious behavior. For example, if you see several failures for a particular user and they have a multifactor authentication requirement configured, the user may have a compromised password. If you see several failures for different users that are related to the same application, you may have an identity provisioning or single sign-on problem that needs to be addressed.

Sending activity log data to Azure Monitor

Azure Monitor is an additional subscription service that can be used to store and analyze logging and auditing data from a variety of sources, including Azure Active Directory, virtual machines, and applications. By connecting Azure AD data to Azure Monitor, you can enable Microsoft Defender to gain access to this data so that you can compare it against security logs, thereby improving risk management:

1. From the Azure portal (`https://portal.azure.com`), enter `Log Analytics workspaces` in the search box.

2. Click **Create**.

3. From the **Subscription** drop-down menu, select an Azure subscription.

4. From the **Resource group** drop-down menu, select an existing resource group or click **Create new** to create a new one.

5. Enter a new workspace **Name** and select a **Region** option for where you want to provision the workspace.

6. Click **Review + Create**.

7. Click **Create**.

Once the workspace has been provisioned, you can connect the activity log to Azure Monitor.

Connecting to Azure Monitor

If you have an Azure subscription with a Log Analytics workspace created and at least Azure AD Premium P1, you can send Azure Active Directory activity log data to Azure Monitor easily by following these steps:

1. From the Azure portal (`https://portal.azure.com`), navigate to Azure Active Directory.

2. Under **Monitoring**, select **Diagnostic settings** and then click **+ Add diagnostic setting**:

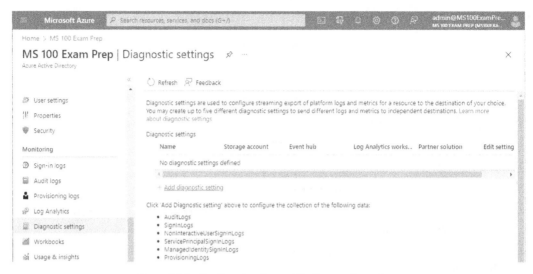

Figure 2.15 – Configuring Azure AD diagnostic settings

3. Under **Logs**, select one or more categories of logs to send to the workspace.

4. Under **Destination details**, check the **Send to Log Analytics workspace** checkbox and then select an Azure **Subscription** and **Log Analytics workspace**. Click **Save** when you have finished selecting these options:

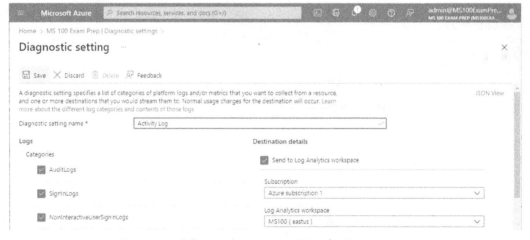

Figure 2.16 – Selecting diagnostics settings for Azure Monitor

After about 15 minutes, new logging event data should begin showing up in the Log Analytics workspace.

Configuring and reviewing reports

With reporting data now flowing into Azure Monitor and Log Analytics, you can review auditing and logging data to gain insights into how your tenant and directory services are being used.

To review this data, you'll need to have access to the Log Analytics workspace where Azure Monitor is sending data, as well as one of the following roles:

- Global Admin
- Reports Reader
- Security Admin
- Security Reader

With that, let's start looking at logs!

Azure AD logs and reports

Azure AD provides several default reports that can be used to identify issues quickly. The core reports are the Audit, Sign-in, and Provisioning logs.

Audit logs

The audit logs are a collection of system activity records for a wide variety of events. These categories can be seen in the following table:

AdministrativeUnit	Agreement	ApplicationManagement
AttributeManagement	Authentication	Authorization
AuthorizationPolicy	CertificateBasedAuthConfiguration	Contact
CrossTenantAccessSettings	CrossTenantIdentitySyncSettings	Device
DeviceConfiguration	DeviceManagement	DeviceTemplate
DirectoryManagement	EntitlementManagement	ExternalUserProfile
GroupManagement	IdentityProtection	KerberosDomain
KeyManagement	Label	Other
PendingExternalUserProfile	PermissionGrantPolicy	Policy
PolicyManagement	PrivateLinkResource	ProvisioningManagement
ResourceManagement	RoleManagement	TaskManagement
UserManagement	WorkflowManagement	

Table 2.2 – Audit log categories

Audit log data can be held for up to 10 years, depending on the license:

- **Office 365 E1 or E3; Microsoft 365 F1 or E3**: 90 days

- **Office 365 E5; Microsoft 365 E5**: 1 year

- **Audit Premium**: 10 years

> **Advanced licensing**
>
> For more information on the variety of SKU mixes for audit retention, see `https://learn.microsoft.com/en-us/microsoft-365/compliance/audit-solutions-overview?source=recommendations&view=o365-worldwide`.

Accessing the audit log data does not require specific licensing, though you will only see audit events for products that you have currently licensed.

Sign-in logs

The Sign-ins activity report provides data regarding sign-in activity for your tenant, including users and other security or service principals. The report includes information regarding the user, the status of the request, the resource name used for the sign-in, whether multi-factor authentication or conditional access was required, as well as regional location and IP address information:

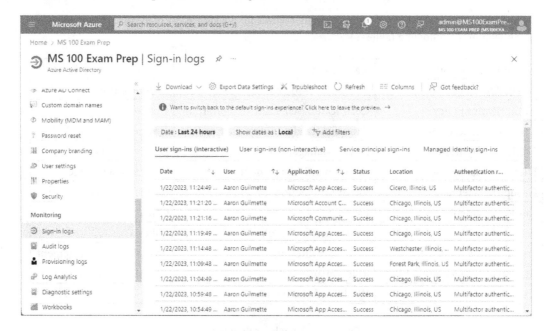

Figure 2.17 – Sign-in logs

Selecting an individual sign-in event brings up advanced details. Each tab contains additional information regarding the sign-in event. See *Figure 2.18*:

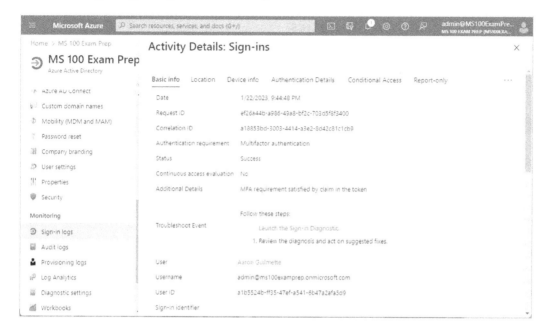

Figure 2.18 – Sign-in activity details

Sign-ins logs are available to all subscriptions, though programmatic access to this data via the Graph API requires either Azure AD Premium P1 or P2.

Provisioning logs

The provisioning logs show data regarding users being provisioned into Azure AD from connected applications or to connected applications from Azure AD provisioning workflows.

To view the provisioning logs, a user must be granted one of the following roles:

- Reports Reader
- Security Reader
- Security Operator
- Security Administrator
- Application Administrator
- Cloud Application Administrator
- Global Administrator

Objects created manually through the Azure AD portal, PowerShell, or Microsoft 365 admin center do not appear here, nor do objects synchronized via Azure AD Connect.

Azure Monitor and Log Analytics

Azure Monitor provides a single, unified hub for diagnostic and monitoring data in Azure and connected applications. The easiest way to start reviewing the logs is to select the **Log Analytics** link under the **Monitoring** section in Azure Active Directory, as shown in *Figure 2.19*:

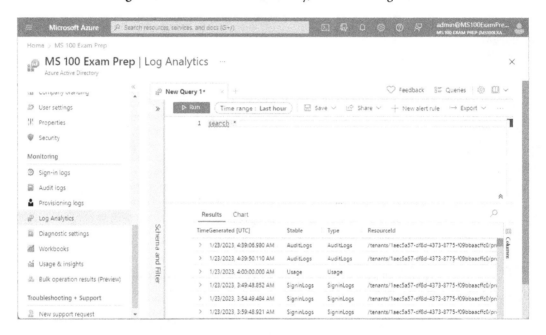

Figure 2.19 – Accessing Log Analytics from the Monitoring section of Azure AD

Log analytics data can be searched using built-in queries or by specifying your own searches in the **Query** window.

For example, you can select built-in queries to begin querying data immediately. *Figure 2.20* shows a query for the *SigninLogs* table, summarizing sign-ins by country:

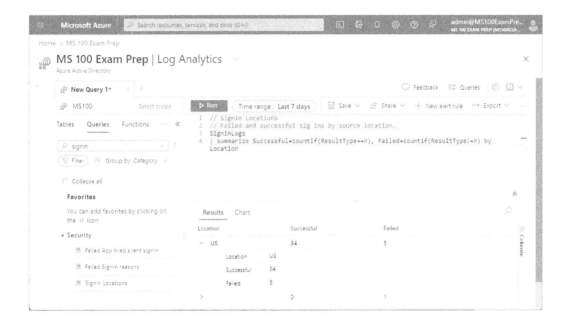

Figure 2.20 – Querying Log Analytics

Deep-dive into Kusto Query Language

Kusto Query Language (KQL) is used to search for and sort through data in Log Analytics. It is an incredibly powerful language but takes some time to learn. KQL is used in Log Analytics, Azure Monitor, and Azure Sentinel. If you want to start learning KQL, you can work through the Log Analytics tutorial at `https://learn.microsoft.com/en-us/azure/azure-monitor/logs/log-analytics-tutorial`.

Reviewing usage metrics

For your organization to get the most benefit from a Microsoft 365 investment, users must adopt the available services and features. You can monitor end user adoption and consumption metrics through a variety of tools, including **Microsoft 365 Usage Metrics**, **Viva Insights** (formerly known as **Workplace Analytics**), and **Adoption Score** (formerly known as **Productivity Score**).

Microsoft 365 usage reports

The Microsoft 365 usage reports are available inside the Microsoft 365 admin center. They are broad reports that can be used to get a high-level snapshot of how your organization uses the Microsoft 365 platform. Report data includes statistics about how many files are stored in SharePoint, how many Exchange mailboxes were active during the reporting period, as well as engagement with other products such as Yammer or Forms:

Figure 2.21 – Microsoft 365 usage reports

Usage reports can be accessed by navigating to the Microsoft 365 admin center (`https://admin.microsoft.com`), expanding **Reports**, and selecting **Usage**.

Viva Insights

Formerly known as Workplace Analytics, Viva Insights provides recommendations about personal and teamwork habits. Viva Insights has four core areas:

- Personal insights
- Teamwork habits
- Organization trends
- Advanced insights

Each of these areas has unique features that are part of the Viva story.

Personal insights

As the name suggests, personal insights are tailored to an individual. Personal insights are private and are only visible to the individual for whom they are intended. Personal insights are best viewed using the Viva Insights app in Microsoft Teams, as shown in *Figure 2.22*:

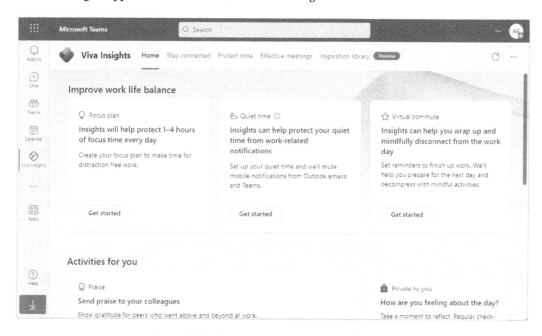

Figure 2.22 – Viva Insights app in Microsoft Teams

The Viva Insights app has functions to allow you to make a focus plan (sometimes referred to as the **protect time** feature), send praise to your colleagues either publicly or privately, and stay connected through AI-based task suggestions and meeting assistance.

The Viva Insights app also features Headspace guided meditation and mindfulness exercises, as well as prompts for taking a break and reflecting on your personal feelings. Using the **Reflection** activity card, you can even set daily reminders to check in on yourself:

Figure 2.23 – Reflection activity card

Viva Insights also has a daily ramp-up and wind-down micro-app called **Virtual commute**, which lets users review upcoming meetings and tasks, block focus time, and initiate a variety of mini-break, meditative, and reflective activities. See *Figure 2.23*:

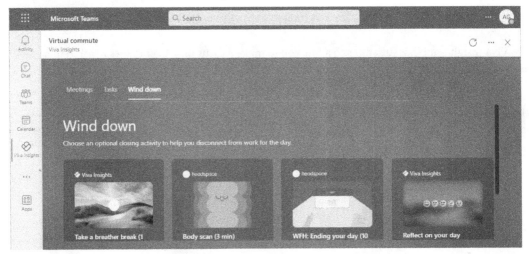

Figure 2.24 – Virtual commute activity card

Together, these insights features can help users manage both their productivity and personal well-being.

Teamwork habits

Viva Insights **Teamwork habits**, part of the premium Viva Insights experience, allows managers to gain additional recommendations for managing people. Teamwork habits helps managers identify regular after-hours work, meeting overload conditions, and a lack of dedicated focus time.

Managers can set up their teams by manually adding users, though they can use the suggested list if the manager property has been configured in Active Directory or Azure Active Directory:

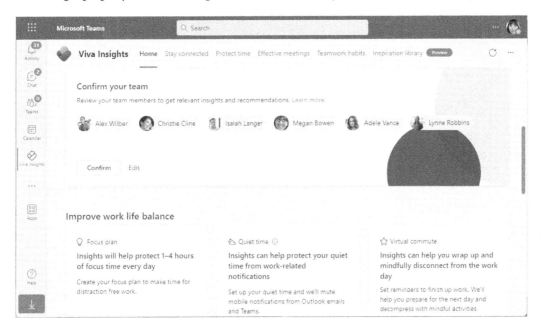

Figure 2.25 – Confirming team members

Three additional core features of Teamwork habits are as follows:

- Scheduling recurring 1:1 time with managed employees
- Gathering quiet hours impact to determine how work habits impact employees outside of their configured working hours
- Shared plans for no-meeting days and shared focus times

Organizations that have the **Teamwork habits** tools available can improve their employees' well-being and work-life balance. The Teamwork habits feature requires a separate Microsoft Viva Insights license.

Organization trends

The **Organization trends** tab shows business leader and manager insights to help understand how to effectively manage your teams, such as identifying work patterns:

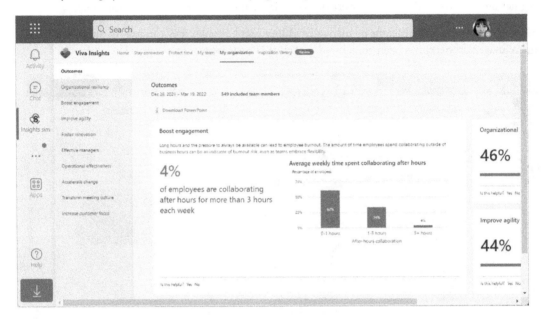

Figure 2.26 – Organization trends

Organization trend data is privacy-oriented, requiring a minimum of 10 people (including the manager) to be in the management chain, either directly or indirectly. In addition, access to organization trends requires granting access to manager insights through the Viva setup.

Advanced insights

Microsoft Viva Advanced Insights is a reporting tool that provides research-based behavioral insights into organizational work patterns, such as hybrid work, work-life balance, and employee well-being.

The Advanced Insights reporting tool comes with several built-in templates and analysis tools to help organizations understand everything, from meeting effectiveness to employee performance trends correlated to manager 1:1 meetings:

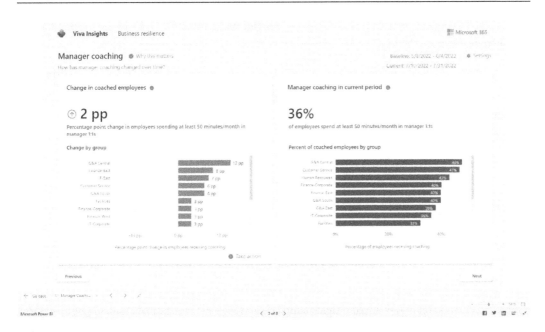

Figure 2.27 – Viva Insights manager coaching report

With large organizational changes such as hybrid and remote work scenarios, it can be important to understand how those work patterns affect performance, including interesting data points such as how much time is spent during meetings multitasking, or how much work is getting done outside normal business hours:

Figure 2.28 – Advanced insights working hours details

The Advanced Insights Power BI report templates provide an analysis of employee engagement and work patterns. Here are the reports:

- **Business resilience**: Overall business report highlighting performance and employee well-being
- **Hybrid workforce experience**: This report highlights how different work modes (onsite, hybrid, and remote) affect workers
- **Manager effectiveness**: This report provides insight into patterns for people managers
- **Meeting effectiveness**: This report captures and displays information on meeting statistics such as how many meetings happen at short notice or how much multitasking occurs during meetings
- **Ways of working**: This data helps answer questions such as, "Are employees receiving enough 1:1 coaching time?" and "Who generates the most work by organizing meetings?"
- **Wellbeing – balance and flexibility**: This reporting data is used to identify whether employees have enough time to focus on core priorities and balance that with breaks and time away from work

For more information on the advanced insights templates and their reporting capabilities, see `https://learn.microsoft.com/en-us/viva/insights/advanced/analyst/templates/introduction-to-templates`.

Adoption Score

Formerly known as **Productivity Score**, **Adoption Score** is a metric that is used to help measure the success of an organization that is using the Microsoft 365 platform. Before Adoption Score can be used, it must be enabled in the Microsoft 365 admin center under **Reports**:

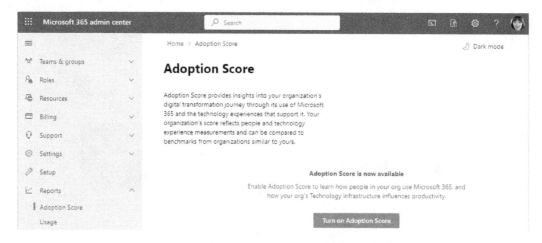

Figure 2.29 – Enabling Adoption Score

Adoption Score provides insights broken into three categories: **people experiences**, **technology experiences**, and **special reports**. When enabling the score, you can select how to calculate people experiences insights:

- **Include all users**
- **Exclude specific users by group**
- **Don't calculate for any users**

Technology experiences insights are shown automatically when you enable the adoption score. If you don't want to collect that data, you can disable the **Endpoint analytics scope** property in the Intune data collection policy.

If you are performing a staged rollout of services using a pilot program, it may be beneficial to limit the reporting scope to groups of users that are part of the pilot.

People experiences

The people experiences insights focus on five categories that show how your users and organization are using the tools in the Microsoft 365 platform. These insight areas are as follows:

- **Communication**: The **Communication** area measures how people communicate with each other, such as via sending emails, instant messages, or posting on communities in Yammer. This area highlights important practices such as using @mentions in emails and marking responses as answers in Yammer. Users need to be licensed for Yammer, Exchange Online, or Teams to be counted in this metric.

- **Content collaboration**: This area measures how people use files in your organization, such as creating or sharing files in OneDrive for Business and SharePoint Online or how email attachments are used (attached files versus a cloud attachment—a link to a file shared in OneDrive or SharePoint). It also captures data about the number of files shared and whether the collaborators are internal or external to the organization. Users need to be licensed for OneDrive for Business, SharePoint, or Exchange Online to be counted in this metric.

- **Mobility**: This area measures what devices and interfaces people use to accomplish their work. For example, a user sending an email from the Outlook desktop app and the Outlook mobile app would be regarded as an individual using the Microsoft 365 apps across multiple platforms. This measurement area also reports on what locations people are working from – whether they are onsite in one of your organization's offices or working remotely. To be counted in this metric, users need to be licensed for Teams, Exchange Online, or Microsoft 365 apps.

- **Meetings**: The **Meetings** area measures how effectively meetings are used across your organization. Meetings are evaluated against practices such as scheduling meetings at least 24 hours in advance, sharing agendas, and the percentage of invitees that show up to the meetings. Other features include measuring interactivity (hand-raising, chat, reactions, or sharing content) during the meeting, as well as whether or not attendees participate via audio or video. Users must be licensed for Microsoft Teams to be included in this metric.

- **Teamwork**: This area is used to measure how people collaborate in Teams and use shared workspaces (such as Teams, channels, Microsoft 365 Groups, and SharePoint sites). To be counted for this metric, users must be licensed for Exchange Online, SharePoint, or Microsoft Teams.

In addition to users requiring licenses to be assigned, they also need to be active in a service at least once every 28 days to get counted for that service. You can use Adoption Score to review how people use the Microsoft 365 service and provide coaching on best practices to get the most out of the platform.

Technology experiences

The technology experiences category focuses on areas relating to the devices that people are using to access Microsoft 365 services:

- **Endpoint analytics**: This area provides insights into the overall performance data of devices that are enrolled in **Intune** or **Configuration Manager** with **tenant attach**. The performance metrics include things such as boot time, how long it takes to sign in and get to a responsive desktop, how much time is spent processing Group Policy, how often applications hang or crash, and the number of active devices that have launched a particular app during the past 14 days. The endpoint analytics reporting has special requirements, such as particular operating system versions of endpoints being either Azure AD joined or hybrid Azure AD joined, as well as licensed for Intune or Microsoft Endpoint Configuration Manager.

- **Network connectivity**: This area provides insights into factors involving network communication between your endpoints and the Microsoft 365 platform. Specific network requirements must be met, such as configuring networks in the Microsoft 365 admin center and enabling location data collection features. For more information on the prerequisites for enabling network connectivity reporting, see `https://learn.microsoft.com/en-us/microsoft-365/enterprise/office-365-network-mac-perf-overview?view=o365-worldwide`.

- **Microsoft 365 Apps**: In this area, you can view insights on how many devices across your organization are up-to-date with their Microsoft 365 app deployments.

The technology experiences score reports can help you gain insight into how devices may affect the overall adoption and satisfaction with Microsoft 365 services.

Special reports

Finally, there is a lightweight version of the **Business Resilience** report (from Viva Insights), which is available to organizations that have at least 100 active Exchange and Viva Insights licenses. This report helps organizational leaders understand how to utilize remote work, how to maintain a work-life balance, the effectiveness of virtual meetings, and how to participate in Yammer communities.

Summary

In this chapter, you learned about a variety of different types of data that is available in the Microsoft 365 environment, including service health, audit and security log data, and adoption and usage metrics. You were also introduced to Viva Insights as part of an employee experience platform to help organizations understand and manage effective employee communications and well-being.

In the next chapter, we will start planning for identity synchronization.

Knowledge check

In this section, we'll test your knowledge of some key elements from this chapter.

Questions

Answer the following questions:

1. What three insight areas does Adoption Score cover?

    A. Technology experiences

    B. Engagement experiences

    C. People experiences

    D. Special reports

    E. License consumption

2. Service health data can be viewed in which location?

    A. Azure Monitor

    B. Microsoft Sentinel

    C. Log Analytics

    D. The health dashboard

3. Which type of data is captured in the Azure AD Provisioning logs?

    A. Enterprise application provisioning activities

    B. Azure AD Connect user provisioning activities

    C. Microsoft Identity Manager provisioning activities

    D. Microsoft 365 Group provisioning activities

4. Which two steps should be taken when creating an incident response plan?

    A. Validate the incident scope details and confirm that your environment is affected

    B. Migrate applications back on-premises

    C. Develop a backup solution in case the service outage or degradation lasts longer than the acceptable time frame for your organization

    D. Immediately begin restoring data from third-party backups or archive locations

5. Microsoft Viva Insights Teamwork habits include suggestions for what two actions?

    A. Virtual happy hours

    B. Scheduling recurring 1:1 time with managed employees

    C. Establishing no-meeting days

    D. Encouraging after-hours work to lessen the workload of coworkers

Answers

The following are the answers to this chapter's questions:

1. A: Technology experiences; C: People experiences; D: Special reports

2. D: The health dashboard

3. A: Enterprise application provisioning activities

4. A: Validate the incident scope details and confirm that your environment is affected; C: Develop a backup solution in case the service outage or degradation lasts longer than the acceptable time frame for your organization

5. B: Scheduling recurring 1:1 time with managed employees; C: Establishing no-meeting days

Part 2:
Planning and Managing User Identity and Roles

In this part, you will learn about the various types of user identity and provisioning strategies, including Azure AD Connect and Azure AD Connect cloud sync. You'll also learn about Azure AD roles and privileged identity management.

This part has the following chapters:

3

Planning Identity Synchronization

The first two chapters introduced you to some of the fundamentals of what a Microsoft 365 tenant is, working with service requests and incident response plans, and monitoring features of the environment.

Now, it's time to start exploring how to start consuming the environment's features. Microsoft 365 is an identity-based platform, meaning that all the services and features that are available are ultimately designed around the concepts of security and identity. Whether you're talking about mailboxes, team sites, or Power Apps, any data is inaccessible without an identity.

This chapter covers the following exam objectives:

- Designing synchronization solutions
- Identifying object source requirements
- Identifying required Azure AD Connect features
- Understanding the prerequisites for Azure AD Connect
- Choosing between Azure AD Connect and Azure AD Connect Cloud Sync
- Planning user sign-in

The topics in this objective drive both security and operations for your environment. By the end of this chapter, you should have an understanding of how to match business requirements to Azure AD identity features.

Designing synchronization solutions

We've already touched on the fact that Microsoft 365 is an identity-driven platform. This means you need to provision some sort of identity for your users to begin accessing the tools and features of the service.

When discussing Azure AD, it's important to understand where identities are stored and how authentication is performed. With Azure AD, three basic identity models are available:

- **Cloud authentication**: Cloud authentication is a model where identities are created in (or synchronized to) Azure AD and the authentication is processed by Azure AD

- **Federated identity**: With federated identity, user objects are synchronized to Azure AD, but the authentication happens in the identity source's directory

- **External identity**: Commonly used for **business-to-business (B2B)** or **business-to-consumer (B2C)** scenarios, external identity is used when a tenant stores a type of reference or a guest object that represents an external user in another directory, such as a business partner's Azure AD environment, Facebook, or Google

For the exam objective, however, we're going to focus on identity models that involve directory synchronization and working with the features surrounding those solutions. **Hybrid identity** is an identity and authentication model that involves both an on-premises identity and a corresponding synchronized cloud identity. With Microsoft 365, you can deploy a hybrid identity solution using **Azure Active Directory Connect** (most commonly referred to as **Azure AD Connect**).

Overview of Azure AD Connect

Azure AD Connect is a directory synchronization tool that has steadily evolved over the past several years to provide increased capabilities in the identity synchronization and authentication management areas. The current Azure AD Connect platform is built on **Microsoft Identity Manager (MIM)**.

At a high level, Azure AD Connect works by connecting to various on-premises and cloud directories, reading in objects such as users and groups, and then provisioning them to another directory. There are several key terms to understand when working with Azure AD Connect, which we'll discuss in this section.

Connected system

Sometimes referred to as a connected directory, a connected system is any directory source that has been configured for use with Azure AD Connect.

Connector

A **connector** is a logical object that represents the configuration necessary to communicate with a connected directory. For example, the Azure AD Connector stores the configuration necessary for Azure AD Connect to read and write data to Azure Active Directory. A connector can contain information about what attributes are available from the connected directory or what server is used when accessing the directory.

Connector space

You can think of the **connector space** as a database table that is used to hold all the objects related to a particular connector. Each connector has its own connector space.

sourceAnchor

Each object has a unique, immutable attribute that stays with it throughout its lifetime. The **sourceAnchor** is an attribute you can use to trace the lineage of an object as it moves between connector spaces and is represented in various connected directories. No two objects can share the same sourceAnchor.

Import

To populate each connector's connector space, Azure AD Connect must read the object data from a source directory. Objects commonly include users, contacts, groups, and devices. The process for reading data is called **import**.

Synchronization

Once objects have been imported into the connector space, a **synchronization** job is executed. Synchronization is responsible for executing logic (called **rules**) that can be used to connect (or **join**, in Azure AD Connect terminology) objects from different directories together or map attributes from between directory objects.

For example, a synchronization rule is responsible for mapping a user's Department property in Active Directory to the Department property in Azure AD. If you have users who are represented in more than one source directory, a synchronization rule can be used to join the two objects together and map their attributes accordingly.

Synchronization also has the idea of **precedence**, meaning that the order of the synchronization rules can (and will) affect the outcome of the processing. Rules configured with higher precedence (which translates to a lower ordinal number when looking at the rules list) means that the outcome of their processing overrides that of lower-precedence (higher-numbered) rules.

Transformation

As part of the synchronization process, Azure AD performs certain computations or evaluations on objects. This process is called **transformation**. Transformations (sometimes called **transforms**) are the actions configured inside synchronization rules and are used to determine how attributes are mapped between objects and what (if any) additional calculations are done between the source and target objects.

For example, you may wish to change the order of a person's name from Firstname, Lastname to Lastname, Firstname. You can perform this update by using a transformation inside a synchronization rule.

Export

The export process is responsible for writing objects (or their updates) to a particular connected directory.

Scope

The term scope is used in a few different places in the context of Azure AD Connect. Scope is broadly used to determine what objects are eligible to be managed as part of Azure AD Connect. Scope can be used in the Azure AD connector configuration to limit which organizational units or domains are imported or exported in the directory. Scope, in the context of an Azure AD synchronization rule, can be used to limit which objects can be affected by a particular synchronization rule.

Metaverse

The metaverse, in simple terms, is a consolidated view of all the objects from connector spaces.

Staging server

Azure AD Connect supports a form of redundancy called a staging server. This server should be configured with the same features, options, settings, and customizations that the primary server has. If the primary server is unavailable for an extended period, you can enable the staging server to continue providing identity synchronization services.

> **Note**
> The staging server is passive and does not actively process exports to Azure AD. Having two active Azure AD Connect servers in a single tenant is not supported.

Now that you understand the basic terminology surrounding Azure AD Connect, let's move on to working with directories.

Understanding Azure AD Connect with a single forest and single tenant

Of all the potential architectures available between Active Directory, Azure AD, and Azure AD Connect, the most common (and easiest) is when Azure AD Connect is used to synchronize data from a single Active Directory forest (including one or more domains in the same forest) into a single Azure Active Directory tenant. This example is depicted in *Figure 3.1*:

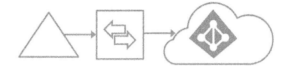

Figure 3.1 – Single forest to single tenant synchronization

> **Exam tip**
>
> If you choose the express installation choice during setup, this is the only supported Azure AD Connect topology. The express installation will automatically configure Password Hash Synchronization.

Understanding Azure AD Connect with multi-forest scenarios

Azure AD Connect also supports several multi-forest scenarios.

In a basic multi-forest scenario, you have one or more on-premises Active Directory forests all contributing unique objects to a single Azure AD tenant.

You might need to support a configuration like this if you have multiple business units within your organization with their own autonomous Active Directory environments that all want to share a single Microsoft 365 environment:

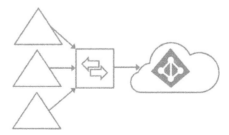

Figure 3.2 – Multiple Active Directory forests contributing to a single Azure AD tenant

There are other organizational scenarios where you may need to support multiple forests. Large organizations sometimes configure multiple directories in what's called a **resource forest** configuration.

In this structure, application resources (such as Microsoft Exchange) are configured in one forest (called the resource forest). A trust relationship is established with another forest containing accounts (intuitively called the **account forest**). The trust allows objects from the account forest to access applications and services in the resource forest. The user objects in the account forests are linked to a corresponding security principal account in the resource forest, thereby granting access to the resource forest. See *Figure 3.3*:

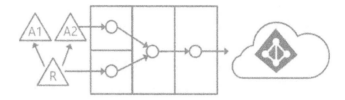

Figure 3.3 – Account forests and a resource forest contributing to a single Azure AD tenant

Another common multi-forest scenario involves two or more on-premises organizations that utilize some other form of directory synchronization (such as **MIM GALSync**) to ensure that each organization's Exchange environment contains a full list of the objects in their partner's directories. This example is shown in *Figure 3.4*:

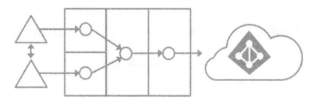

Figure 3.4 – Multiple forests with on-premises synchronization to a single Azure AD tenant

In this scenario, users have a single primary account that they use for accessing services and resources. That account is represented in the partner organization's directory as a contact object.

Multiple forests, multiple users, multiple options

Multi-forest configurations can be quite tricky. During the Azure AD Connect setup, you'll be prompted to select how your users are represented across the organization. You have two core options: **Users are represented only once across all directories** and **User identities exist across multiple directories**.

The first option is straightforward – it's a scenario where users only have one object.

The second option, though, has two additional choices: to match using **Mail attribute** or **ObjectSID and msExchangeMasterAccountSID attributes**.

In an on-premises directory synchronization scenario (which Microsoft refers to as **full mesh**), users may be represented by several objects, such as a security principal (user account), as well as a contact object in other forests. For this scenario, you would choose to match users based on the mail attribute.

In a resource forest configuration, users typically have more than one identity: an identity in the account forest that is linked to a corresponding account in the resource forest. Typically, the account in the resource forest is set to disabled. In an Exchange resource forest scenario, the objects are linked by copying the **ObjectSID** value from the user object in the account forest to the **msExchangeMasterAccountSID** value of the user object in the resource forest. With an Exchange resource forest design, you'll want to select the **ObjectSID and msExchangeMasterAccountSID attributes** option.

Understanding Azure AD Connect with multi-tenant scenarios

In more complex scenarios, you can synchronize objects from one (or more) on-premises forests to one (or more) Azure AD tenants, as shown in *Figure 3.5*:

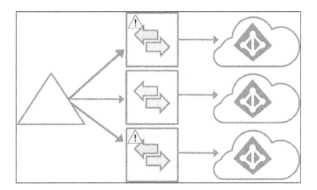

Figure 3.5 – Synchronization to multiple Azure AD tenants

This is relatively new, from a supported topologies perspective. This is a potential solution if you need to support multiple tenants in your organization. Microsoft, however, recommends trying to consolidate to a single tenant where possible.

There are some important caveats with this design, primarily the following:

- You need to deploy an Azure AD Connect server to communicate with each tenant.
- While the same object can be in scope for multiple Azure AD Connect instances, Exchange hybrid writeback, device writeback, and group writeback are only supported by one tenant. If you configure those writeback features for more than one tenant and have the same object in scope for those Azure AD Connect servers, you will enter a race condition where the object will get continuously updated errantly.
- You can have Password Write-back enabled on multiple tenants for the same user object.
- Hybrid Azure AD Join and Seamless SSO can only be configured with one tenant.
- You cannot configure the same custom domain in more than one tenant.

As previously mentioned, Microsoft recommends trying to consolidate into a single tenant to get the best experience. And, regardless of the Azure AD Connect topologies selected, it is not supported to deploy more than one active Azure AD Connect server to a single tenant. If you need to connect multiple on-premises systems to a single Azure AD tenant, you can achieve that with a single Azure AD Connect server.

Identifying object source requirements

Since the purpose of Azure AD Connect is synchronizing user, group, contact, and device objects to Azure AD, you'll need to make sure your objects meet the minimum requirements.

Microsoft has guidance surrounding preparing user objects for synchronization. Some attributes (specifically those that are used to identify the user throughout the system) must be unique throughout the organization. For example, you cannot have two users that have the same **userPrincipalName** value.

The following attributes should be prepared before synchronizing the directory to Azure AD:

Attribute	Constraints	Must Be Unique	Required
displayName	≤ 256 characters		X
givenName	≤ 64 characters		
mail	≤ 113 characters ≤ 64 characters before the @ symbol Adheres to RFC 822/2822/5322 standard	X	

Attribute	Constraints	Must Be Unique	Required
mailNickName	≤ 64 characters Cannot start with a "." Cannot contain certain characters such as &	X	
proxyAddresses	≤ 256 characters per value No spaces Diacritical marks are prohibited	X	
sAMAccountName	≤ 20 characters	X	X
sn	≤ 64 characters		
targetAddress	≤ 256 characters No spaces Includes prefix (such as SMTP:) Value after the prefix adheres to the RFC 822/2822/5322 standard after the prefix	X	
userPrincipalName	≤ 113 characters Must use a routable domain name Unicode characters are converted into underscores	X	X

Table 3.1 – Azure AD Connect attributes

As you can see, very few attributes are required for an object to synchronize. Each attribute that is synchronized does have some core requirements around formatting, including length and allowed characters. Several attributes (such as **mailNickname**, **userPrincipalName**, **mail**, **sAMAccountName**, and **proxyAddresses**) must contain unique values – that is, no other object in the directory of any type can share those values.

Further reading

You can learn more about the required and supported values for attributes at `https://learn.microsoft.com/en-us/powershell/module/exchange/set-mailbox` and `https://learn.microsoft.com/en-us/microsoft-365/enterprise/prepare-for-directory-synchronization`.

When preparing to synchronize your directory, Microsoft recommends performing the following procedures:

- Use the IdFix tool (`https://aka.ms/idfix`) to detect errors such as invalid characters in on-premises identities. Values that contain invalid characters will cause object synchronization errors.

- Configure a user's **userPrincipalName** (**UPN**) to be the same as their primary SMTP address. While it's not required to have parity between UPN and SMTP addresses, it is recommended to help minimize the number of unique values that users have to remember.

You shouldn't install and configure directory synchronization until you have resolved the issues identified by IdFix.

Identifying required Azure AD Connect features

Depending on your organization's requirements for onboarding to Microsoft 365 as well as additional features or services that are included with your subscription, you may want (or need) to enable or configure additional Azure AD Connect features.

The following table illustrates features that can be enabled through Azure AD Connect setup:

Feature	Description
Device Writeback	Synchronizes Azure AD-joined devices back to on-premises Active Directory
Directory Extensions	Enables the synchronization of additional on-premises attributes
Federation	Enables authentication federation with Microsoft Active Directory Federation Services or PingFederate
Hybrid Azure AD Join	Enables on-premises domain-joined devices to be synchronized and automatically joined to Azure AD
Password Hash Synchronization	Enables hashing the on-premises password to be synchronized to Azure AD; can be used for authentication, a backup option for authentication, or Leaked Credential Detection

Feature	Description
Pass-through Authentication	An authentication method where passwords are validated on-premises through the Azure AD Connect service's connection to the Azure Service Bus
Unified Group Writeback	Enables cloud-based Microsoft 365 Groups to be written back to on-premises Active Directory

Table 3.2 – Azure AD Connect features

There are several additional features available post-installation for Azure AD Connect, such as managing **duplicate attribute resiliency** and **user principal name soft-matching**, both of which are used to manage how Azure AD handles conflicts and connect cloud accounts to on-premises accounts.

> **Further reading**
>
> More detailed information about the Azure AD Connect optional features, such as duplicate attribute resiliency, is available here: `https://learn.microsoft.com/en-us/azure/active-directory/hybrid/how-to-connect-syncservice-features`.

Understanding the prerequisites for Azure AD Connect

The Azure AD Connect synchronization has several prerequisites, including supported hardware and software, as well as permissions required for various synchronization options.

The Azure AD prerequisites can be broken down into seven sections:

- Azure AD
- On-premises Active Directory
- SQL Server
- Azure AD Connect server hardware requirements
- Azure AD Connect server software requirements
- Accounts and security
- Connectivity

Let's quickly review the requirements.

Azure AD

The first set of requirements surrounds your Azure AD environment:

- You must have an Azure AD tenant (any Azure AD or Microsoft 365 subscription is sufficient)
- You should have one or more verified domains in Azure AD

> **Note**
>
> The Microsoft Azure AD Connect documentation (`https://learn.microsoft.com/en-us/azure/active-directory/hybrid/how-to-connect-install-prerequisites`) lists a verified domain as a requirement, but functionally, you can install and configure Azure AD Connect synchronization without a verified domain. The user interface will display a warning, but you can proceed. Objects will receive a managed domain name (`onmicrosoft.com`) suffix when they are synchronized.

On-premises Active Directory

Before you install Azure AD Connect, you will also need to make sure that Active Directory meets certain requirements as well:

- You must have at least one on-premises Active Directory environment with Windows Server 2003 or later forest functional level and schema. The NetBIOS name of the forest or domain cannot have a period in it.
- The domain controller that Azure AD Connect uses must be writeable. **Read-only domain controllers (RODCs)** are not supported for use with Azure AD Connect. RODCs are permitted in the environment, but Azure AD Connect should be installed in an Active Directory site without RODCs.

SQL Server

In addition to the core prerequisites to install and configure Azure AD Connect, you should be aware of limitations regarding the size of the database.

By default, Azure AD Connect installs SQL Server 2019 Express for use with the Azure AD Connect database. Express editions of SQL are limited to a 10 GB database, which is sufficient for managing synchronization for approximately 100,000 objects. If the sum of objects in all of your connected directories is larger than 100,000 objects, you will need to configure Azure AD Connect during installation to connect to a full version of SQL Server.

> **Exam tip**
>
> SQL database server sizing and performance requirements are outside the scope of the MS-100 exam.

Azure AD Connect Server hardware components

Azure AD Connect's hardware requirements are largely dictated by the scale of the environment:

Number of Objects in Active Directory	CPU	Installed Memory	Available Hard Disk Space
Up to 50,000	1.6 GHz	6 GB	70 GB
50,000 – 100,000	1.6 GHz	16 GB	100 GB
100,000 – 300,000	1.6 GHz	32 GB	300 GB
300,000 – 600,000	1.6 GHz	32 GB	450 GB
Over 600,000	1.6 GHz	32 GB	500 GB

Table 3.3 – Azure AD Connect server hardware requirements

As previously mentioned, Azure AD Connect deployments that are used to synchronize more than 100,000 objects will require their own SQL Server. The memory and disk space requirements in *Table 3.3* are for Azure AD Connect only and do not reflect the additional SQL Server sizing requirements.

Azure AD Connect server software components

Azure AD Connect has requirements specific to the minimum operating system versions, as well as other software components:

- Currently, you can deploy to Windows Server 2016 or Windows Server 2019 (but not Server 2022 yet). You cannot deploy to Small Business Server or Windows Server Essentials editions before 2019.

- The PowerShell execution policy for the server should be set to RemoteSigned or Unrestricted.

  - You must not have PowerShell Transcription enabled through Group Policy if you plan on using Azure AD Connect to configure **Active Directory Federation Services** (**AD FS**).

> **Note**
>
> This is a change from the original product documentation. Previously, PowerShell Transcription would cause the installation to abort.

  - The server used for Azure AD Connect must have a full GUI installed. It doesn't support deployment to any edition of Windows Server Core.

  - Ensure you have PowerShell 5.0 or later as well as .NET Framework 4.5.1 or later installed.

  - Azure AD Connect checks for the **MachineAccessRestriction**, **MachineLaunchRestriction**, and **DefaultLaunchPermission** values in the **Distributed COM** (**DCOM**) configuration. If those values are missing or corrupt, the installation will fail.

While it is not required, Microsoft recommends forcing the use of TLS 1.2 for .NET Framework components. This can be configured by setting the `HKLM\SOFTWARE\Microsoft\.NETFramework\ v4.0.30319\SchUseStrongCrypto` registry value to `DWORD:00000001`.

AD FS

If you are using the Azure AD Connect installation wizard to configure AD FS, there are additional requirements that must be met:

- If you are using Azure AD Connect to configure AD FS, the federation and **web application proxy** (**WAP**) servers must already have TLS/SSL certificates installed and the servers must be accessible via WinRM.

- AD FS server hosts must be Windows Server 2012 R2 or later.

- The AD FS farm servers *must be* domain-joined. The AD FS web application proxy servers *must not be* domain-joined.

- AD FS also has specific name resolution requirements. The internal DNS domain must use A records for the federation server farm (external DNS can use A records or CNAME records).

> **Further information**
>
> While it is not covered by the MS-100 exam, per se, it's important to note that externally, DNS will point to the AD FS WAP servers using the name deployed on the SSL/TLS certificate (such as `sts.contoso.com` or `adfs.contoso.com`). However, the AD FS WAP servers need to resolve the AD FS farm name to the internal farm servers, not to themselves. This is frequently accomplished by configuring a host's file on the AD FS WAP servers.

Accounts and security

To successfully configure Azure AD Connect, you must have access to privileged accounts:

- You must have either an Azure AD Global Administrator or Hybrid Identity Administrator account to configure synchronization. These credentials are used to create a service account in Azure AD that's used to provision and synchronize objects.

- If you use the Express setup option or upgrade from the legacy DirSync product, the installation account must be a member of Enterprise Admins in the local Active Directory.

- If you are configuring Azure AD Connect with a service account, the account must have the following permissions delegated:

  - Write permissions to Active Directory (if any hybrid writeback features are enabled, such as Exchange hybrid writeback, password writeback, group writeback, or device writeback)

- If password hash synchronization is deployed, the service account must be delegated the special permissions called **Replicating Directory Changes** and **Replicating Directory Changes All** to read the password data from Active Directory

Connectivity

Azure AD Connect needs to be able to communicate with both on-premises directories as well as Azure AD:

- Azure AD Connect must be able to resolve DNS for both internet and intranet locations.
- Azure AD Connect must be able to communicate with the root domain of all configured forests.
- If your network requires a proxy to connect to the internet, you must update the .NET Framework's `machine.config` file with the appropriate proxy server address and port. If your proxy server requires authentication, you must use a custom installation and specify a domain-member service account.

If your environment meets the minimum requirements for deploying Azure AD Connect, you can download the components and begin the installation. You can download the most recent version of Azure AD Connect from `https://aka.ms/aadconnect`.

Choosing between Azure AD Connect and Azure AD Connect Cloud Sync

Azure AD Cloud Sync is the next evolution of the directory synchronization product. While it does not yet have full parity with Azure AD Connect features, Azure AD Connect Cloud Sync (sometimes referred to as **Cloud Sync**) can provide additional features and benefits that Azure AD Connect cannot:

- While Azure AD Connect requires on-premises connectivity between the Azure AD Connect server and all connected forests, Azure AD Connect Cloud Sync can import identities from forests that do not have site-to-site connectivity. This makes Cloud Sync advantageous when dealing with mergers and acquisitions as well as organizations that have multiple, disconnected business units.
- Lightweight on-premises provisioning agents with cloud-managed sync configuration. Multiple sync agents can be installed to provide fault tolerance and redundancy for password hash synchronization customers.

However, Cloud Sync provides fewer overall features. The following list identifies the core feature gaps:

- Cloud Sync does not support on-premises LDAP directories.
- Cloud Sync does not support device objects.
- Pass-through authentication is unavailable with Cloud Sync.

- Advanced filtering and scoping (such as by using object attributes) are not supported with Cloud Sync, nor are advanced configurations of custom synchronization rules.

- Azure AD Connect Cloud Sync does not support more than 150,000 objects per AD domain, nor does it support **Azure AD Domain Services (Azure AD DS)**. Since Cloud Sync is limited to 150,000 objects, it does not support large groups (up to 250,000 members).

- Cloud Sync does not support Exchange hybrid writeback or group writeback.

- Cloud Sync cannot merge object attributes from multiple source domains.

A full comparison of features is available at `https://learn.microsoft.com/en-us/azure/active-directory/cloud-sync/what-is-cloud-sync`. As you can see from the previous lists, Azure AD Connect Cloud Sync is potentially a good option for organizations that don't have more than 150,000 objects in any single domain, don't require object or property writeback, and don't need to heavily customize synchronization rules.

Planning user sign-in

The final step in planning your hybrid identity solution is around what type of sign-in experience you want to deploy for your users. As discussed briefly in the *Designing synchronization solutions* section, there are three core methods for managing user sign-in:

- Password hash synchronization
- Pass-through authentication
- Federation

While all three of these solutions utilize some sort of identity synchronization technology, knowing the features and capabilities of each will help you choose the option that's right for your organization.

Let's explore each of these options in a little more detail.

Password hash synchronization

Password hash synchronization (commonly referred to as **PHS**) is the Microsoft-recommended identity solution. In addition to synchronizing the core identity object data, PHS also synchronizes password hash values to the account objects in Azure AD. This ensures that users can use the same password to access local Active Directory resources, as well as Azure AD services.

> **Further reading**
>
> The security behind Azure AD Password Hash Synchronization is complex, involving multiple hashing algorithms. For a deeper understanding of how Password Hash Synchronization protects user data, see `https://learn.microsoft.com/en-us/azure/active-directory/hybrid/how-to-connect-password-hash-synchronization`.

When a user logs in to a tenant that has PHS configured, every part of the authentication takes place in Azure AD. This is advantageous because the organization has no reliance on the availability of any on-premises infrastructure for ongoing authentication. Once an identity and its password hash have been synchronized, the on-premises directory isn't needed until the on-premises object is updated again (such as an additional email address, a change in the display name, or a new password).

In addition, PHS enables an advanced Azure AD Premium P2 security feature: leaked credential detection. With this feature, Microsoft continuously checks various dark websites for organizational identity data that may have been compromised.

As mentioned in the *Accounts and security* section, password hash synchronization requires the service account to have the **Replicating Directory Changes** and **Replicating Directory Changes All** rights in the on-premises directory.

Password hash synchronization is a cloud authentication solution.

Pass-through authentication

Similar to password hash synchronization, **pass-through authentication** (**PTA**) relies on synchronizing objects to Azure AD. Unlike PHS, however, the actual password validation happens on-premises. PTA relies upon an agent installed on-premises, which periodically checks Azure for an authentication request.

When Azure AD Connect is configured with PTA, a secure channel is established between the **Azure Service Bus** and the lightweight PTA agent. For redundancy, you can deploy multiple PTA agents in your environment.

> **Note**
> From a networking perspective, Azure AD Connect's communication is outbound only to the Azure Service Bus. Unlike federation, PTA does not require inbound connectivity.

When a user requests access to an Azure AD resource, the logon request is stored on the Azure Service Bus. This request is encrypted with the public key of each of the PTA agents. The agents check the Service Bus for a request, bring the request back on-premises, decrypt it with the agent's private key, and then process the request against an on-premises domain controller. The result of the validation (either success or failure) is then sent back to the Azure Service Bus, where Azure AD retrieves the response and then either grants or denies the logon request.

PTA is a potential solution for organizations that want as much benefit from cloud authentication as possible but may have organizational requirements for on-premises credential validation or the enforcement of Active Directory logon hours.

Due to its on-premises password validation component, if none of the on-premises authentication agents can connect to both the Azure Service Bus and local Active Directory, users will be unable to log in.

Microsoft categorized PTA as a cloud authentication solution.

Federation

With federated identity solutions, Azure AD is configured to refer authentication requests to an on-premises service to validate login data. When a federated user attempts to log on to an Azure AD resource, Azure AD redirects the login session to an organization-managed web service. Users then enter their credentials in this organization-managed application, which, in turn, validates the logon details against the on-premises directory.

Some organizations may require federated identity due to specific regulations, the need to use smartcard-based login, or third-party multi-factor authentication products. Due to its on-premises password validation component, if on-premises services (such as federation farm servers, load balancers, web application proxy servers, or domain controllers) are unavailable, users will be unable to log in to Azure AD.

You can use the following flowchart to understand which solution is appropriate for you:

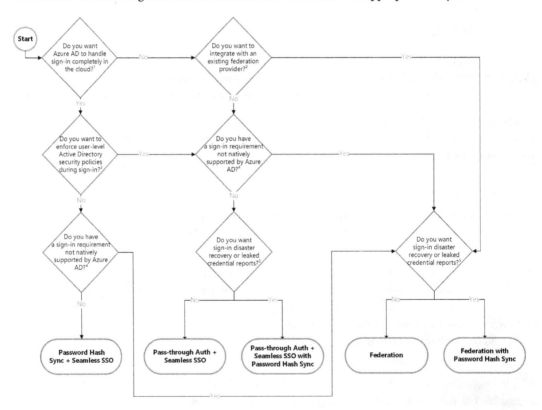

Figure 3.6 – Authentication selection decision flowchart

Once you have selected an identity and authentication mechanism for your tenant, you can begin preparing your environment for hybrid authentication. Regardless of the method selected for authenticating hybrid identity, Azure AD Connect can be used to configure it.

Summary

In this chapter, you learned how to plan for a hybrid identity deployment, including choosing an authentication method (such as password hash sync, pass-through authentication, or federation) and understanding the various requirements and capabilities of identity synchronization tools. You also learned the basic terminology associated with the Azure AD Connect synchronization engine.

In the next chapter, we will begin configuring Azure AD Connect.

Knowledge check

In this section, we'll test your knowledge of some key elements from this chapter.

Questions

Answer the following questions:

1. Which two authentication or sign-in methods validate user passwords on-premises?

    A. Password hash synchronization

    B. Pass-through authentication

    C. Federation

    D. Hybrid identity

2. Which two rights are necessary for password hash synchronization?

    A. Replicating Directory Changes

    B. Replicating Directory Changes Password

    C. Replicating Directory Changes All

    D. Replicating Directory Changes Advanced

3. Which feature, service, or component is a consolidated view of all objects from the connected systems?

    A. Connector space

    B. sourceAnchor

    C. Connected system

    D. Metaverse

4. You have 75,000 objects in your Active Directory environment and need to recommend a solution for Azure AD Connect. You should recommend the simplest option that supports your environment.

    A. An Azure AD Connect server with local SQL Server Express

    B. An Azure AD Connect server with local or remote SQL Server Analysis Services

    C. Azure AD Connect with database stored in a local or remote standalone SQL server

    D. Azure AD Connect configured with WID database

5. Azure AD Connect setup can configure which two federation services?

    A. Azure Active Directory Federation Services

    B. Active Directory Federation Services

    C. OKTA Federation Services

    D. PingFederate

Answers

The following are the answers to this chapter's questions:

1. B: Pass-through authentication; C: Federation

2. A: Replicating Directory Changes; C: Replicating Directory Changes All

3. D: Metaverse

4. A: Azure AD Connect with local SQL Server Express

5. B: Active Directory Federation Services; D: PingFederate

4

Implementing and Managing Identity Synchronization with Azure AD

In *Chapter 3*, you learned about the foundational hybrid identity concepts. As we move forward with this chapter, we'll move from concept to implementation.

In this chapter, we're going to step through basic configuration and troubleshooting tasks for Azure AD Connect and Azure AD Connect cloud sync.

This chapter covers the following exam objectives:

- Preparing for identity synchronization by using IdFix
- Configuring and managing directory synchronization by using Azure AD Connect cloud sync
- Configuring and managing directory synchronization by using Azure AD Connect
- Configuring Azure AD Connect object filters
- Monitoring synchronization by using Azure AD Connect Health
- Troubleshooting Azure AD Connect synchronization

The topics in this chapter will help you understand, step by step, what it takes to deploy and manage directory synchronization.

Preparing for identity synchronization by using IdFix

IdFix is Microsoft's tool for detecting common issues with on-premises AD identity data. While it doesn't fix all errors, it is able to identify and remediate data formatting errors so that objects have valid data to synchronize.

IdFix supports the following features:

- Transaction rollback
- Verbose logging
- Exporting data to the CSV and LDF formats for offline review and editing

To get started with the tool, follow these steps:

1. Navigate to `https://aka.ms/idfix`.
2. Scroll to the bottom of the page and click **Next**.
3. Review the prerequisites for the tool. Scroll to the bottom of the page and click **Next**.
4. Click **setup.exe** to download the file and start the installation.
5. After the installation wizard starts, click **Install**.
6. Acknowledge the IdFix privacy statement by clicking **OK**.
7. IdFix, by default, targets the entire directory. You can select **Settings** (the gear icon) to change the options for IdFix. You can edit the filter to scope to certain object types. You can also select the search base to specify a starting point for IdFix to begin its query. After modifying any settings, click **OK**.

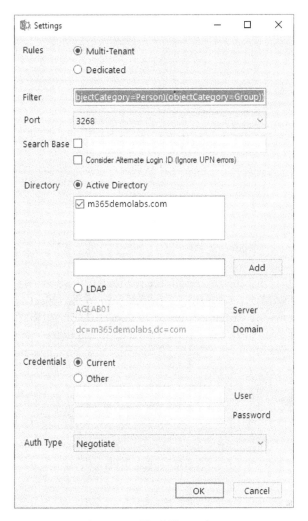

Figure 4.1 – The IdFix settings

8.   Click **Query** to connect to AD and begin the analysis.

Schema warning

If you receive a schema warning, such as the one in *Figure 4.2*, you can click **Yes** to proceed or click **No** to return to the IdFix tool. The schema warning is generally presented when attributes are present in the AD schema but have not been marked for replication (usually because Exchange Server has not been installed or replication hasn't completed successfully in your organization for an extended period of time). If you receive this error, you should check to ensure that you have at least run the Exchange Server setup with the /PrepareSchema and /PrepareAD switches and have validated that AD replication is working correctly.

Figure 4.2 – The IdFix schema warning

After IdFix has analyzed the environment, results are returned to the data grid, shown in *Figure 4.3*. The **DISTINGUISHEDNAME** column shows the full path to the object in question, while the **ATTRIBUTE** column shows the attribute or property impacted. The **ERROR** column shows what type of error was encountered (such as an invalid character or duplicate object value). The **VALUE** column shows the existing value and the **UPDATE** column shows any suggested value.

DISTINGUISHEDNAM	COMMONNAME	OBJECTCLASS	ATTRIBUTE	ERROR	VALUE	UPDATE	ACTION	
CN=E'Lane A Eman...	E'Lane A Emanuel	user	userPrincipalName	Character	E'Lane.A.Emanuel...	ELane.A.Emanuel@...	EDIT	∨
CN=E'Lane C Baer,...	E'Lane C Baer	user	userPrincipalName	Character	E'Lane.C.Baer@m3...	ELane.C.Baer@m36...		∨
CN=E'Lane H Lovell,...	E'Lane H Lovell	user	userPrincipalName	Character	E'Lane.H.Lovell@m...	ELane.H.Lovell@m3...		∨
CN=E'Lane J Monte...	E'Lane J Montemayor	user	userPrincipalName	Character	E'Lane.J.Montemay...	ELane.J.Montemayo...		∨
CN=E'Lane K Harmo...	E'Lane K Harmon	user	userPrincipalName	Character	E'Lane.K.Harmon@...	ELane.K.Harmon@...		∨
CN=E'Lane M Holida...	E'Lane M Holiday	user	userPrincipalName	Character	E'Lane.M.Holiday@...	ELane.M.Holiday@...		∨
CN=E'Lane P Beaty,...	E'Lane P Beaty	user	userPrincipalName	Character	E'Lane.P.Beaty@m3...	ELane.P.Beaty@m3...		∨
CN=E'Lane T Cutler,...	E'Lane T Cutler	user	userPrincipalName	Character	E'Lane.T.Cutler@m...	ELane.T.Cutler@m3...		∨
CN=E'Lane T Franci...	E'Lane T Francis	user	userPrincipalName	Character	E'Lane.T.Francis@...	ELane.T.Francis@m...		∨
CN=E'Lane V Popp,...	E'Lane V Popp	user	userPrincipalName	Character	E'Lane.V.Popp@m3...	ELane.V.Popp@m3...		∨
CN=Engineering Eng...	Engineering Enginee...	group	sAMAccountName	Duplicate	Engineering Engine...	Engineering Enginee...		∨
CN=Engineering Eng...	Engineering Enginee...	group	sAMAccountName	Duplicate	Engineering Engine...	Engineering Enginee...		∨
CN=Engineering Eng...	Engineering Enginee...	group	sAMAccountName	Duplicate	Engineering Engine...	Engineering Enginee...		∨
CN=Engineering Eng...	Engineering Enginee...	group	sAMAccountName	Duplicate	Engineering Engine...	Engineering Enginee...		∨
CN=Engineering Eng...	Engineering Engineer	group	sAMAccountName	Duplicate	Engineering Engineer	Engineering Engineer		∨
CN=Engineering Eng...	Engineering Engineer	group	sAMAccountName	Duplicate	Engineering Engineer	Engineering Engineer		∨
CN=Engineering Ma...	Engineering Manage...	group	sAMAccountName	Duplicate	Engineering Manag...	Engineering Manage...		∨
CN=Engineering Ma...	Engineering Manage...	group	sAMAccountName	Duplicate	Engineering Manag...	Engineering Manage...		∨
CN=Engineering Ma...	Engineering Manager	group	sAMAccountName	Duplicate	Engineering Manager	Engineering Manager		∨
CN=Engineering Ma...	Engineering Manager	group	sAMAccountName	Duplicate	Engineering Manager	Engineering Manager		∨
CN=Engineering Res...	Engineering Resear...	group	sAMAccountName	Duplicate	Engineering Resear...	Engineering Researc...		∨

Total Error Count: 250

Figure 4.3 – The IdFix data grid

After you have investigated an object, you can choose to accept the suggested value in the **UPDATE** column (if one exists). You can also choose to either enter or edit a new value in the **UPDATE** column.

Once you're done investigating or updating an object, you can use the dropdown in the **ACTION** column to mark an object:

- Selecting **EDIT** indicates that you want to configure the object attribute with the value in the **UPDATE** column

- Selecting **COMPLETE** indicates that you want to leave the object as is

- Selecting **REMOVE** instructs IdFix to clear the offending attribute

In addition, you can select **Accept** to accept any suggested values in the **UPDATE** column. Choosing this option will configure all objects with a value in the **UPDATE** column to **EDIT**, indicating that the changes are ready to be processed.

Once you have configured an action for each object, select **Apply** to instruct IdFix to make the changes.

1. IdFix will process the changes. Transactions are written to a log that can be imported and used to roll back any mistakes.

2. Once you have ensured that your on-premises directory data is ready to synchronize to Azure AD, you can deploy and configure one of the Azure AD Connect synchronization products.

Configuring and managing directory synchronization by using Azure AD Connect

Azure AD Connect has a long history, originally starting as DirSync to support the deployment of Microsoft **Business Productivity Online Suite (BPOS)** in 2007.

If you are familiar with **Microsoft Identity Manager (MIM)**, you'll notice a lot of similarities between that and the current Azure AD Connect platform. As you learned in *Chapter 3*, Azure AD Connect allows you to connect to multiple directory sources and provision those objects to Azure AD.

Installing the synchronization service

The first step to deploying Azure AD Connect is gathering the requirements of your environment, as outlined in *Chapter 3*. These requirements can impact the prerequisites for deployment (such as additional memory or a standalone SQL Server environment). As part of the planning process, you'll also want to identify which sign-in method will be employed (password hash synchronization, pass-through authentication, or federation).

Exam tip

To perform the express installation, you'll need an Enterprise Administrator credential to the on-premises Active Directory forest so that the installer can create a service account and delegate the correct permissions. By default, the on-premises service account is created in the CN=Users container and named MSOL_<string>.

You'll also need an account that has either the Global Administrator or Hybrid Identity Administrator role in Azure AD, which Azure AD Connect will use to create a cloud synchronization service account. By default, the cloud service account is named Sync_<AADConnectServerName>.

With that information in hand, it's time to start deploying Azure AD Connect:

1. On the server where Azure AD Connect will be deployed, download the latest version of the Azure AD Connect setup files (https://aka.ms/aad-connect) and launch the installer.

2. Agree to the installation terms and select **Continue**.

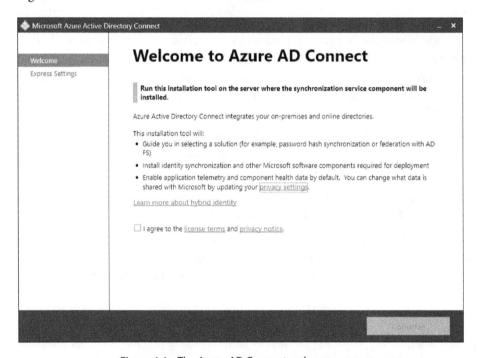

Figure 4.4 – The Azure AD Connect welcome page

3. Review the **Express Settings** page. You can choose **Customize** if you want to configure Azure AD Connect to use the pass-through or federated authentication methods, group-based filtering, or a custom SQL Server installation. *While the sign-in methods and other features can be changed after installation, it is not possible to enable group-based filtering or change the SQL Server location after setup.*

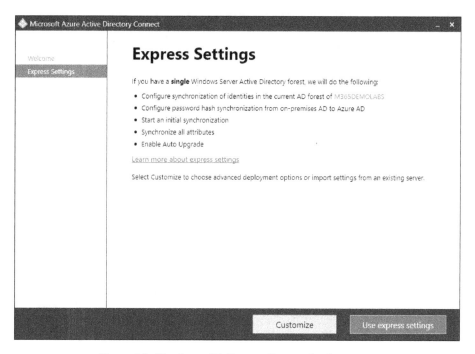

Figure 4.5 – The Azure AD Connect Express Settings page

Installation notes

If you have other domains in your AD forest, they must all be reachable from the Azure AD Connect server or installation will fail. You can perform a custom installation to specify which domains to include in synchronization.

4. On the **Connect to Azure AD** page, enter a credential that has either the Global Administrator or Hybrid Identity Administrator role in Azure AD. Click **Next**.

5. On the **Connect to AD DS** page, enter an Enterprise Administrator credential and click **Next**.

6. Verify the configuration settings. By default, the Exchange hybrid scenario is not enabled. If you have an on-premises Exchange environment that you will migrate to Microsoft 365, select the **Exchange hybrid deployment** option to include the Exchange-specific attributes. If you want to perform additional configuration tasks before synchronizing users, clear the **Start the synchronization process when configuration completes.** checkbox.

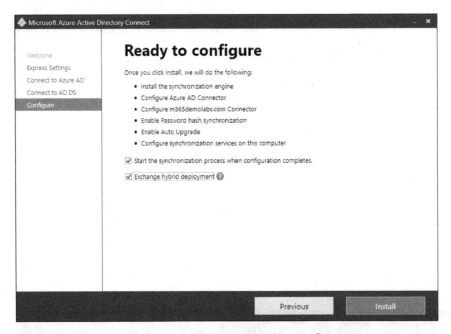

Figure 4.6 – The Azure AD Connect Ready to configure page

7. Click **Install**.

8. Review the **Configuration complete** page and click **Exit**.

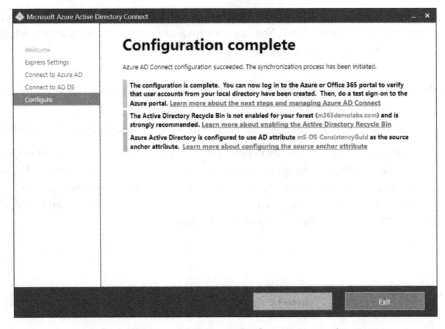

Figure 4.7 – The Azure AD Connect Configuration complete page

If you selected the **Start the synchronization process when configuration completes.** checkbox, you can review the Azure AD portal to verify that users have been synchronized.

Configuring Azure AD Connect filters

If you need to exclude objects from Azure AD Connect's synchronization scope, you can do so through a number of different methods:

- Domain and organizational unit-based filtering
- Group-based filtering
- Attribute-based filtering

Let's quickly examine these.

Domain and organizational unit-based filtering

With this method, you can deselect large portions of your directory by modifying the list of domains or organizational units that are selected for synchronization. While there are several ways to do this, the easiest way is through the Azure AD Connect setup and configuration tool:

1. To launch the Azure AD Connect configuration tool, double-click the **Azure AD Connect** icon on the desktop of the server where Azure AD Connect is installed. After it launches, click **Configure**.

2. On the **Additional tasks** page, select **Customize synchronization options** and then click **Next**.

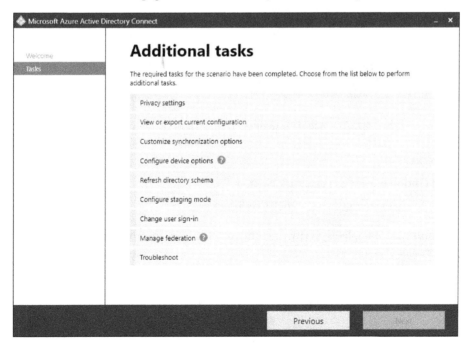

Figure 4.8 – The Additional tasks page

3. On the **Connect to Azure AD** page, enter a credential with either the Global Administrator or Hybrid Identity Administrator role and click **Next**.

4. On the **Connect your directories** page, click **Next**.

5. On the **Domain and OU filtering** page, select the **Sync selected domains and OUs** radio button, and then select or clear objects to include or exclude from synchronization.

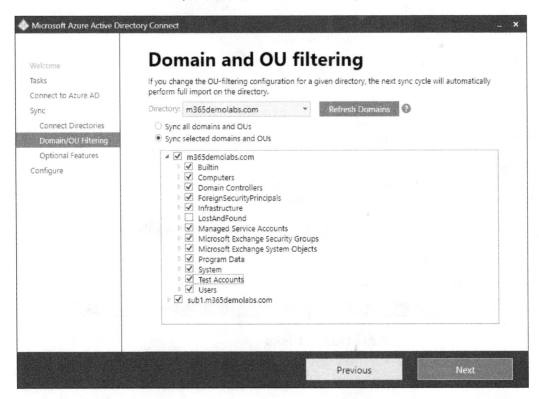

Figure 4.9 – The Azure AD Connect Domain and OU filtering page

6. Click **Next**.

7. On the **Optional features** page, click **Next**.

8. On the **Ready to configure** page, click **Configure**.

After synchronization completes, verify that only objects from in-scope organizational units or domains are present in Azure AD.

Group-based filtering

Azure AD Connect only supports the configuration of group-based filtering if you choose to customize the Azure AD Connect setup. It is not available if you perform an express installation.

That being said, if you've chosen a custom installation, you can choose to limit the synchronization scope to a single group. On the **Filter users and devices** page of the configuration wizard, select the **Synchronize selected** radio button and then enter the name or **distinguished name** (**DN**) of a group that contains the users and devices to be synchronized.

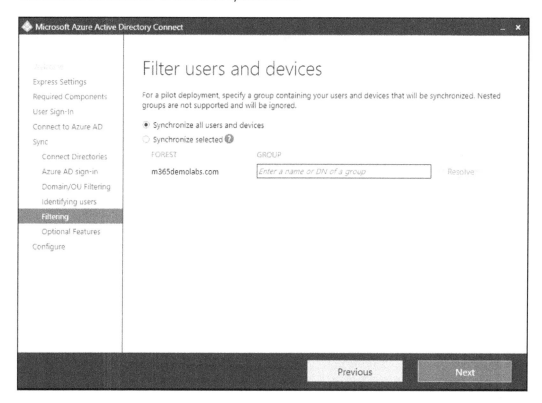

Figure 4.10 – The Filter users and devices page

With group-based filtering, only direct members of the group are synchronized. Users, groups, contacts, or devices nested inside other groups are not resolved or synchronized.

Microsoft recommends group-based filtering for piloting purposes only.

Attribute-based filtering

Another way to filter objects to Azure AD is through the use of an attribute filter. This advanced method requires creating a custom synchronization rule in the Azure AD Connect Synchronization Rules Editor.

To create an attribute-based filtering rule, select an attribute that isn't currently being used by your organization for another purpose. You can use this attribute as a scoping filter to exclude objects.

The following procedure can be used to create a simple filtering rule:

1. On the server running Azure AD Connect, launch the Synchronization Rules Editor.

2. Under **Direction**, select **Inbound**, and then click **Add new rule**.

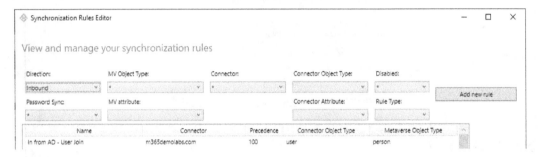

Figure 4.11 – Synchronization Rules Editor

3. Provide a name and a description for the rule.

4. Under **Connected System**, select the object that represents your on-premises Active Directory forest.

5. Under **Connected System Object Type**, select **user**.

6. Under **Metaverse Object Type**, select **person**.

7. Under **Link Type**, select **Join**.

8. In the **Precedence** text field, enter an unused number (such as 50). Click **Next**.

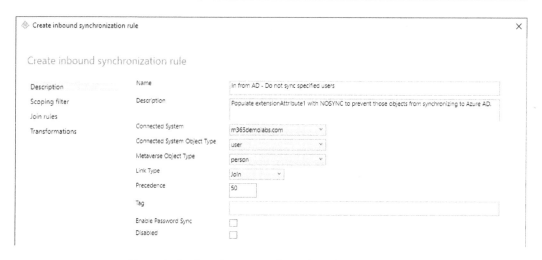

Figure 4.12 – Creating a new inbound synchronization rule

9.   On the **Scoping filter** page, click **Add group** and then click **Add clause**.

10. Under **Attribute**, select **extensionAttribute1** (or whichever unused attribute you have selected).

11. Under **Operator**, select **EQUAL**.

12. In the **Value** text field, enter NOSYNC and then click **Next**.

Figure 4.13 – Configuring a scoping filter for extensionAttribute1

13. On the **Join rules** page, click **Next** without adding any parameters.

14. On the **Transformations** page, click **Add transformation**.

15. Under **FlowType**, select **Constant**.

16. Under **Target Attribute**, select **cloudFiltered**.

17. In the **Source** text field, enter the value `True`. Click **Add transformation**.

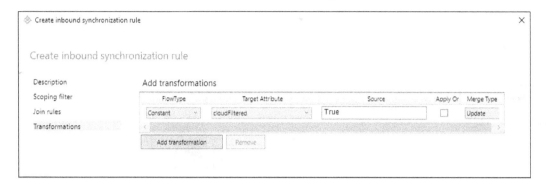

Figure 4.14 – Adding a transformation for the cloudFiltered attribute

18. Acknowledge the warning that a full import will be required by clicking **OK**.

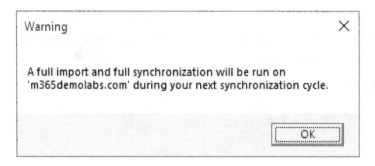

Figure 4.15 – The warning for full import and synchronization

After modifying a synchronization rule, a full import and full synchronization is required. You don't have to perform any special steps, however; Azure AD Connect is aware of the update and will automatically perform the necessary full imports and synchronizations.

Monitoring synchronization by using Azure AD Connect Health

Azure AD Connect Health is a premium feature of the Azure AD license. Azure AD Connect Health has separate agent features for Azure AD Connect, Azure AD Health for Directory Services, and Azure AD Health for **Active Directory Federation Services (AD FS)**.

Azure AD Connect Health

You can see the Azure AD Connect Health portal at `https://aka.ms/aadconnecthealth`. From there, you will be able to view basic details about your environment as well as obtain agent installation packages. See *Figure 4.16*.

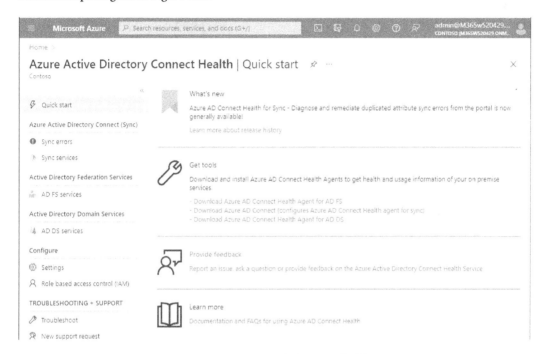

Figure 4.16 – Azure AD Connect Health

While the Azure AD Connect Health agent for sync is included in the Azure AD Connect installation, the health agents for DS and AD FS are separate installations and must be downloaded separately:

- Azure AD Connect Health Agent for DS: `https://go.microsoft.com/fwlink/?LinkID=820540`

- Azure AD Connect Health Agent for AD FS: `https://go.microsoft.com/fwlink/?LinkID=518973`

If you do not have AD FS deployed in your environment, you do not need to deploy the AD FS agents.

Azure AD Connect Health for sync

The core health product, Azure AD Connect Health for sync, shows the current health of your synchronization environment, including object synchronization problems and data-related errors.

You can view the health status and identified errors by selecting **Sync errors** under **Azure Active Directory Connect (Sync)** on the Azure AD Connect Health portal (`https://aka.ms/aadconnecthealth`).

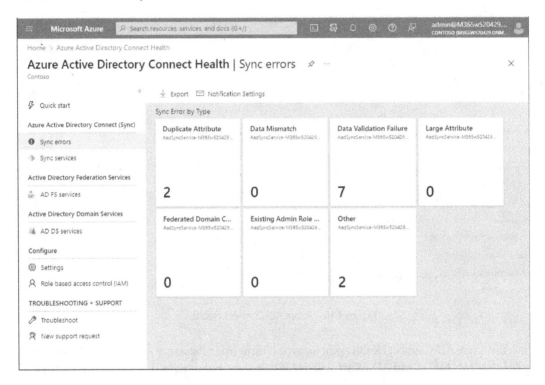

Figure 4.17 – Azure AD Connect Health sync errors

Selecting an error type will allow you to drill down into individual errors. In the example in *Figure 4.18*, Azure AD Connect Health has detected two objects with the same address:

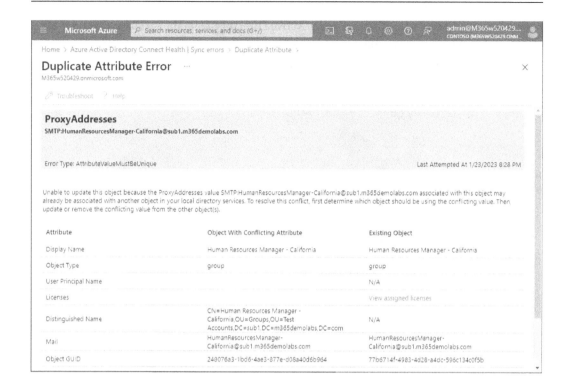

Figure 4.18 – Azure AD Connect Health error details

You can use this information to identify and troubleshoot on-premises objects.

Azure AD Connect Health for Directory Services

Microsoft recommends deploying Azure AD Connect Health for Directory Services agents on all domain controllers you want to monitor, or at least one for each domain.

The Azure AD Connect Health agent deployment is relatively straightforward, asking only for a credential to complete the installation. Once the installation has completed, you can review details about your domain controller health in the Azure AD Connect Health portal at https://aka. ms/aadconnecthealth.

On the Azure AD Connect Health page, under **Active Directory Domain Services**, select **AD DS services**, as shown in *Figure 4.19*, and then select a domain to view the details.

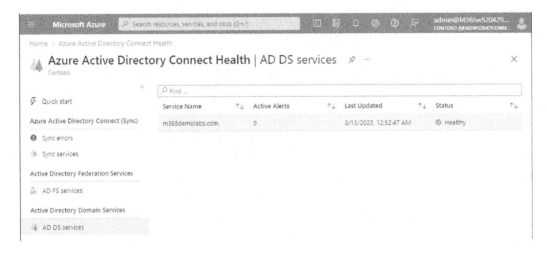

Figure 4.19 – Azure AD Connect Health AD DS services

The health services agents display a variety of details about the environment, including replication errors, LDAP bind operations, NTLM authentication operations, and Kerberos authentication operations.

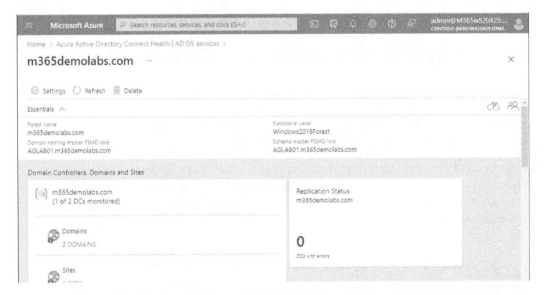

Figure 4.20 – The Azure AD Connect Health for AD Directory Services details page

Errors that are detected here should be resolved in your on-premises Active Directory environment.

Azure AD Connect Health for AD FS

In addition to gathering and reporting information for your on-premises Active Directory and synchronization services, Azure AD Connect Health also supports AD FS.

To get the most out of Azure AD Connect Health for AD FS, you'll need to enable auditing, which involves three steps:

1. Ensure that the AD FS farm service account has been granted the **Generate security audits** right in the security policy (**Local Policies | User Rights Assignment | Generate security audits**).

2. From an elevated command prompt, run the following command: `auditpol.exe /set / subcategory:{0CCE9222-69AE-11D9-BED3-505054503030} /failure:enable /success:enable`.

3. On the AD FS primary farm server, open an elevated PowerShell prompt and run the following command: `Set-AdfsProperties -AuditLevel Verbose`.

Then, you can deploy the agents to your servers.

After deploying the agents to your federation and proxy servers, you will see information reported in the Azure AD Connect Health portal under **Active Directory Federation Services**, as shown in *Figure 4.21*:

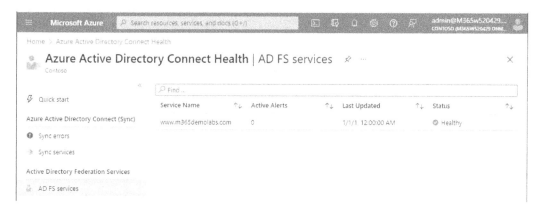

Figure 4.21 – Azure AD Connect Health for AD FS

In addition to diagnostic information, the health services for AD FS can also provide usage analytics and performance monitoring, as well as failed logins and information regarding risky sign-ins.

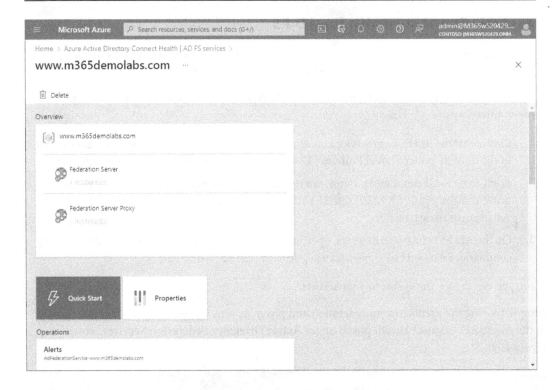

Figure 4.22 – Azure AD Connect Health for AD FS

Azure AD Connect Health is a valuable premium service that can help keep you on top of the health and performance aspects of your hybrid identity deployment.

Troubleshooting Azure AD Connect synchronization

While things normally operate smoothly, there may be times when objects become misconfigured or services go offline unexpectedly. You can troubleshoot common issues with Azure AD Connect's built-in troubleshooting tools.

To launch the troubleshooting tool, follow these steps:

1. Launch the Azure AD Connect configuration tool on the desktop of the server where Azure AD Connect is installed.

2. Click **Configure**.

3. On the **Additional tasks** page, select **Troubleshoot** and then click **Next**.

4. On the **Welcome to AADConnect Troubleshooting** page, select **Launch**.

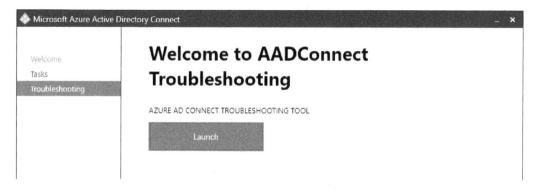

Figure 4.23 – Launching the AADConnect Troubleshooting tool

5. Select the appropriate troubleshooting options from the menu shown in *Figure 4.24*:

Figure 4.24 – The AADConnect Troubleshooting menu

The AADConnect Troubleshooting tool provides several specific troubleshooters, such as diagnosing attribute or group membership synchronization, password hash synchronization, as well as service account permissions.

Most object or attribute troubleshooting routines will require the object's DN to continue.

> **Further reading**
>
> For more information on the tests that can be performed by the AADConnect Troubleshooting tool, see https://learn.microsoft.com/en-us/azure/active-directory/hybrid/tshoot-connect-objectsync.

Configuring and managing directory synchronization by using Azure AD Connect cloud sync

Azure AD Connect cloud sync is a new synchronization platform that allows you to manage directory synchronization from the Azure portal. Depending on your organization's goals and environments, Azure AD Connect cloud sync can be a lightweight, flexible option that allows you to begin directory synchronization quickly.

Exam tip

To perform the installation, you'll need either a Domain Administrator or Enterprise Administrator credential to the on-premises Active Directory forest so that the installer can create the **group Managed Service Account (gMSA)**. You'll also need an account that has either the Global Administrator or Hybrid Identity Administrator role in Azure AD.

Microsoft recommends configuring a unique identity in Azure AD with the Hybrid Identity Administrator role for Azure AD Connect cloud sync.

Installing the provisioning agent

To begin installing Azure AD Connect cloud sync, follow these steps:

1. Log on to a server where you wish to install the Azure AD Connect cloud sync provisioning agent.

2. Navigate to the Azure portal (`https://portal.azure.com`) and select **Active Directory | Azure AD Connect**.

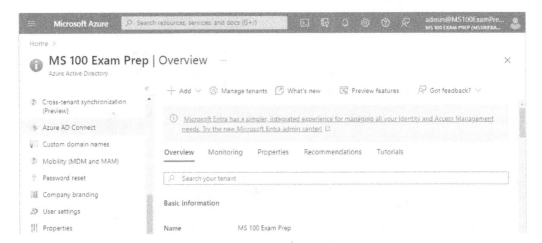

Figure 4.25 – Azure AD Connect in the Azure portal

3. From the navigation menu, select **Cloud sync**.

4. Under **Monitor**, select **Agents**.

5. Select **Download on-premises agent**.

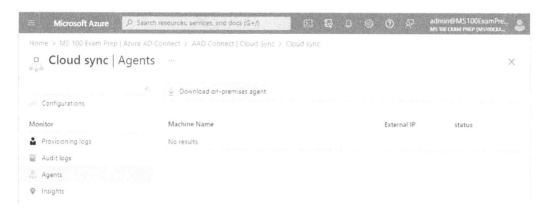

Figure 4.26 – Download on-premises agent for Azure AD Connect cloud sync

6. On the **Azure AD Provisioning Agent** flyout, select **Accept terms & download** to begin the download.

7. Open the AADConnectProvisioningAgentSetup.exe file to begin the installation.

8. Agree to the licensing terms and click **Install** to deploy the Microsoft Azure AD Connect provisioning package.

9. After the software installation is complete, the configuration wizard will launch. Click **Next** on the splash page to begin the configuration.

10. On the **Select Extension** page, choose the **HR-driven provisioning (Workday and SuccessFactors) / Azure AD Connect Cloud Sync** radio button and click **Next**.

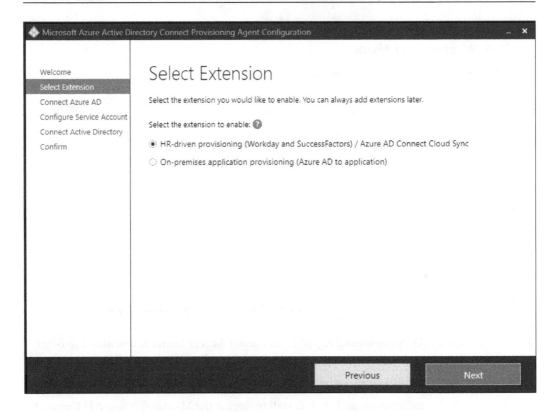

Figure 4.27 – The Azure AD Connect cloud sync Select Extension page

11. On the **Connect Azure AD** page, click **Authenticate** to sign in to Azure AD.

12. On the **Configure Service Account** page, select the **Create gMSA** radio button to instruct the setup process to provision a new gMSA in the format of DOMAIN\provAgentgMSA. Enter either a Domain Administrator or Enterprise Administrator credential and click **Next**.

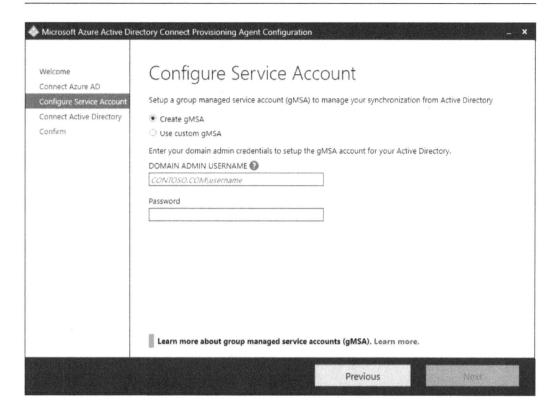

Figure 4.28 – Configuring an Azure AD Connect cloud sync service account

Creating a custom gMSA

You can also create a gMSA if desired. The custom service account will need to be delegated permissions to read all properties on all `User`, `inetOrgPerson`, `computer`, `device`, `Group`, `foreignSecurityPrincipal`, and `Contact` objects, as well as being able to create and delete user objects. For more information, see `https://learn.microsoft.com/en-us/azure/active-directory/cloud-sync/how-to-prerequisites?tabs=public-cloud#custom-gmsa-account`.

13. On the **Connect Active Directory** page, click **Add Directory** and provide the domain credentials to add the directory to the configuration. When finished, click **Next**.

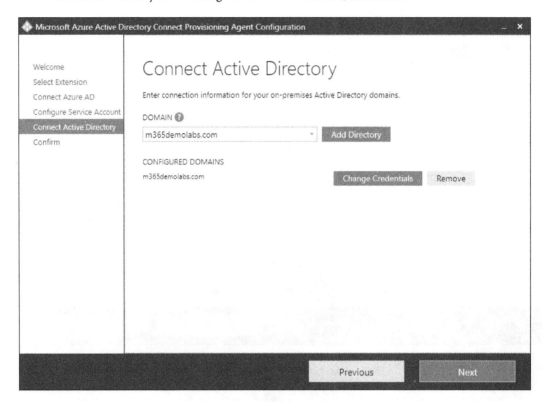

Figure 4.29 – Adding a directory to Azure AD Connect cloud sync

14. Review the details on the **Agent configuration** page and click **Confirm** to deploy the provisioning agent. When finished, click **Exit**.

After the agent has been deployed, you will need to continue in the Azure AD portal.

Configuring the provisioning service

In order to complete the Azure AD Connect cloud sync deployment, you'll need to set up a new configuration in the Azure portal:

1. Navigate to the Azure portal (https://portal.azure.com) and select **Active Directory | Azure AD Connect**.

2. Select **Cloud sync** from the navigation menu and then, on the **Configurations** tab, select **New configuration**.

3. On the **New cloud sync configuration** page, select which domains you would like to synchronize to Azure AD. If desired, select the **Enable password hash sync** checkbox. The password hash sync checkbox on this page only enables the feature; it does not configure password hash sync as a sign-in method (see *Figure 4.30*).

Exam tip

Azure AD Connect cloud sync does not support using password hash sync for `InetOrgPerson` objects.

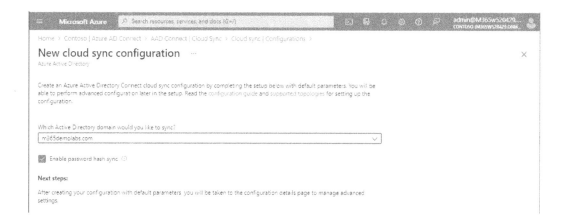

Figure 4.30 – Creating a new Azure AD Connect cloud sync configuration

4. Scroll to the bottom of the page and click **Create** to complete the basic configuration.

The Azure AD Connect cloud sync configuration has been completed, but it is not yet enabled and ready to start provisioning users. In the next series of steps, you can customize the service before fully enabling it.

Customizing the provisioning service

Like the on-premises Azure AD Connect service, Azure AD Connect cloud sync features the ability to perform scoping (including or excluding objects from synchronization) as well as attribute mapping.

After creating a new configuration, you should be redirected to the properties of the configuration, as shown in *Figure 4.31*:

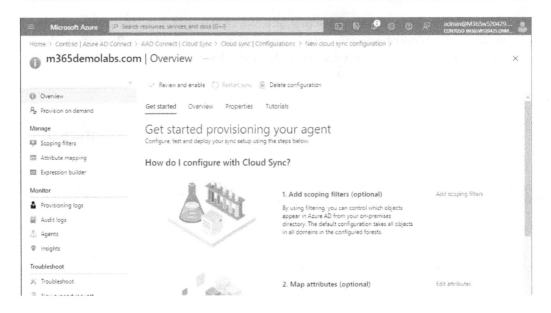

Figure 4.31 – The provisioning agent overview page

From this page, you can set up the scoping filters and attribute mappings to customize your environment. By default, Azure AD Connect cloud sync will include all objects in the connected forest and domains for synchronization.

Scoping filters

By selecting **Scoping filters** under **Manage**, you can configure what objects should be included for synchronization to Azure AD. You can specify a list of security groups or select organizational units, but not both (see *Figure 4.32*).

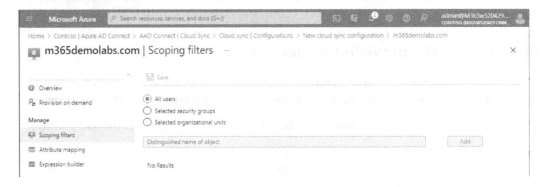

Figure 4.32 – Azure AD Connect cloud sync scoping filters

There are a few important caveats when using scoping filters with Azure AD Connect cloud sync:

- When using group-based scoping, nested objects beyond the first level will not be included in scope
- You can only include 59 separate OUs or security groups as scoping filters

It's also important to note that using security groups to perform scoping is only recommended for piloting scenarios.

Attribute mapping

Another customization option available involves mapping attribute values between on-premises and cloud objects. As with Azure AD Connect, you can configure how cloud attributes are populated – whether it's from a source attribute, a constant value, or some sort of expression.

Azure AD Connect cloud sync comes with a default attribute mapping flow, as shown in *Figure 4.33*:

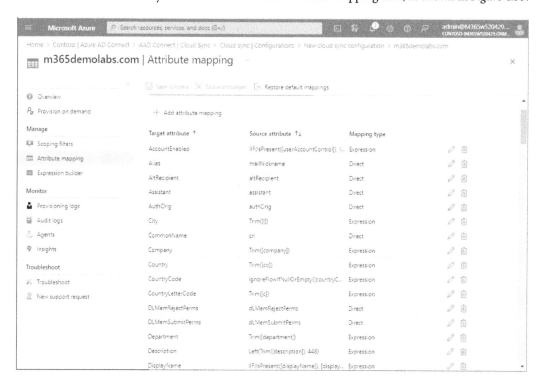

Figure 4.33 – Azure AD Connect cloud sync attribute mappings

You can select an existing attribute to modify or create a new attribute flow. One of the basic configuration features for many attributes is to configure a default value (if the on-premises value is blank), allowing you to make certain that cloud attributes are populated with values.

In *Figure 4.34*, the **Country** attribute has been selected and updated with the default value, US. This ensures that if a user's on-premises **Country** attribute is blank, the corresponding cloud attribute will be populated with a valid entry.

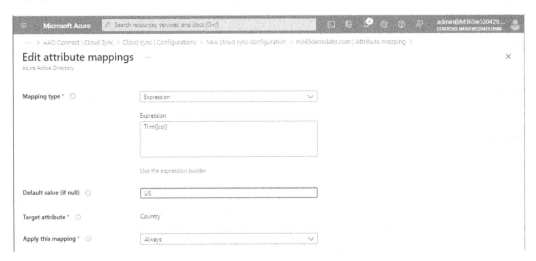

Figure 4.34 – Edit attribute mappings in Azure AD Connect cloud sync

Azure AD Connect cloud sync also features an expression builder, allowing you to create your own custom attribute flows.

Unlike Azure AD Connect, however, attribute mappings and expressions cannot be used to merge attributes from different domains or forests, nor does Azure AD Connect cloud sync support synchronization rules or attribute flow precedence. If you require that level of customization, you should deploy Azure AD Connect instead.

Once you have finished customizing the scoping filters and attribute flows, you can return to the **Overview** page and enable synchronization by selecting **Review and enable**.

Summary

In this chapter, you built on the skills from *Chapter 3* and learned how to deploy identity synchronization and authentication solutions. You learned how to configure filtering for both Azure AD Connect and Azure AD Connect cloud sync, as well as deploy and manage the health agents for diagnostics and troubleshooting.

In the next chapter, we'll learn how to manage identities, groups, and licensing.

Knowledge check

In this section, we'll test your knowledge of some key elements from this chapter.

Questions

1. When installing Azure AD Connect cloud sync, which two roles, rights, or permissions are necessary for the on-premises Active Directory environment? Each answer represents a complete solution.

    A. Hybrid Identity Administrator

    B. Server Administrator

    C. Domain Administrator

    D. Enterprise Administrator

2. Azure AD Connect cloud sync supports group-based scoping filters.

    A. True

    B. False

3. You are trying to install the agent for Azure Active Directory Health for sync. Where is it located?

    A. In the Azure AD Health portal

    B. In the Azure AD Connect installation package

    C. In the Microsoft Download Center

    D. In the Microsoft 365 admin center

4. You have determined that you need to run the Azure AD Connect troubleshooting tool. Where do you launch it?

    A. In the Azure portal

    B. In the Azure AD Connect Health portal

    C. In the Azure AD Connect configuration wizard

    D. In the Azure AD Connect synchronization service

5. You have deployed Azure AD Connect and want to prevent it from synchronizing an organizational unit with test objects. Where can you do this easily?

    A. The Azure AD portal

    B. The Microsoft 365 admin center

    C. The Azure AD Synchronization Rules Editor

    D. The Azure AD Connect configuration wizard

Answers

1. C: Domain Administrator and D: Enterprise Administrator

2. A: True

3. B: In the Azure AD Connect installation package

4. C: The Azure AD Connect configuration wizard

5. D: The Azure AD Connect configuration wizard

Planning and Managing Azure AD Identities

As you've seen throughout this book, identity is the foundation of Azure AD. Without it, people wouldn't be able to access services. Azure AD identity covers a broad range of objects, including cloud-only accounts, synchronized accounts, and external accounts (as well as groups, devices, and contacts).

Each of these types of objects has a purpose, and one is generally more suited to a business case than another.

In this chapter, we're going to look at the following topics, as they relate to the *MS-100* exam objectives:

- Creating and managing users
- Creating and managing guest users
- Creating and managing groups
- Managing and monitoring Microsoft 365 license allocations
- Performing bulk user management

By the end of this chapter, you should be comfortable articulating the differences between the different kinds of objects and familiar with methods for provisioning and managing them.

Let's get started!

Creating and managing users

Creating and managing users is central to administrating an information system—whether that system is an application on a small network, an enterprise-scale directory, or a cloud service hosted by a SaaS provider. In any instance, identities are used by people, applications, and devices to authenticate and perform activities.

In the context of Azure AD, there are three core types of identity:

- Cloud-based users

- Synchronized users

- Guest users

When planning out identity scenarios, it's important to understand the benefits, features, drawbacks, or capabilities associated with each type of identity and authentication scheme—including ease of provisioning, integration with existing directory or security products, requirements for on-premises infrastructure, and network availability.

In this section, we'll learn about managing each of these kinds of users.

Creating and managing cloud users

From an Azure AD perspective, cloud users are the easiest type of object to understand and manage. When you create an Azure AD or Microsoft 365 tenant, one of the first things you set up is your administrator user identity (in the form of user@tenant.onmicrosoft.com). This identity is stored in the Azure AD directory partition for your Microsoft 365 tenant. When we talk about Azure AD cloud users, we're talking about users whose primary source of identity is in Azure AD.

> **Exam tip**
>
> Cloud users can be assigned to any domain that is verified in the Microsoft 365 tenant with a single caveat—the domain must be in **managed** mode. If a domain has been federated (such as with AD FS or PingFederate), users can only be assigned that domain when they are provisioned in the on-premises system.

The **initial** domain (or **tenant** domain) will always be a cloud-only domain since Azure AD will always be the source of authority for it. When you add domains to a tenant, the domains are initially configured as **managed**—that is, Azure AD is used to manage the identity store.

One benefit of configuring cloud-only users is that there is no dependency on any other infrastructure or identity service. For many small organizations, cloud-only identity is the perfect solution because it requires no hardware or software investment other than a Microsoft 365 subscription. Correspondingly, a drawback of cloud-only users is the lack of integration with on-premises directory solutions.

> **Exam tip**
>
> As a best practice, Microsoft recommends maintaining at least one cloud-only account in case you lose access to any on-premises environment.

The easiest way to provision cloud users is through the Microsoft 365 admin center (https://admin.microsoft.com). To configure a user, expand **Users**, select **Active Users**, and then click **Add a user**. The wizard, shown in *Figure 5.1*, will prompt you to configure an account.

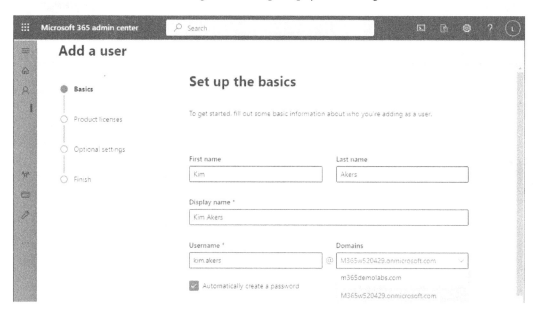

Figure 5.1 – Adding a new cloud user

You can configure the name properties for a user as well as assign them any licenses and a location through the **Add a user** wizard's workflow, as shown in *Figure 5.2*:

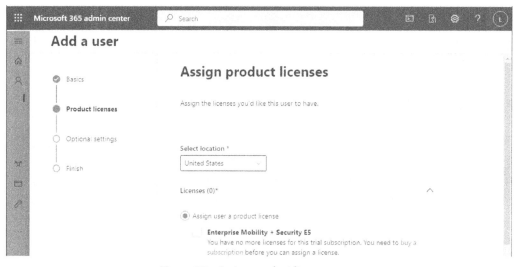

Figure 5.2 – Assign product licenses page

On the **Optional settings** page, you can also configure additional properties such as security roles, job title and department, addresses, and phone numbers, as shown in *Figure 5.3*.

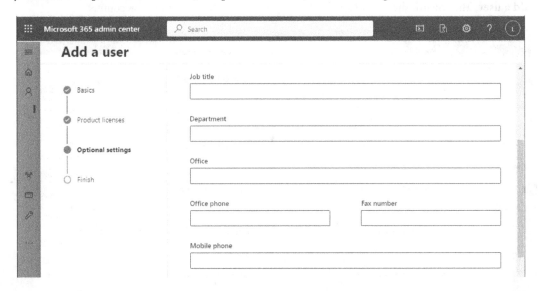

Figure 5.3 – Add a user profile information

You can also add users through the Azure AD portal (`https://aad.portal.azure.com`). The Azure AD portal is arranged much differently from the Microsoft 365 admin center, due largely to the number of different types of resources and services that can be managed there. There are several differences in managing users and objects between the two interfaces; the Microsoft 365 admin center is a much more menu-driven experience, prompting administrators to configure common options and features inside the provisioning workflow.

Once you've logged in to the Azure AD portal, select **Users** and then select **New user**. The interface, shown in *Figure 5.4*, offers the opportunity to populate similar fields to those in the admin center.

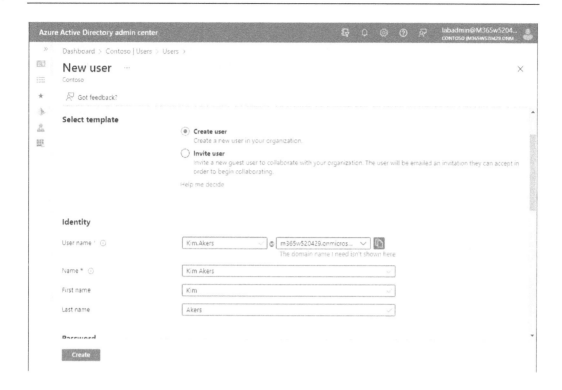

Figure 5.4 – Creating a user through the Azure AD portal

Most organizations that are using Azure from a cloud-only identity perspective will likely provision objects inside the Microsoft 365 admin center.

Creating and managing synchronized users

As you saw in *Chapter 3* and *Chapter 4*, the process of identity synchronization replicates your on-premises identity in Azure AD. Whether you are using Azure AD Connect sync, Azure AD Connect Cloud sync, or a third-party product, the process is largely the same: an on-premises agent or service connects to both Active Directory and Azure Active Directory, reads the objects from Active Directory and recreates a corresponding object in Azure AD.

During this provisioning process, the on-premises and cloud objects are linked through a unique, immutable attribute, which stays the same throughout the life cycle of the object.

Exam tip

Originally, an on-premises object was linked to its corresponding cloud object by converting the on-premise object's `objectGUID` attribute value into a `base64` string, and stored in the cloud object's `ImmutableID` attribute. Modern versions of Azure AD Connect use the `ms-DS-ConsistencyGuid` attribute instead. The `ms-DS-ConsistencyGuid` value is blank by default; after Azure AD Connect is configured to use `ms-DS-ConsistencyGuid` as the source anchor during setup, an object's `objectGUID` value is copied to the `ms-DS-ConsistencyGuid` attribute. Since a new `objectGUID` attribute is generated every time an object is created, a static value such as `ms-DS-ConsistencyGuid` helps organizations maintain the relationship between identities through the Active Directory domain migrations that happen as part of business mergers, acquisitions, and divestitures.

After Azure AD Connect has been deployed, you can create a new synchronized identity by creating a new user in the on-premises Active Directory. See *Figure 5.5*.

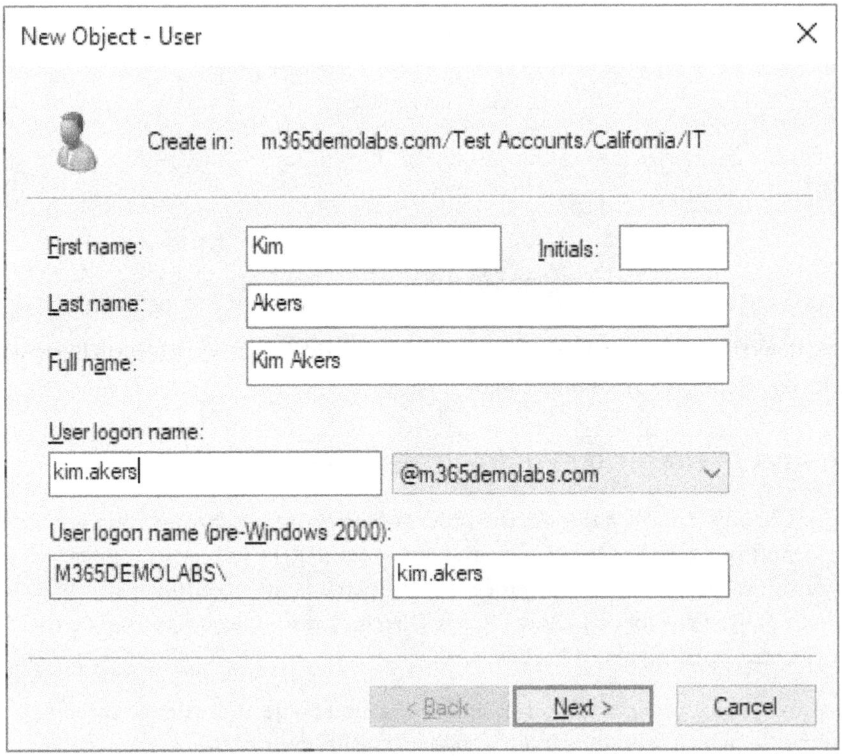

Figure 5.5 – Creating a new user through Active Directory Users and Computers

After synchronization completes, the new user account is ready to sign into the service. From the Microsoft 365 admin center, it's simple to visually distinguish between cloud and synchronized accounts. *Figure 5.6* shows both a cloud user and a synchronized user.

Figure 5.6 – Displaying cloud and synchronized users

Under the **Sync status** column, a cloud user is represented by a cloud icon, while a synchronized user is represented by a notebook icon.

Creating and managing guest users

Guest users are special accounts that have limited rights in the Azure AD environment. In most contexts, guest users are synonymous with Azure **Business-to-Business (B2B)** identities, so that's the reference point that we'll use to discuss them.

Azure B2B guest accounts are generally created through an **invitation** process, such as inviting someone from an external organization to participate in a Microsoft SharePoint site, collaborate on a document in OneDrive, or access files in a Teams channel. When an invitation is sent, an Azure identity object is created in the inviting organization's tenant and an invitation email is sent to the external recipient. After the recipient clicks on the link in the invitation email, the recipient is directed to an Azure sign-in flow, which prompts them to enter credentials corresponding to their own identity source (whether that's another Azure AD or Microsoft 365 tenant, a consumer account (such as Microsoft, Google, or Facebook), or another third-party issuer that uses a SAML/WS-Fed-based identity provider. The process of the recipient accepting the invitation is called **redemption**.

More about guests

While guests are typically part of an invitation process, with the new Azure AD cross-tenant synchronization feature (currently in preview), you can automate the provisioning of guest objects between trusted tenants similar to how you would with your own directory synchronization. Microsoft recommends this feature only for Azure AD tenants that belong to the same organization. For more information on the new cross-tenant sync feature, see `https://learn.microsoft.com/en-us/azure/active-directory/multi-tenant-organizations/cross-tenant-synchronization-overview`.

While guest users can be viewed and edited in the Microsoft 365 admin center, they can only be provisioned through the Azure AD portal. Clicking **Add a guest user** in the Microsoft 365 admin center transfers you over to the Azure AD portal to complete the invitation process.

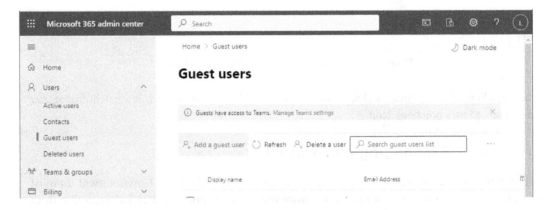

Figure 5.7 – Guest users administration in Microsoft 365 admin center

After either logging in to the Azure AD portal or being redirected there by the Microsoft 365 admin, center you can begin the process of inviting guests. To invite a new guest user from the Azure AD portal, click **New user** and then select **Invite external user**.

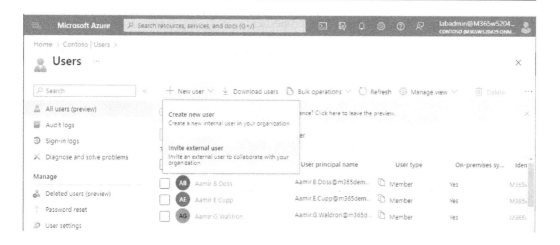

Figure 5.8 – Inviting a new guest user

The user interface elements for inviting a guest user are very similar to those for creating a new cloud user. The main differences are in the selection of the template and, in the case of a guest user, you have the opportunity to supply message content (which will be included as part of the email invitation sent). See *Figure 5.9*.

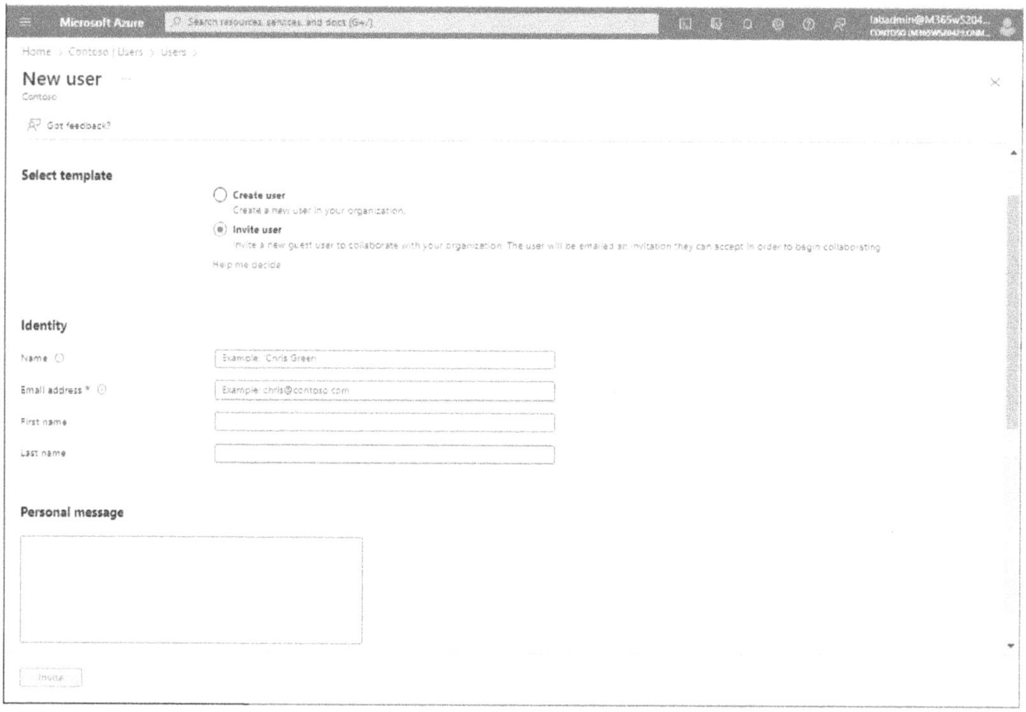

Figure 5.9 – Configuring the guest invitation

Once a guest has been invited, take note of the properties:

- The guest identity's **User principal name** value is formatted as `emailalias_domain.com#EXT#@tenantname.onmicrosoft.com`

- **User type** is set to **Guest**

- Initially, the **Identities** property on the **Overview** tab is set to **tenant.onmicrosoft.com**

- The invitation state is set to **PendingAcceptance**

See *Figure 5.10* for reference.

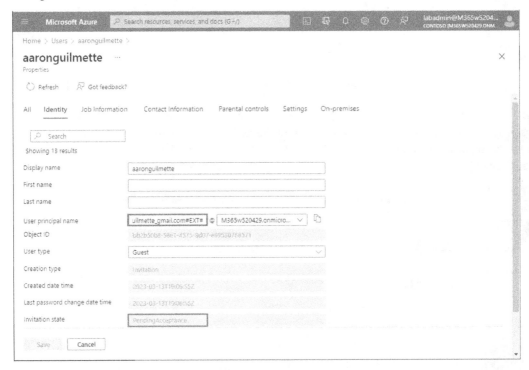

Figure 5.10 – Newly invited guest user

Upon receiving and accepting the invitation, the recipient is prompted to read and accept certain terms and grant permissions:

- Receive profile data including name, email address, and photo

- Collect and log activity including logins, data that has been accessed, and content associated with apps and resources in the inviting tenant

- Use profile and activity data by making it available to other apps inside the organization

- Administer the guest user account

Figure 5.11 – Invitation redemption consent

After consenting, the invitation state in the Azure portal is updated from **PendingAcceptance** to **Accepted**. Additionally, depending on what identity source the guest user is authenticated against, the **Identity** property could be updated to one of several possible values:

- **External Azure AD**: An Azure AD identity from another organization

- **Microsoft Account**: An MSA account ID associated with Hotmail, Outlook.com, Xbox, LiveID, or other Microsoft consumer properties

- **Google.com**: A user identity associated with Google's consumer products (such as Gmail) or a Google Workspace offering

- **Facebook.com**: A user identity authenticated by the Facebook service

- **{issuer URI}**: Another SAML/WS-Fed-based identity provider

Guest users can be assigned licenses, granted access to apps, and delegated administrative roles inside the inviter's tenant.

Creating and managing groups

Groups are directory objects used to perform operations, grant rights or permissions, or communicate with one or more users collectively. In Azure Active Directory, there are several kinds of groups:

- **Security groups** – This type of group is typically used for granting permissions to resources, either on-premises or in Azure AD.

- **Distribution lists or distribution groups** – These groups are usually used for sending emails to multiple recipients, though they can also sometimes be used to restrict the scope of rules or for filtering purposes in Azure AD, SharePoint Online, and Exchange Online.

- **Microsoft 365 groups** – Formerly called **modern groups** (and sometimes still referred to as **unified groups**), Microsoft 365 groups are an all-purpose group type that can be used as a security group for assigning permissions to resources or a distribution group for handling email. Microsoft 365 groups are special objects that are connected to SharePoint Online sites and form the basis for teams in Microsoft Teams. In addition, each Microsoft 365 group is connected to an Exchange group mailbox, allowing it to store persistent messages (such as email or, in the case of Microsoft Teams, channel conversations). Microsoft 365 groups are only available in Azure AD. There is no on-premises corollary.

Each of these groups has certain capabilities and benefits. One or more types of groups may be appropriate for a specific task. In Azure Active Directory, security groups can be mail-enabled (or not), while distribution groups and Microsoft 365 groups are always mail-enabled.

In Azure Active Directory, any of the cloud-based groups can be configured to have their membership be **assigned** or **dynamic**. With assigned membership, an administrator is responsible for periodically updating group members. Dynamic groups are built by creating an object query that is periodically used to add or remove members. For example, you may choose to create a dynamic group called *Sales* that automatically includes users whose job title or department value is set to *Sales*. Groups in Azure AD can contain users, contacts, devices, and other groups. Groups can be converted between assigned and dynamic membership.

When working with groups, there are several important things to remember:

- An Azure AD tenant can have groups that are synchronized from on-premises environments as well as cloud-only groups.

- Both security and distribution groups can be synchronized from on-premises environments. The exception to this is on-premises dynamic distribution groups. Because they can be based on queries that aren't possible in Azure AD, they are not synchronized. You will have to either recreate the dynamic groups in Azure AD using supported query parameters or modify the on-premises group to be based on assigned membership.

- Microsoft 365 groups, due to their unique construction, cannot be a member of a group nor can they have other groups of any type nested in them.

- Microsoft 365 groups are the only type of object with a cloud source of authority that can be written back on-premises.

With all of that said, let's take a look at administering groups in Azure AD!

The Microsoft 365 admin center

For most Azure AD group administration use cases, you'll probably use the Microsoft 365 admin center. To configure groups in the Microsoft 365 admin center, follow these steps:

1. Navigate to the Microsoft 365 admin center (`https://admin.microsoft.com`). Expand **Teams & groups** and then select **Active teams & groups**.

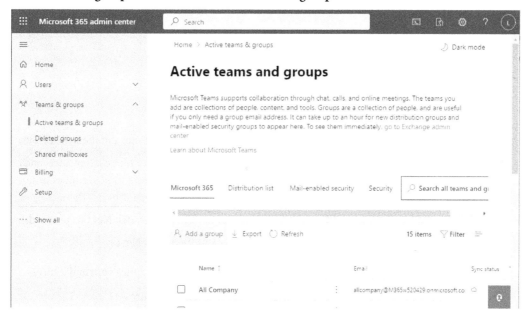

Figure 5.12 – Active teams and groups

2. Click **Add a group**.

3. On the **Group type** page, select the type of group you wish to create. With the exception of **Security** groups, all group types will require essentially the same information (non-mail-enabled security groups do not allow you to add owners or members in the workflow, though they can be added later). If you select a **Microsoft 365** group as your group type, you'll also have the option at the end of the wizard to create a Microsoft Teams team from the group.

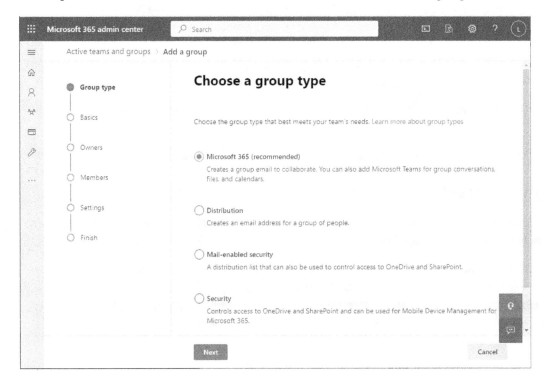

Figure 5.13 – Choose a group type

4. On the **Basics** page, enter a name and an optional description for the group, and then click **Next**.

5. On the **Owners** page, click **Assign owners** to assign at least a single owner. Microsoft recommends having at least two owners (in case one leaves the organization or is absent for a period of time). The owner cannot be an external guest. Click **Next** when finished.

6. On the **Members** page, click **Add members**. This is an optional step. Click **Next** to proceed.

7. On the **Settings** page, configure settings for the group and then click **Next**:

   - For distribution groups and mail-enabled security groups, this includes an email address.

   - For Microsoft 365 and security groups, this includes assigning Azure AD roles. The option does not appear for mail-enabled security groups, though it can be added later.

- For distribution groups, this includes the ability for users outside the org to email the groups (Microsoft 365 groups must have this setting configured manually in the Exchange properties for the group object afterward).

- For Microsoft 365 groups, you can also configure privacy settings (either **Public** or **Private**). Public groups can be browsed and joined by anyone while private groups require an owner to add additional members.

- Also for Microsoft 365 groups, you can choose to convert the group into a team, though users must have a Teams license assigned to access the group.

8. On the **Finish** page, review the settings and click **Create group**.

After the group has been created, you can modify its settings in either the Microsoft 365 admin center or Azure AD portal, as shown in *Figure 5.14*:

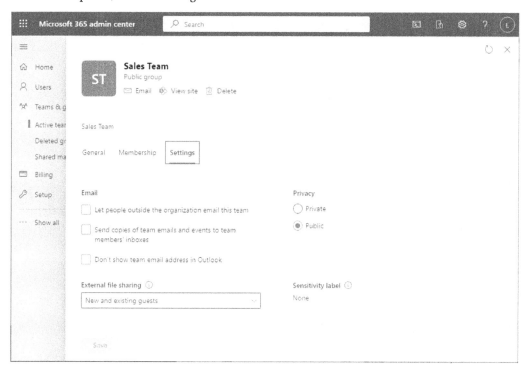

Figure 5.14 – Modifying the settings of a Microsoft 365 group

As you can see in *Figure 5.14*, Microsoft 365 groups have some additional properties (such as determining whether to send copies of emails received by the group mailbox to individual team mailboxes or associate them with a **sensitivity label**).

The Azure AD portal

The Azure AD portal is the other interface that is used to create and manage groups. As with the user creation options, the Azure AD portal provides a slimmed-down feel without the wizard experience of the Microsoft 365 admin center.

To create and manage groups in the Azure AD portal, follow these steps:

1. Navigate to the Azure AD portal (`https://aad.portal.azure.com`) and select **Groups**.

2. With the default **All groups** navigation item selected, click **New group**.

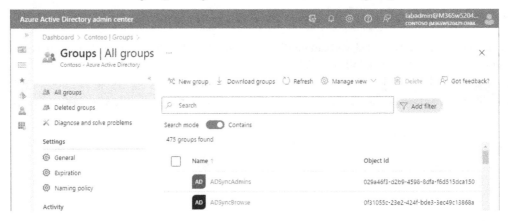

Figure 5.15 – Azure AD all groups

3. On the **New Group** page, specify either **Security** or **Microsoft 365** for **Group type**, enter a name in the **Group name** field, and optionally, provide a description in the **Group description** field. If you've selected **Microsoft 365** as the group type, you will also be required to enter **Group email address**. The security groups created in the Azure portal are not mail-enabled.

Figure 5.16 – New Group page

4. You can choose whether or not Azure AD security roles can be assigned to the group. If you select **Yes**, then the group must have an assigned membership.

5. Under **Membership type**, you can select **Assigned**, **Dynamic User**, or **Dynamic Device** (if it is a security group). If it is a Microsoft 365 group, you can choose from **Assigned** or **Dynamic user**. Security groups with assigned membership can have all supported object types, but dynamic groups are constrained to a single object type.

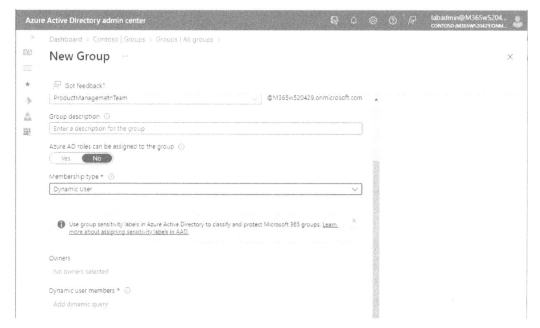

Figure 5.17 – Creating a new dynamic group

6. If you select a group with an **Assigned** membership type, you can add **Owners** and **Members**. If you select a group with either of the dynamic membership types, you must add a dynamic query, as shown in *Figure 5.17*.

7. To configure a dynamic query, click **Add dynamic query**.

8. On the **Configure Rules** tab of the **Dynamic membership rules** page, configure an expression that represents the users or devices you want to have included in the group. For example, to create a user membership rule that looks for the value *Engineering* in either the **jobTitle** or **department** user attributes, select the appropriate property, select **Equals** or **Contains** under **Operator**, and then enter the value Engineering.

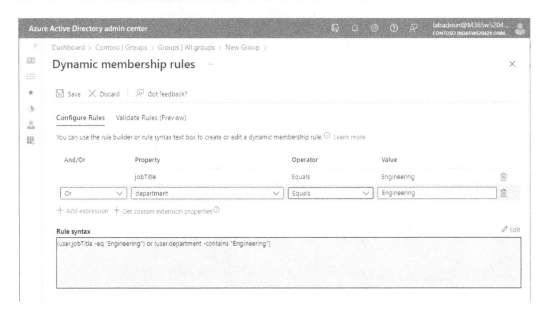

Figure 5.18 – Creating a dynamic membership rule

9. You can view the construction of the rule in the **Rule syntax** output box. If necessary, you can edit the rule free-form to create a more complex rule type.

10. You can select the **Validate Rules (Preview)** tab and add users you think should be in-scope or out-of-scope to verify that the rule is working correctly. Click **Add users** and then select users from the picker. In this example, **Aamir E Cupp** and **Abagael R Rauch** were selected. Aamir's job title is *Manager* and his department is *Sales*, so the expected result is that he is not included in the group. Abagael's job title is *Scientist* but her department is *Engineering*. Based on the way the query is constructed, she is included in the group. See *Figure 5.19*.

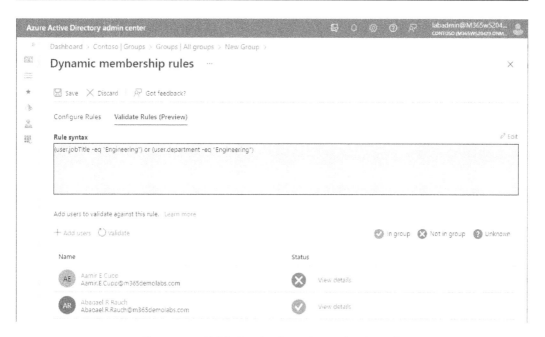

Figure 5.19 – Validating the dynamic membership rule

11. When you have finished editing the rule, click **Save**.

12. Click **Create** to create the new group.

Using the Azure AD portal, you can also update the membership rules for existing groups or change a group's membership from **Assigned** to **Dynamic** by selecting the group and then editing the details in its **Properties** menu, as shown in *Figure 5.20*.

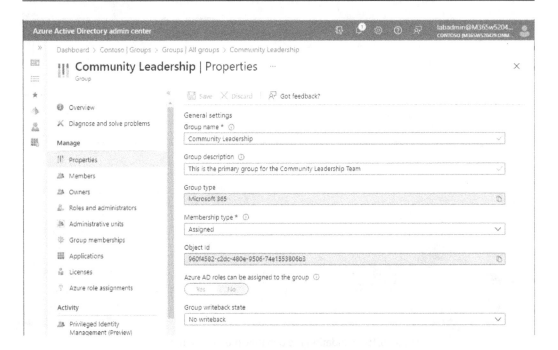

Figure 5.20 – Editing a group

If you change a group from **Assigned** to **Dynamic** membership, you'll need to create a query. It's important to note, though, that you cannot change a group's type (for example, from **Security** to **Microsoft 365**) or whether a group is eligible for Azure AD role assignment—those options can only be selected when creating a group.

> **Note**
>
> Microsoft Entra is the new umbrella product that covers Microsoft identity management and governance. Currently, the Microsoft Entra admin center (`https://entra.microsoft.com`) maps to specific blades or tabs inside the Azure portal and doesn't really display anything new. Over the next year or two, anticipate that Microsoft will begin emphasizing the Entra admin center experience over the Azure portal experience for identity management tasks.

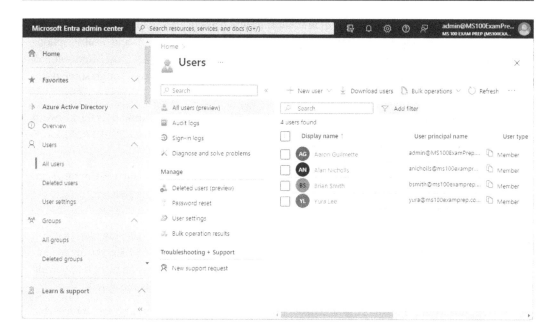

Figure 5.21 – Entra admin center

Managing and monitoring Microsoft 365 license allocations

If identity is the foundation for security in the Microsoft 365 platform, licensing is the entitlement engine that is used to grant identities access to the tools and applications.

Every Microsoft 365 service is tied to a license—whether that's individual product licenses for Exchange Online or SharePoint Online or bundled offerings such as Microsoft 365 E3, which include multiple services.

In Microsoft terminology, there are a number of key terms to be aware of:

- **Licensing plans**: In broad terms, a licensing plan is any purchased licensing item. For example, standalone Exchange Online P2 and Microsoft 365 E3 are both examples of licensing plans.

- **Services**: Also known as **service plans**, these are the individual services that exist inside of a licensing plan. For example, Exchange Online P2 has a single Exchange Online P2 service plan, while Microsoft 365 E3 has an Exchange Online service plan, a Microsoft 365 Apps service plan, a SharePoint Online service plan, and so on.

- **Licenses**: This is the actual number of individual license plans of a particular type that you have purchased. For example, If you have 5 subscriptions to Exchange Online P2 and 5 subscriptions to Microsoft 365 E3, you have 10 licenses (or 5 each of Exchange Online P2 and Microsoft 365 E3). Licenses are frequently mapped 1:1 with users or service principals, though some users may have more than one license plan associated with them.

- **SkuPartNumber**: When reviewing licensing in PowerShell, the SkuPartNumber is the keyword that maps to a licensing plan. For example, Office 365 E3 is represented by the `ENTERPRISEPACK` `SkuPartNumber`.

- **AccountSkuId**: The AccountSkuId is the combination of your tenant name (such as Contoso) and the SkuPartNumber or licensing plan. For example, the Office 365 E3 licensing plan belonging to the `contoso.onmicrosoft.com` tenant has an AccountSkuId of `contoso:ENTERPRISEPACK`.

- **ConsumedUnits**: Consumed units represent the number of items in a licensing plan that you have assigned to users. For example, if you have assigned a Microsoft 365 E3 licensing plan to three users, you have three ConsumedUnits of the Microsoft 365 E3 licensing plan. If reviewing licensing from the Azure AD portal, this field is sometimes displayed as **Assigned**.

- **ActiveUnits**: Number of units that you have purchased for a particular licensing plan. If reviewing licensing from the Azure AD portal, this field is sometimes displayed as **Total**.

- **WarningUnits**: Number of units that you haven't renewed purchasing for in a particular license plan. These units will be expired after the 30-day grace period. If reviewing licensing in the Azure AD portal, this field is also sometimes displayed as **Expiring soon**.

You can easily view purchased licensing plan details in the Microsoft 365 admin center under **Billing | Licenses**:

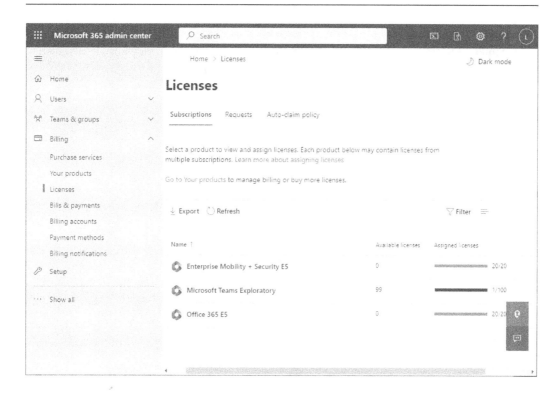

Figure 5.22 – License details in the Microsoft 365 admin center

You can assign licenses in many ways:

- Through the **Licenses** page in the Microsoft 365 admin center (**Microsoft 365 admin center | Billing | Licenses**)

- In the properties of a user on the **Active users** page in the Microsoft 365 admin center (**Microsoft 365 admin center | Users | Active Users | User properties**)

- To users through the **Licenses** page in the Azure AD portal (**Azure AD Portal | Azure AD | Licenses | Licensed users**)

- To users through the **User** properties page in the Azure AD portal (**Azure AD Portal | Azure AD | Users | User properties**)

- To groups through group-based licensing (**Azure AD Portal | Azure AD | Licenses | Licensed groups**)

- Through PowerShell cmdlets such as `Set-MsolUserLicense`

Each licensing method provides you with similar options for assigning license plans to users, including assigning multiple license plans or selectively enabling service plans inside an individual license plan.

For example, in the Microsoft 365 admin center, you can view and modify a user's licenses on the **Licenses and apps** tab of their profile.

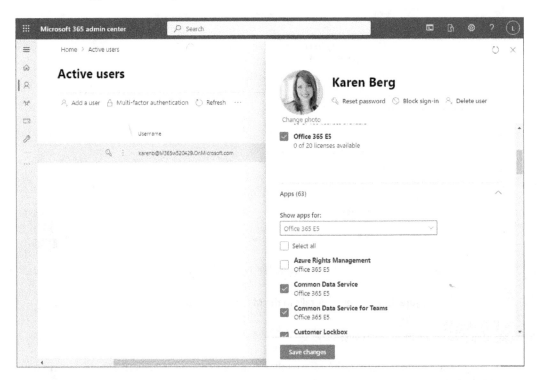

Figure 5.23 – User license management

As you can see in *Figure 5.23*, the user has the **Office 365 E5** licensing plan enabled as well as individual services such as **Common Data Service**, **Common Data Service for Teams**, and **Customer Lockbox**, while the **Azure Rights Management** service plan for this licensing plan is disabled.

> **Note**
>
> In order to assign licenses, a **usage location** is required. The usage location is used to determine what service plans and features are available for a given user. Any user that does not have a usage location set will inherit the location of the Azure AD tenant.

Many organizations choose to use group-based licensing automation. Group-based licensing allows you to specify one or more licenses to be assigned to one or more users or security groups.

To configure group-based licensing, you can follow these steps:

1. Navigate to the Azure AD portal (`https://portal.azure.com`). Select **Azure AD | Licenses**.

2. Under **Manage**, select **All products**.

3. Select one or more licenses that you want to assign as a unit to a group and then click **Assign**.

Figure 5.24 – Assign selected licenses to a group

4. On the **Users and groups** tab, click **Add users and groups** and select one or more security groups from the list. You can only select security groups or mail-enabled security groups. The security groups can be cloud-only or synchronized.

5. Click the **Assignment options** tab.

6. Select which services you want to enable for each licensing plan by sliding the toggle to either **Off** or **On**.

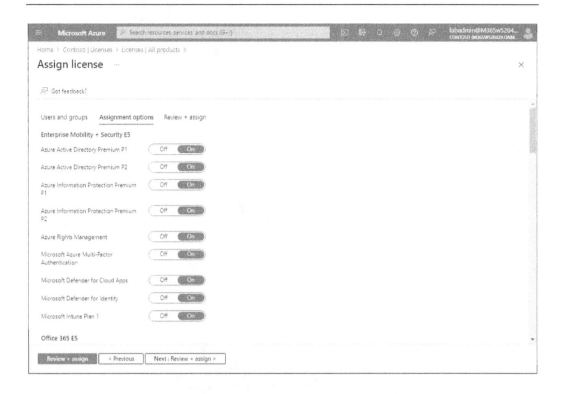

Figure 5.25 – Configuring assignment options

7.   When finished, click **Review + assign**.

8.   Confirm the configuration. When ready, click **Assign**.

Further reading

For more information on configuring group-based licensing, see `https://learn.`
`microsoft.com/en-us/azure/active-directory/fundamentals/active-`
`directory-licensing-whatis-azure-portal`.

Next, we'll look at how to perform bulk user management operations in Microsoft 365.

Performing bulk user management

While many organizations will deploy a hybrid identity solution and manage accounts on-premises, you may face scenarios where you need to manage cloud identities or guests in bulk (such as creating bulk guest user invitations or during a tenant-to-tenant migration procedure).

These operations can be performed in several ways, including through the Microsoft 365 admin center, the Azure AD portal, and various PowerShell commands.

The Microsoft 365 admin center

The Microsoft 365 admin center allows you to perform bulk user additions, either interactively or by uploading a specially formatted **Comma-Separated Values** (**CSV**) file.

To begin the process, select **Add multiple users** on the **Active users** page of the Microsoft 365 admin center, as shown in *Figure 5.26*.

Figure 5.26 – Active users page

On the **Add multiple users** flyout, you can choose to either enter basic details interactively (up to 249 users) or you can download a CSV template, which has more fields that can be populated.

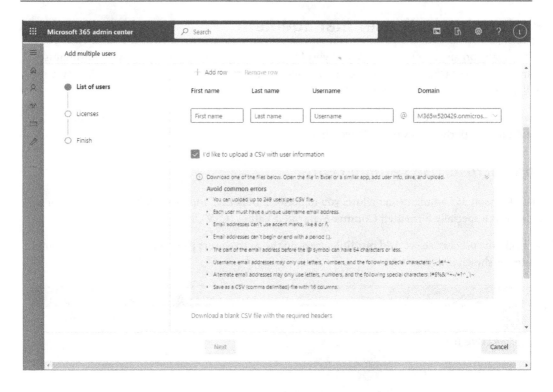

Figure 5.27 – Configuring the bulk user upload

If you choose to work with a bulk user template, you can edit it in any text editor that supports CSV files. You must preserve the first row, which has the fields or header information. You can add up to 249 users, each on their own row.

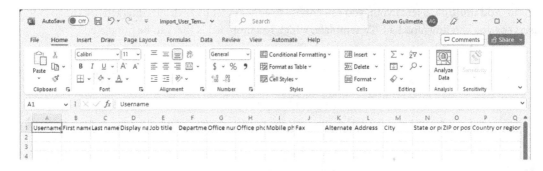

Figure 5.28 – Microsoft 365 admin center bulk user template

After you have either added the users in the admin center flyout or into the CSV and uploaded it, you can click **Next** to go to the next page of the wizard.

On the **Licenses** page, you can assign a location, licensing plan, and, optionally, the individual services that will be enabled. When you've completed your selections, click **Next** to proceed to the confirmation page and click **Add users** to submit the operation.

The Azure AD portal

Bulk operations can also be performed through the Microsoft Azure AD portal. In contrast to only the create option provided by the Microsoft 365 admin center, the Azure AD portal supports **Bulk create**, **Bulk invite** (for guest users), and **Bulk delete** operations.

Figure 5.29 – Bulk operations menu in Azure AD portal

To get started, you'll need to use one of the templates provided in the Azure AD portal. On the **Users** blade, select **Bulk operations** and then choose the appropriate operation.

> **Note**
>
> The templates in the Microsoft 365 admin center and Azure AD portal are *not* interchangeable. You'll need to use the correct template for the interface that you're working with.

On the corresponding flyout, you'll have the option to download a template. Once downloaded, you can edit in any app that supports CSV files. See *Figure 5.30*.

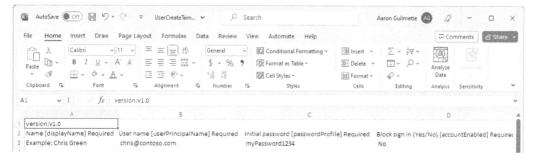

Figure 5.30 – Azure AD bulk user create template

It's important to note that the first two rows of any of the templates must be preserved and not modified in any way. Each identity to be modified is included in a separate row, starting at row 3. The first four fields (**displayName**, **userPrincipalName**, **passwordProfile**, and **accountEnabled**) are required. All other fields are optional.

When finished, you can upload the CSV back to the same flyout in the Azure portal to process the request.

PowerShell

By far, the most flexible option for managing bulk users is through Windows PowerShell. There are currently three different PowerShell modules that can be used:

- **MSOnline module**
- **Azure AD module**
- **Azure AD Graph module**

Both the MSOnline module and the Azure AD module will eventually be deprecated and replaced by the Azure AD Graph module. The modules work similarly, though the cmdlet names, parameters, syntax, and overall capabilities are different.

> **Note**
> Microsoft has announced that the legacy Azure AD module will be deprecated starting in June 2023 and recommends updating scripts to use the newer Azure AD Graph-based cmdlets. For more information, see `https://learn.microsoft.com/en-us/azure/active-directory/fundamentals/whats-deprecated-azure-ad`.

Installing modules

Each of the modules can be installed running the `Install-Module` cmdlet from an elevated PowerShell prompt on your system:

- **MSOnline**: `Install-Module MSOnline`
- **Azure AD**: `Install-Module AzureAD`
- **Microsoft Graph**: `Install-Module Microsoft.Graph`

Once the modules have been installed, you can begin connecting to Azure AD and performing operations.

Connecting to Azure AD

Each module has a slightly different syntax for connecting to Azure AD. We'll go over them here.

- **MSOnline**: `Connect-MsolService`
- **Azure AD**: `Connect-AzureAD`
- **Microsoft Graph**: `Connect-MgGraph -Scopes "User.ReadWrite.All"`

In each of these cases, you'll need to provide credentials with the appropriate rights to create users (such as Global Administrator or User Administrator). In the case of the Microsoft Graph cmdlets, you'll also need to consent to the permissions scope.

Working with PowerShell

When working with bulk users via PowerShell, you're free to collect, organize, and manipulate the data in whatever way works best for you. For example, if you need to gather a list of user objects and their properties, you can use one of the modules' `Get-*` cmdlets. You can choose to store, view, or manipulate the data in a variety of ways—for example, saving it to a variable, displaying it to the console (screen), exporting it to a file, or passing the data through to another command.

PowerShell supports a processing concept called **piping**. Piping can be used to redirect the output of one command into another command. It can be used to process intermediary computations or steps without writing data to disk.

Let's look at some common examples of how you might interact with one or more objects in bulk.

Retrieving user data

Let's say you need to retrieve a list of all users in your organization that meet certain criteria (such as members of the *Project Management* department).

Using the MSOnline cmdlets, you could accomplish this using the following `Get-MsolUser` cmdlet:

```
Get-Msoluser -MaxResults 10 -Department "Project Management" | Select
DisplayName,UserPrincipalName,Department
```

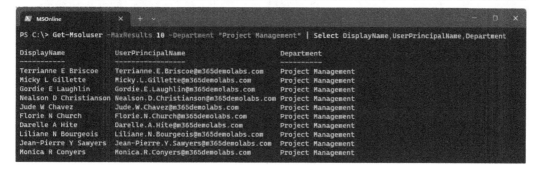

Figure 5.31 – Get-MsolUser cmdlet

To perform the same action with the Azure AD module, you would need to modify the syntax slightly:

```
Get-AzureADUser -Top 10 -Filter "Department eq 'Project Management'" |
Select DisplayName,UserPrincipalName,Department
```

```
PS C:\> Get-AzureADUser -Top 10 -Filter "Department eq 'Project Management'" | Select DisplayName,UserPrincipalName,Depa
rtment

DisplayName                UserPrincipalName                       Department
-----------                -----------------                       ----------
Terrianne E Briscoe        Terrianne.E.Briscoe@m365demolabs.com    Project Management
Micky L Gillette           Micky.L.Gillette@m365demolabs.com       Project Management
Gordie E Laughlin          Gordie.E.Laughlin@m365demolabs.com      Project Management
Nealson D Christianson     Nealson.D.Christianson@m365demolabs.com Project Management
Jude W Chavez              Jude.W.Chavez@m365demolabs.com          Project Management
Florie N Church            Florie.N.Church@m365demolabs.com        Project Management
Darelle A Hite             Darelle.A.Hite@m365demolabs.com         Project Management
Liliane N Bourgeois        Liliane.N.Bourgeois@m365demolabs.com    Project Management
Jean-Pierre Y Sawyers      Jean-Pierre.Y.Sawyers@m365demolabs.com  Project Management
Monica R Conyers           Monica.R.Conyers@m365demolabs.com       Project Management
```

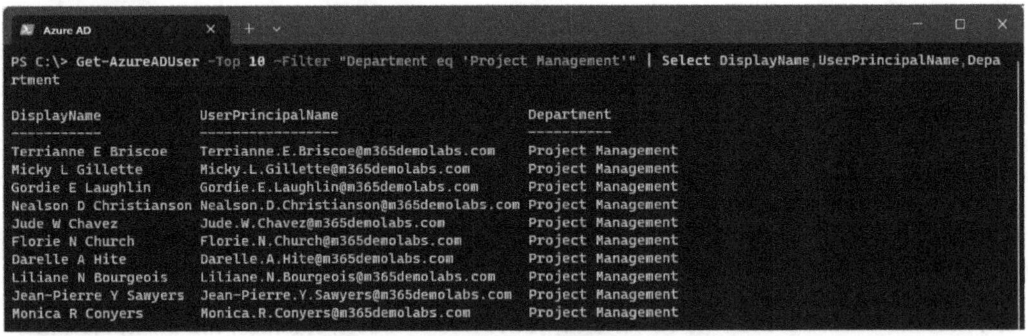

Figure 5.32 – Get-AzureADUser cmdlet

Finally, working with the Microsoft Graph module, you'd need to use the following syntax:

```
Get-MgUser -Filter "Department eq 'Project Management'"
-Top 10 -ConsistencyLevel Eventual -Property
DisplayName,UserPrincipalName,Department | Select
DisplayName,UserPrincipalName,Department
```

```
PS C:\> Get-MgUser -Filter "Department eq 'Project Management'" -Top 10 -ConsistencyLevel Eventual -Property DisplayName
,UserPrincipalName,Department | Select DisplayName,UserPrincipalName,Department

DisplayName                UserPrincipalName                       Department
-----------                -----------------                       ----------
Terrianne E Briscoe        Terrianne.E.Briscoe@m365demolabs.com    Project Management
Micky L Gillette           Micky.L.Gillette@m365demolabs.com       Project Management
Gordie E Laughlin          Gordie.E.Laughlin@m365demolabs.com      Project Management
Nealson D Christianson     Nealson.D.Christianson@m365demolabs.com Project Management
Jude W Chavez              Jude.W.Chavez@m365demolabs.com          Project Management
Florie N Church            Florie.N.Church@m365demolabs.com        Project Management
Darelle A Hite             Darelle.A.Hite@m365demolabs.com         Project Management
Liliane N Bourgeois        Liliane.N.Bourgeois@m365demolabs.com    Project Management
Jean-Pierre Y Sawyers      Jean-Pierre.Y.Sawyers@m365demolabs.com  Project Management
Monica R Conyers           Monica.R.Conyers@m365demolabs.com       Project Management
```

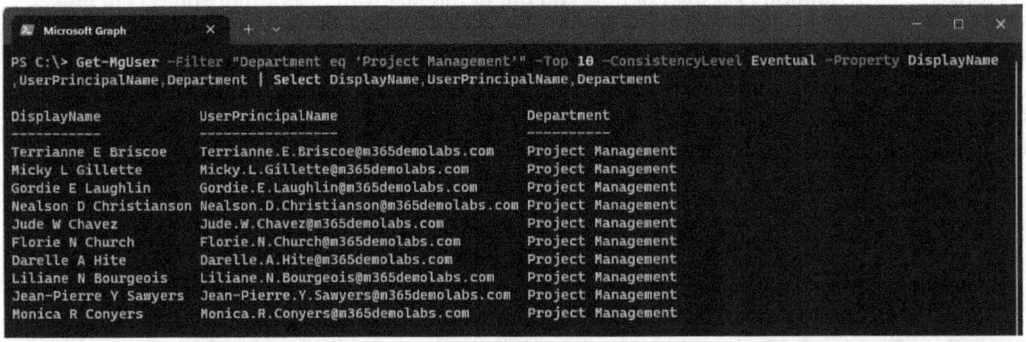

Figure 5.33 – Get-MgUser cmdlet

Updating users

One of the most common bulk administration tasks, after reporting, is updating objects. Let's say we needed to assign licenses to this group of users, but they didn't have their usage location set. In order to assign the proper license plans and service plans, we'll need to configure the correct location.

Using the MSOnline cmdlets, we could retrieve our list of users and then, through piping, use the output of the `Get-MsolUser` cmdlet as the input for the `Set-MsolUser` cmdlet:

```
Get-Msoluser -MaxResults 10 -Department "Project Management" |
Set-MsolUser -UsageLocation US
```

Figure 5.34 – Updating UsageLocation with Set-MsolUser

The Azure AD cmdlets also support piping input:

```
Get-AzureADUser -Top 10 -Filter "Department eq 'Project Management'" |
Set-AzureADUser -UsageLocation US
```

Figure 5.35 – Updating UsageLocation with Set-AzureADUser

Finally, you can also use the `Set-MgUser` cmdlet to update user objects with the Microsoft Graph PowerShell, though the pipeline syntax is a little different still. In this example, the piped data is processed using a `Foreach` command, instructing PowerShell to loop through the list of users returned, substituting the actual individual object (represented by $_) and the property of the object to be retrieved (represented by .id)

```
Get-MgUser -Filter "Department eq 'Project Management'" -Top 5
-ConsistencyLevel Eventual -Property * | Foreach { Update-MgUser
-UserId $_.id -UsageLocation US }
```

Figure 5.36 – Updating UsageLocation with Update-MgUser

Updating licenses

License management is also a task that is often performed via scripting.

In order to determine the licensing plan to assign, you'll need to retrieve the list of valid products using the `Get-MsolAccountSku` cmdlet. After that, you can assign a license using the following format – `tenant:LICENSINGPLAN`:

```
Get-MsolAccountSku
Set-MsolUserLicense -UserPrincipalName Aamir.b.doss@m365demolabs.com
-AddLicenses "M365w520429:TEAMS_EXPLORATORY"
```

Figure 5.37 – Adding a license to a user

To assign a license with the Azure AD PowerShell is a bit more complicated, as it involves creating a special licensing object. In this example, we'll assign the user named `Aamir` the `TEAMS_EXPLORATORY` license:

```
Get-AzureADSubscribedSku
$TeamsSku = Get-AzureADSubscribedSku | ? { $_.SkuPartNumber -eq
"TEAMS_EXPLORATORY" }
$License = New-Object -TypeName Microsoft.Open.AzureAD.Model.
AssignedLicense
$License.SkuId = $TeamsSku.SkuId
$LicenseToAssign = New-Object -TypeName Microsoft.Open.AzureAD.Model.
AssignedLicenses
$LicenseToAssign.AddLicenses = $License
Set-AzureADUserLicense -ObjectId Aamir.E.Cupp@m365demolabs.com
-AssignedLicenses $LicenseToAssign
```

Figure 5.38 – Adding a license with the Set-AzureADUserLicense cmdlet

In the final license example, we'll use the Microsoft Graph PowerShell cmdlets. They work similarly to the Azure AD cmdlet, but the syntax requires a hash table to hold the license `SkuId` property:

```
$user = get-mguser -UserId karenb@M365w520429.OnMicrosoft.com
-Property *
$TeamsSku = Get-MgSubscribedSku -all | Where SkuPartNumber -eq "TEAMS_
EXPLORATORY"
```

```
Set-MgUserLicense -UserId $user.Id -AddLicenses @{SkuId = $TeamsSku.
SkuId} -RemoveLicenses @()
```

Figure 5.39 – Adding a license with the Set-MgUserLicense cmdlet

Depending on your licensing scenario, managing through one of the PowerShell interfaces may be the most efficient way to craft custom license configurations.

> **Further reading**
>
> Managing licenses can be a complex topic, especially when considering options for enabling or disabling individual service plans within a license or replacing licensing options for users. You can see more in-depth information regarding the different capabilities of PowerShell-based licensing at https://learn.microsoft.com/en-us/microsoft-365/enterprise/ view-licenses-and-services-with-microsoft-365-powershell.

Creating users

There are several scenarios where you may need to bulk-create users or contacts or bulk-invite users to your tenant. Frequently, when these operations are required, you will be working with source data stored in a **CSV** text file.

Previously, in the *Performing bulk user management* section, you used a specially formatted CSV to import objects into the Microsoft 365 admin center. You can use a similarly formatted CSV to perform the action with PowerShell.

In this set of examples, we've entered a few names into a CSV file (as shown in *Figure 5.40*) to demonstrate bulk user processing. While some of the administrative interfaces (such as the Microsoft 365 admin center) limit you to a maximum of 249 objects, you can process thousands of objects with PowerShell—the only real limitation is the memory on your computer.

Figure 5.40 – Bulk user template

First, we'll perform the operation with the MSOnline cmdlets. We'll begin by importing the CSV source file and storing it as a variable. Then, with a `Foreach` command, we'll iterate through the lines in the CSV, using the values stored in the `$User` variable to provide the input for each of the parameters:

```
$Users = Import-Csv -Path C:\temp\ImportUsers.csv
Foreach ($User in $Users) { New-MsolUser -UserPrincipalName $User.
UserPrincipalName -FirstName $User.FirstName -LastName $User.LastName
-DisplayName $User.DisplayName -Title $User.JobTitle -Department
$User.Department -UsageLocation $User.UsageLocation -Country US }
```

Figure 5.41 – Bulk creating users with New-MsolUser

Next, we'll look at doing the same thing with the Azure AD cmdlets. As with the other examples in this section, you'll see that the syntax follows a pattern, but there are other required parameters that must be specified. In the case of `New-AzureADUser`, that means a `PasswordProfile` object (which is used to specify a password) and `MailNickName` must be supplied:

```
$Users = Import-Csv C:\temp\ImportUsers.csv
$PasswordProfile = New-Object -TypeName Microsoft.Open.AzureAD.Model.
PasswordProfile
$PasswordProfile.Password = "P@ssw0rd123"
Foreach ($User in $Users) { New-AzureADUser -UserPrincipalName $User.
UserPrincipalName -GivenName $User.FirstName -Surname $User.LastName
```

```
-DisplayName $User.DisplayName -JobTitle $User.JobTitle -Department
$User.Department -UsageLocation $User.UsageLocation -Country
$User.UsageLocation -AccountEnabled $True -MailNickname $User.
UserPrincipalName.Split("@")[0] -PasswordProfile $PasswordProfile }
```

```
PS C:\> $Users = Import-Csv C:\temp\ImportUsers.csv
PS C:\> $PasswordProfile = New-Object -TypeName Microsoft.Open.AzureAD.Model.PasswordProfile
PS C:\> $PasswordProfile.Password = "P@ssw0rd123"
PS C:\> Foreach ($User in $Users) { New-AzureADUser -UserPrincipalName $User.UserPrincipalName -GivenName $User.FirstNam
e -Surname $User.LastName -DisplayName $User.DisplayName -JobTitle $User.JobTitle -Department $User.Department -UsageLoc
ation $User.UsageLocation -Country $User.Country -AccountEnabled $True -MailNickname $User.UserPrincipalName.Split("@")[
0] -PasswordProfile $PasswordProfile }


ObjectId                                DisplayName       UserPrincipalName               UserType
--------                                -----------       -----------------               --------
fb2754d2-605d-4e0f-bb0a-18d9c8912bf9    Robert Smith      robert.smith@m365demolabs.com   Member
7848058c-df77-4e46-a4b0-b60759164bfb    Grant Roberts     grant.roberts@m365demolabs.com  Member
```

Figure 5.42 – Creating new users with New-AzureADUser

Finally, we'll look at bulk user creation with the Microsoft Graph-based New-MgUser cmdlet. It has very similar parameters to the New-AzureADUser cmdlet, with the main differences being how the $PasswordProfile object is created and that the AccountEnabled parameter does not require an argument:

```
$Users = Import-Csv C:\Temp\ImportUsers.csv
$PasswordProfile = @{ Password = "P@ssw0rd123" }
PS C:\> Foreach ($User in $Users) { New-MgUser -UserPrincipalName
$User.UserPrincipalName -GivenName $User.FirstName -Surname $User.
LastName -DisplayName $User.DisplayName -JobTitle $User.JobTitle
-Department $User.Department -UsageLocation $User.UsageLocation
-Country $User.UsageLocation -AccountEnabled -MailNickname $User.
UserPrincipalName.Split("@")[0] -PasswordProfile $PasswordProfile }
```

```
PS C:\> $Users = Import-Csv C:\Temp\ImportUsers.csv
PS C:\> $PasswordProfile = @{ Password = "P@ssw0rd123" }
PS C:\> Foreach ($User in $Users) { New-MgUser -UserPrincipalName $User.UserPrincipalName -GivenName $User.FirstName -Su
rname $User.LastName -DisplayName $User.DisplayName -JobTitle $User.JobTitle -Department $User.Department -UsageLocation
 $User.UsageLocation -Country $User.UsageLocation -AccountEnabled -MailNickname $User.UserPrincipalName.Split("@")[0] -P
asswordProfile $PasswordProfile }


Id                                      DisplayName       Mail UserPrincipalName               UserType
--                                      -----------       ---- -----------------               --------
fb0618c1-6972-4f2d-bdee-5e25eafec28a    Robert Smith           robert.smith@m365demolabs.com
f73211cd-446d-4e49-9c60-685164ad4066    Grant Roberts          grant.roberts@m365demolabs.com
```

Figure 5.43 – Creating new users with the New-MgUser cmdlet

As you can see, the flexibility and capability of the PowerShell interface allow you to do far more than what's available in the graphical administration centers—with the trade-off that the parameters and syntax for the various modules can vary greatly.

> **Further reading**
>
> We only touched the surface in describing the capabilities of the various PowerShell modules. You can learn more about all of the available modules and their associated cmdlets and best practices at `https://learn.microsoft.com/en-us/powershell/`.

Summary

In this chapter, you learned some of the basics of administering objects on the Microsoft 365 platform, whether those objects were on-premises or cloud-only. Managing identity is a large part of the Microsoft 365 administration experience, so it's important to have a firm grasp on the variety of tools and methods for provisioning, licensing, and updating objects.

In the next chapter, we'll learn how to manage roles in Microsoft 365.

Knowledge check

In this section, we'll test your knowledge of some key elements from this chapter.

Questions

1. You need to quickly add 500 cloud users to your tenant. Which two methods would be most effective?

    A. Adding users in bulk through Forefront Identity Manager

    B. Adding users in bulk through the Azure AD portal

    C. Adding users in bulk add through Microsoft Azure AD PowerShell

    D. Adding users in bulk to on-premises Active Directory

2. Which command should you use to connect to Microsoft Online (MSOnline) through PowerShell?

    A. `Connect-AzureAD`

    B. `Connect-MsolService`

    C. `Connect-MsGraph`

    D. `Connect-MgGraph`

3. You need to retrieve information about a user from the Microsoft Graph PowerShell. Which command would you use?

   A. `Get-MgUser`

   B. `Get-MsUser`

   C. `Get-MsolUser`

   D. `Get-User`

4. When provisioning hybrid identity or synchronized users, what interface should you use?

   A. Azure AD

   B. Azure AD Connect Sync Service

   C. Azure AD Connect Synchronization Rules Engine

   D. Active Directory Users and Computers

5. The purchasing administrator for your organization has asked you for a snapshot of how many licenses are currently being consumed. Which two locations can be used to easily obtain this information?

   A. **Microsoft 365 admin center | Reports | Usage**

   B. **Microsoft 365 admin center | Billing | Your products**

   C. **Microsoft 365 admin center | Billing | Licenses**

   D. **Microsoft 365 admin center | Reports | Adoption**

Answers

1. B: Adding users in bulk through the Azure AD portal; and C: Adding users in bulk through Microsoft Azure AD PowerShell

2. B: `Connect-MsolService`

3. A: `Get-MgUser`

4. D: Active Directory Users and Computers

5. B: **Microsoft 365 admin center | Billing | Your products**; and C: **Microsoft 365 admin center | Billing | Licenses**

6
Planning and Managing Roles in Microsoft 365

In the previous chapter, you became familiar with provisioning and managing identities. In this chapter, we're going to address how to grant those identities roles in the Microsoft 365 platform.

Each of these types of objects has a purpose, and one is generally more suited to a business case than another.

In this chapter, we're going to look at the following topics as they relate to the MS-100 exam objectives:

- Understanding roles
- Planning for role assignments
- Managing roles in the Microsoft 365 admin center
- Managing administrative units
- Planning and implementing privileged identity management

By the end of this chapter, you should be able to describe Azure AD roles and other security management concepts. You should also understand how to assign roles.

Let's get started!

Understanding roles

Azure AD roles are used to delegate permissions to perform tasks in Azure AD and Microsoft 365. Most people are familiar with the Global Administrator role, as it is the first role that's established when you create a tenant. However, there are dozens of other roles available that can be used to provide a refined level of delegation throughout the environment. As the number of applications and services available in Microsoft 365 has grown, so has the number of security roles.

Roles for applications, services, and functions are intuitively named and generally split into two groups, *Administrator* and *Reader*, though there are some roles that have additional levels of permission associated with them (such as *Printer Technician* or *Attack Simulator Payload Author*).

If you're reading the chapters of this book in order, you'll already be familiar with the Global Administrator role (also called the *Company Administrator* role in some legacy interfaces). The Global Administrator role is able to administer all parts of an organization, including creating and modifying users or groups and delegating other administrative roles. In most cases, users with the Global Administrator role can access and modify all parts of an individual Microsoft 365 service – for example, editing Exchange transport rules, creating SharePoint Online sites, or setting up directory synchronization.

> **Further reading**
>
> There are currently over 70 built-in administrative roles specific to Azure AD services and applications. For an up-to-date list of the roles available, see `https://learn.microsoft.com/en-us/azure/active-directory/roles/permissions-reference`.

For the MS-100 exam, you should plan on becoming familiar with the core Microsoft 365 and Azure AD roles:

Roles	Role description
Global Administrator	Can manage all aspects of Azure AD and Microsoft 365 services
Hybrid Identity Administrator	Can manage Azure AD Connect and Azure AD Connect cloud sync configuration settings, including **Pass-Through Authentication (PTA)**, **Password Hash Synchronization (PHS)**, **Seamless Single Sign-On (Seamless SSO)**, and federation settings
Billing Administrator	Can perform billing tasks such as updating payment information
Compliance Administrator	Can read and manage the compliance configuration and reporting in Azure AD and Microsoft 365
Exchange Administrator	Can manage all aspects of the Exchange Online service
Guest Inviter	Can invite guest users regardless of the "members can invite guests" setting
Office Apps Administrator	Can manage Office apps, including policy and settings management
Privileged Authentication Administrator	Can view, set, or update authentication method information for all users, including other administrators

Roles	Role description
Reports Reader	Can read sign-in and audit reports
Security Administrator	Can read and manage security-related features in the Microsoft 365 Defender portal, Azure AD Identity Protection, Azure Information Protection, Microsoft Purview compliance portal, and Azure Active Directory Authentication
Security Reader	Can read security information and reports in Azure AD and Office 365
SharePoint Administrator	Can manage all aspects of the SharePoint service
Teams Administrator	Can manage all aspects of the Microsoft Teams service
User Administrator	Can manage all aspects of users and groups, including resetting passwords for limited admins

Table 6.1 – Core Azure AD and Microsoft 365 roles

Planning for role assignments

One of the core tenets of security is the use of a least-privilege model. *Least privilege* means delegating the minimum level of permissions to accomplish a particular task. In the context of Microsoft 365 and Azure AD, this translates to using the built-in roles for services, applications, and features where possible, instead of granting the Global Administrator role. Limiting the administrative scope for services based on roles is commonly referred to as **role-based access control** (**RBAC**).

In order to help organizations plan for a least-privileged deployment, Microsoft currently maintains this list of least-privileged roles necessary to accomplish certain tasks, grouped by application or content area: `https://learn.microsoft.com/en-us/azure/active-directory/roles/delegate-by-task`.

When planning role assignments in your organization, you can choose to assign roles directly to users or via a specially designated Azure AD group. If you want to use groups for role assignment, you must configure the **isAssignableToRole** property during the group creation. For example, in *Figure 6.1*, the **Azure AD roles can be assigned to the group** toggle needs to be set to **Yes** in order for the group to be provisioned with that capability. It cannot be configured afterward.

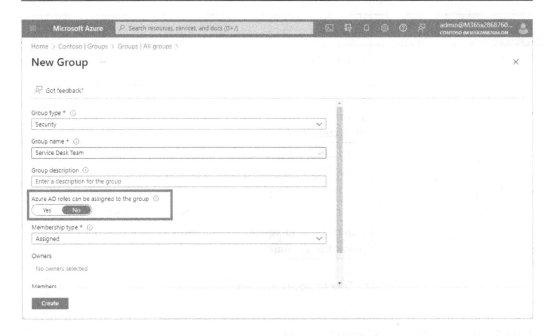

Figure 6.1 – Configuring the isAssignableToRole property on a new group

As you learned in *Chapter 5*, Azure AD groups configured to be role-eligible must have assigned membership. As soon as you move the slider to configure a role-assignable group, the ability to change the membership type is grayed out to prevent you from accidentally elevating a user to a privileged role.

Managing roles in the Microsoft 365 admin center

Roles can be easily managed within the Microsoft 365 admin center by expanding the navigation menu, expanding **Roles**, and then selecting **Role assignments**.

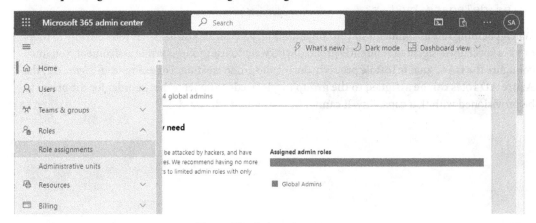

Figure 6.2 – Role assignments

Roles are displayed across four tabs, **Azure AD**, **Exchange**, **Intune**, and **Billing**, as shown in *Figure 6.3*:

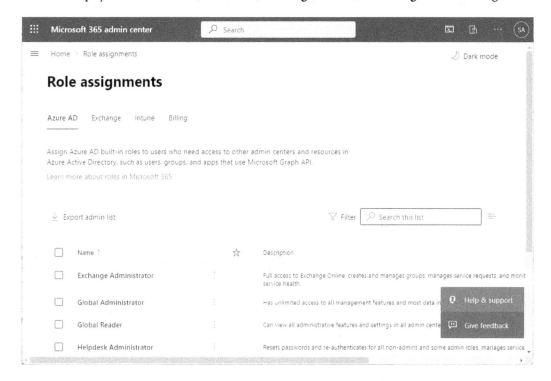

Figure 6.3 – The Role assignments page

To add people to a role, simply select the role from the list, choose the **Assigned** tab, and then add either users or groups to the particular role.

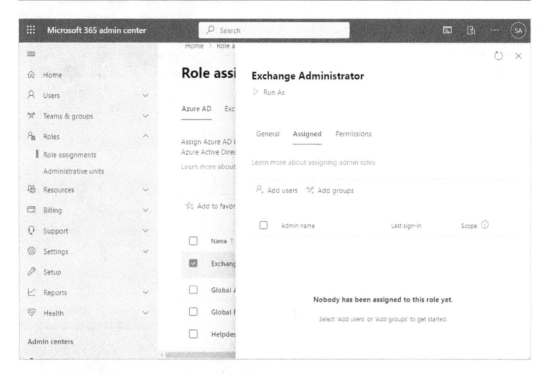

Figure 6.4 – Making role assignments

Depending on the role being granted through this interface, you may be able to use Microsoft 365 groups, role-assignable security groups, or mail-enabled security groups.

Managing administrative units

Administrative units are collections of users and devices that can be delegated to certain administrators. In on-premises AD, you can choose to delegate control of administrative functions, using the delegation of Control Wizard in Active Directory Users and Computers or the Active Directory Administrative Center. Unlike on-premises AD, Azure AD is not hierarchical. The delegation must be achieved by defining boundaries and then controlling which users or devices are placed inside the boundaries.

Administrative units can be role-scoped – that is, administrators can both be granted administrative roles (such as Helpdesk Administrator) and be limited to administrative tasks only for assigned administrative units.

Creating administrative units

In the following example, we'll create an administrative unit called `California` that will be used to hold users in that region. During creation, we'll configure administrators to be able to perform role-scoped activities inside that administrative unit:

1. Navigate to the Microsoft 365 admin center (`https://admin.microsoft.com`) and log in with a Global Administrator credential.

2. Expand **Roles** | **Role assignments** and click **Administrative units**.

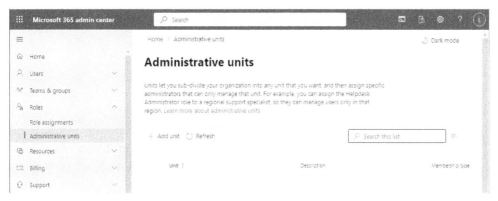

Figure 6.5 – The Administrative units page

3. Click **Add unit**.

4. On the **Basics** page, enter a name and description, and then click **Next**.

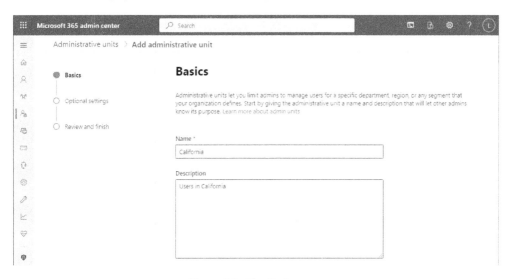

Figure 6.6 – The Basics page

5. On the **Optional settings | Add members** page, you can add members to the administrative unit or click **Next** to proceed.

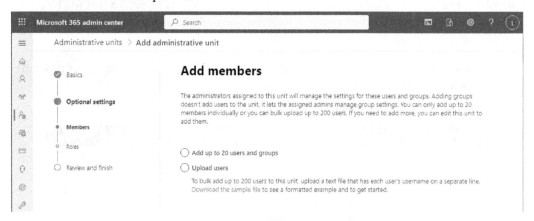

Figure 6.7 – The Add members page

6. On the **Assign admins to scoped roles** page, review the roles listed. Not all roles can be scoped to administrative units. In this example, select the checkbox next to **User Administrator**, and then click the role name itself.

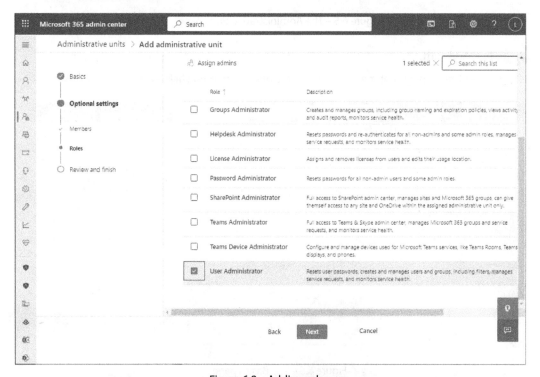

Figure 6.8 – Adding roles

7. On the **User Administrator** flyout, click the **Assigned** tab.

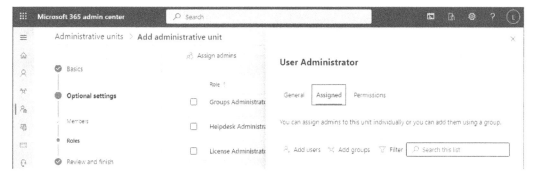

Figure 6.9 – The User Administrator flyout

8. Click **Add users** or **Add groups** to assign administrators to this role. Click **Close** when finished.

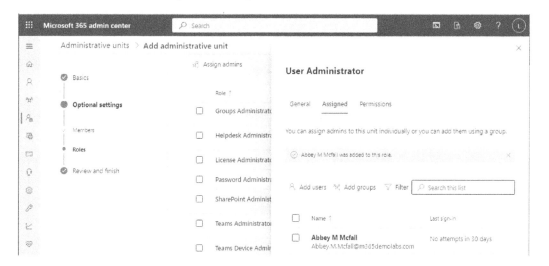

Figure 6.10 – Adding users to a role

9. On the **Assign admins to scoped roles** page, click **Next**.

10. On the **Review and finish** page, review your selections, make any changes, and then click **Add**.

11. Click **Done** to return to the **Administrative units** page.

One of the features of role-scoped administration is being able to limit what users or objects can be impacted by a particular administrator. As you saw during the configuration, only a subset of the roles available in the tenant honor administrative unit scoping.

Viewing and updating administrative units

After creating administrative units, you can review them and modify their members and administrators from either the Azure AD portal or the Microsoft 365 admin center under **Roles | Administrative units**.

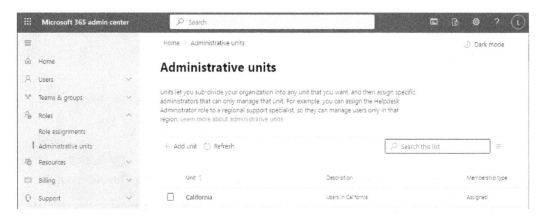

Figure 6.11 – Viewing administrative units

By selecting a group, you can assign users and groups to the administrative unit.

While you can assign groups to administrative units, it does not automatically add the group member objects to the administrative scope – it only enables managing the properties of the group. You need to add the members of the group to the administrative unit directly in order for them to be in scope.

> **Note**
>
> **Dynamic administrative units** are a preview feature that allows you to use filters and queries to automatically populate administrative units. Like dynamic groups, dynamic administrative units can only have one object type (users or devices). Dynamic administrative units can only be configured in the Azure AD portal at this time.

As you define administrative structures and delegation for your organization, you'll need to understand the limits of scoping controls. For instance, assigning an administrator to both an administrative unit as well as an Exchange or SharePoint Administrator role means that while they can only make modifications to users in their administrative unit, they can potentially make changes to application settings that affect users tenant-wide.

> **Note**
>
> Some applications, such as Exchange Online, support additional RBAC scoping controls to offer fine-grained service administration.

Planning and implementing privileged identity management

Privileged identity management (**PIM**) is the logical next step in RBAC and least-privileged identity management. While RBAC addresses *what amount of privilege is needed to accomplish a task*, PIM addresses the idea of *how long this level of privilege is required*.

Sometimes called **just-in-time** (**JIT**) access, PIM is a feature that allows users to request elevation to Azure AD roles or resources for limited periods of time to perform administrative tasks. At the end of the period, the roles and privileges are revoked, returning the user account to their pre-elevation access rights.

> **Note**
>
> PIM is an Azure AD Premium P2 feature and is included with Microsoft 365 E5 or Enterprise Mobility + Security E5.

PIM has a few key terms that you'll need to understand:

- **Assignment**: This describes how the user is granted the role. In the case of **eligible**, it means a user has to perform an action to use the role, such as requesting elevation or asking for an approval. In the case of **active**, it means the user doesn't have to do anything to request the role.

- **Duration**: This describes how long a particular assignment is active. It can be **permanent** (no expiration date) or **time-bound**, meaning it will only be active for a specific period of time.

For example, John is a full-time employee and needs to periodically be able perform functions in the Exchange Administrator role. His assignment would be *eligible*, while its duration would be *permanent*.

In another example, Kay is a temporary worker whose contract ends on July 31. She periodically needs to be elevated to be able to perform user administration functions. Her assignment would be *eligible*, while the duration would have an end date of July 31.

PIM for Azure AD roles and Azure resources can be configured in the Azure AD portal under the **Identity Governance** blade, as shown in *Figure 6.12*:

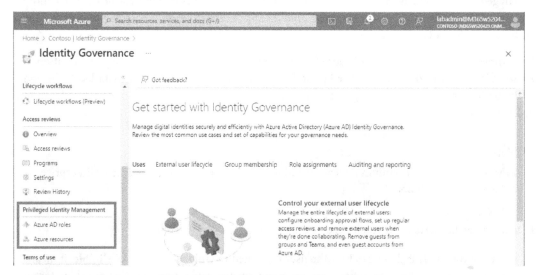

Figure 6.12 – Privileged Identity Management

Next, we'll look at configuring a simple assignment.

Creating a role assignment

You can configure PIM for a role by following this procedure:

1. Navigate to the Azure AD portal (`https://portal.azure.com`). Enter `Identity Governance` into the search bar and select the **Identity Governance** option.

2. Under **Privileged Identity Management**, select **Azure AD** roles.

3. Under **Manage**, select **Roles**.

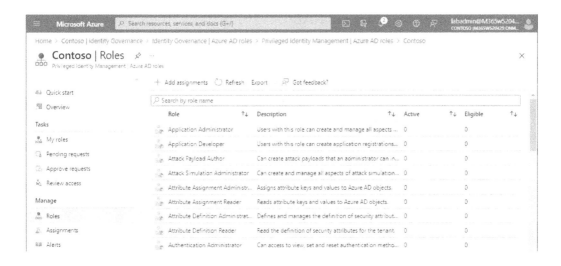

Figure 6.13 – Role assignments

4. Select the role you wish to configure an assignment for, such as the **Exchange Administrator** role.

5. Click **Add assignments**.

6. On the **Membership** tab of the **Add assignments** page, under **Select member(s)**, click **No member selected** to bring up the **Select a member** flyout.

7. On the **Select a member** flyout, choose one or more members and click **Select**.

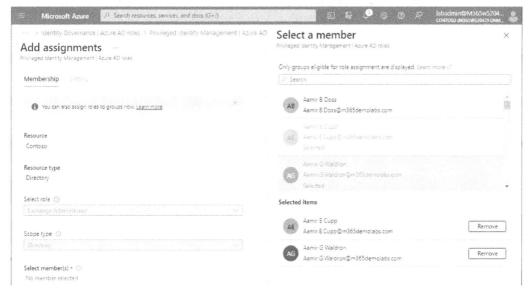

Figure 6.14 – Selecting members

8. On the **Add assignments** page, click **Next**.

9. On the **Setting** tab of the assignment page, select an assignment type, such as **Eligible**. In this instance, if you want users to be eligible to request elevation for the duration of the time period that their account is enabled, select **Permanently eligible**. Click **Assign**.

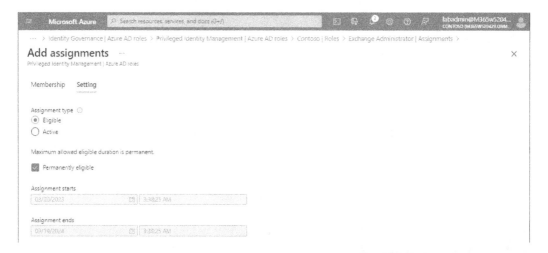

Figure 6.15 – Configuring the assignment type and eligibility duration

10. Click **Assign**.

From this point, the users that you have selected can activate their role assignment from the Azure AD portal.

Reviewing role assignments

You can review all of the assignments that you've created in the Azure AD portal. To view the role assignments, navigate to the **Identity Governance** blade and then select **Azure AD roles | Assignments**.

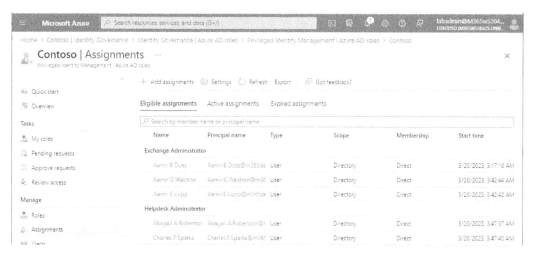

Figure 6.16 – Viewing role assignments

Under the **Eligible** assignments tab, assignments are listed under their respective Azure AD roles. The **Active assignments** tab lists individuals with various role assignments, including their end dates and whether they're permanent.

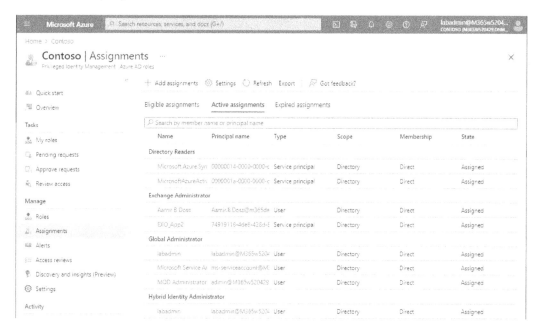

Figure 6.17 – Viewing active assignments

Alerting

PIM also has built-in alerting functions. The alerts are designed to provide notifications if certain risk conditions are detected. Several of the role alerts have sliders for notifications that can be used to tune the alerts for your organization. Alerts are accessed through the Azure AD portal | **Identity Governance** | the **Alerts** page. By clicking on the gear icon, you can see all of the pre-configured alerts and edit them to your requirements.

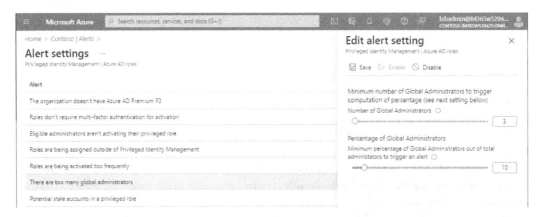

Figure 6.18 – Viewing the PIM alert settings

PIM is a tool to help reduce the surface area of your organization. By reducing the number of accounts with standing privileges, you can greatly reduce the risks presented by compromised administration accounts.

Summary

In this chapter, you learned about what it means to manage Azure AD from a least-privilege perspective. Reducing the scope and privileges used to administer an environment can greatly reduce the possible impacts of administrative actions – whether those are unintentional or targeted attacks by malicious users.

In the next chapter, we'll explore authentication options and configurations in the Microsoft 365 platform.

Knowledge check

In this section, we'll test your knowledge of some key elements from this chapter.

Questions

1. What is RBAC?

    A. Really broad administrator control

    B. Role-based administrative center

    C. Role-based access control

    D. Role-based administrative control

2. Which technology is sometimes referred to as just-in-time access control?

    A. RBAC

    B. PIM

    C. PAM

    D. LDAP

3. What configuration object is responsible for containing users, groups, and devices for delegated control in Azure AD?

    A. Administrative units

    B. Role-based access control

    C. Privileged identity management

    D. Organizational units

4. The first user created in a new Microsoft 365 tenant is granted which role?

    A. Exchange Administrator

    B. Identity Administrator

    C. Hybrid Identity Administrator

    D. Global Administrator

5. PIM is required to deploy administrative units.

    A. True

    B. False

Answers

1. C: Role-based access control
2. B: PIM
3. A: Administrative units
4. D: Global Administrator
5. B: False

Part 3:
Managing Access and Authentication

This part introduces you to concepts for secure and password-less authentication methods, such as Windows Hello for Business and FIDO2 tokens. You'll learn about implementing self-service password reset, multi-factor authentication, and Azure AD Identity Protection features. Finally, you'll explore application access provisioning and security.

This part has the following chapters:

- *Chapter 7, Planning and Implementing Authentication*
- *Chapter 8, Planning and Implementing Secure Access*
- *Chapter 9, Planning and Implementing Application Access*

7
Planning and Implementing Authentication

Over the course of the last few chapters, you've learned a lot about identity, synchronization, and sign-in methods – all part of the Microsoft 365 foundation. In this chapter, we'll shift gears from how you configure the service for a sign-in method to how you implement authentication on the user-facing side.

We're going to tackle authentication mechanisms and methods by covering the following topics:

- Choosing an authentication mechanism
- Configuring and managing multi-factor authentication
- Implementing and managing authentication methods
- Implementing and managing self-service password reset
- Implementing and managing Azure AD password protection
- Investigating and resolving authentication issues

By the end of this chapter, you should be able to describe the various authentication methods and supporting tools, as well as have an understanding of where to go to troubleshoot authentication issues.

Let's go!

Choosing an authentication mechanism

Everyone is familiar with using an identity and a corresponding password to log in to a device, service, application, or website. While Microsoft 365 supports traditional username and password authentication mechanisms, there are newer methods that provide fewer opportunities for malicious users to compromise identities, applications, and devices.

Microsoft has long advocated for using **multi-factor authentication (MFA)** as part of the login process to help secure identities – that is, using some sort of supplementary login tool (such as a token, authenticator app, phone call, or text message) to confirm the login process. The weakest link in this chain is the password; interfaces unable to leverage the MFA process are more susceptible to bad actors.

With Microsoft's newest **password-less** technologies, users get the advantage of MFA (something you have, something you know) without the frustration of remembering complex passwords. Microsoft supports several different approaches to password-less login, including **Windows Hello for Business (WHFB)**, the Microsoft Authenticator app, and FIDO2-compatible security keys or tokens.

Microsoft password-less options are based on a **public key infrastructure (PKI)** design, comprised of a **private key** (managed and stored by the user's device) and a **public key** saved in Azure AD. The keys are linked and only work with each other. When an entity (be it a user or device) establishes a public/private **key pair**, the public key can be broadly distributed to all other entities that the owner of the key pair wishes to communicate with.

Each key has two purposes:

- The public key is used to *encrypt* data. Only the corresponding private key can *decrypt* it.
- The private key is used to *sign* data. Only the corresponding public key can *authenticate* or verify the signature, offering proof that a particular private key produced it.

For example, let's say you establish a public/private key pair and you wish to conduct secure email communication. You distribute the public key to everyone who you will communicate with. You might even add it to your email signature, post it on a blog, or store it in a directory where others can look it up.

The following examples demonstrate possible uses for public key cryptography in the context of email:

- You're sending out an important product announcement update on behalf of your organization and you want people to be certain it's authentic. You sign the email with your private key. Recipients who already have your public key (or who can retrieve it from your website or a directory) can use the public key to check the signature on your email. Since only your private key matches that well-known public key, recipients can be assured that your private key was used to sign the content.
- You're in the process of acquiring financing for a new business venture. The lender has prepared documents for you to review. Since they contain sensitive financial information, the lender wants to make sure that only you can open them. They encrypt the content with your public key and email you the documents. Since only your private key is able to decrypt the content, both entities can be assured that the content will be unreadable to anyone else.

Those types of scenarios are analogous to what happens when using PKI-based sign-on methods such as Windows Hello, but instead of signing and encrypting email, it's used for authentication data.

In this section, we'll explore a little bit about each of these mechanisms to help you decide which is appropriate for your organization.

Windows Hello for Business

Microsoft's recommended solution for password-less authentication is Windows Hello for Business. It's designed for users that have their own dedicated PC. When logging in, the user presents a biometric or PIN code to unlock the device.

Windows Hello for Business supports a variety of biometric logins, including facial recognition and fingerprint scanner. Devices configured to use Windows Hello can be recognized because they have the Windows Hello smiley face greeting at the top:

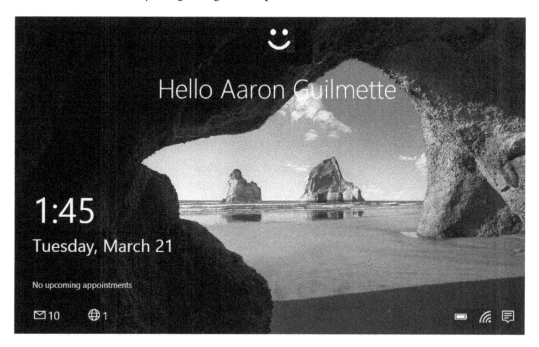

Figure 7.1 – Windows Hello for Business sign-on screen

After configuring Windows Hello, the sign-in flow follows this sequence, as depicted in *Figure 7.2*:

Figure 7.2 – Windows Hello authentication sequence

The steps are as follows:

1. User signs in with either biometrics or PIN (if the configured biometric input can't be accessed), which unlocks the WHFB private key. The key is then passed to the **Cloud authentication security support provider**, also known as the **Cloud AP**, part of the on-device security package.

2. The Cloud AP requests a **nonce** (single-use random number) from Azure AD.

3. Azure AD sends the nonce to the Cloud AP on the endpoint.

4. The Cloud AP signs the nonce with the user's private key and returns the signed nonce to Azure AD.

5. Azure AD decrypts and validates the signed nonce with the user's public key. After it's validated, Azure ID issues a **primary refresh token** (**PRT**) with the session key, encrypts it using the device's public transport key, and sends that to the Cloud AP.

6. The Cloud AP decrypts the PRT/session key using the device's transport private key and then uses the **Trusted Platform Module** (**TPM**) to store the session key.

    The Cloud AP returns a successful response to Windows, allowing the user to log in to complete.

Windows Hello for Business is available to be deployed as a cloud-only or hybrid identity solution and can be used for both Windows login as well as for logging in to Microsoft 365 services. Windows Hello-based authentication is tied to a unique device, meaning you have to set it up individually for each device that you will be using.

Microsoft Authenticator app

Many administrators and users are already familiar with the Microsoft Authenticator mobile device app, using it for MFA. The Authenticator app can also be used as a password-less sign-in option. When used as a password-less option, Microsoft Authenticator can use number-matching, where the sign-in screen displays a number that the user enters and confirms with their PIN or biometric data (see *Figure 7.3*):

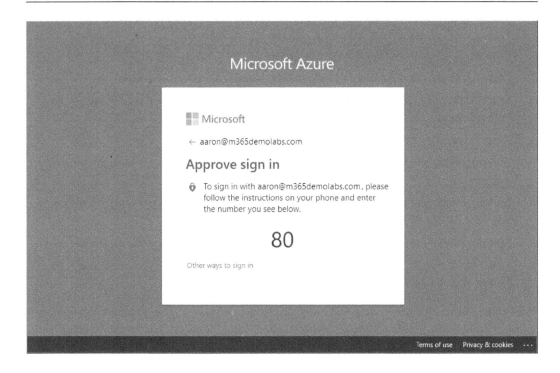

Figure 7.3 – Password-less authentication dialog with Microsoft Authenticator

The data flow using the Authenticator app follows the same general pattern as Windows Hello, as shown in *Figure 7.4*:

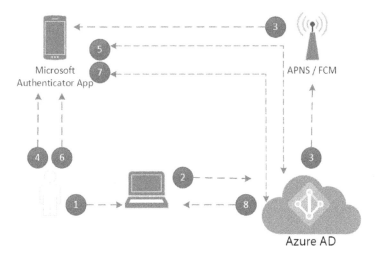

Figure 7.4 – Microsoft Authenticator authentication sequence

The steps are as follows:

1. The user enters their username on the device.

2. Azure AD detects that the user is configured for password-less authentication.

3. Azure AD sends a notification to the Authenticator app on the user's configured Apple or Android device.

4. The user launches the Authenticator app.

5. The Authenticator app connects to Azure AD and receives the proof-of-presence challenge and nonce.

6. The user completes the challenge on their mobile device and then confirms their identity with biometric data or a PIN, unlocking the private key.

7. The private key is used to sign the nonce and the Authenticator app returns the data to Azure AD.

8. Azure AD decrypts the data with the user's public key, performs validation, and then returns the sign-in token to the original device where the login was started.

While WHFB has specific hardware requirements (such as a Windows Hello-compatible camera or fingerprint reader), the password-less Microsoft Authenticator has a very low barrier to entry. The Authenticator app is free for iOS and Android devices and works not only with Microsoft 365 services but also with any service that supports a soft-token app or device.

FIDO2 security keys

Physical tokens, such as the **Fast Identity Online 2 (FIDO2)**-based token or security key, are another password-less option that can be used. While the Microsoft Authenticator app is a soft token, FIDO2 tokens are physical pieces of hardware that are typically either connected to the computer (in the form of a USB device) or that communicate wirelessly (via Bluetooth or NFC).

You can access the security key login process during a browser session by selecting the **Sign in with Windows Hello or a security key** option from the sign-in page:

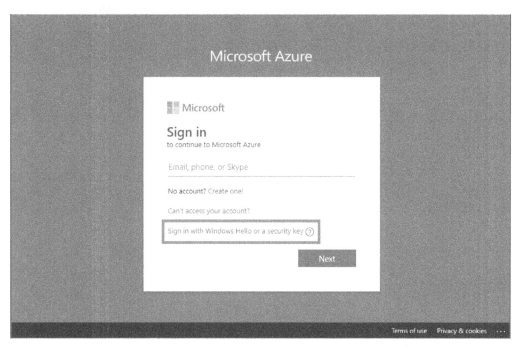

Figure 7.5 – Password-less authentication dialog with FIDO2 security token

The data flow for a FIDO2-based login follows a similar pattern as both WHFB and the Microsoft Authenticator app. For example, to log on to a device using FIDO2, this process is followed:

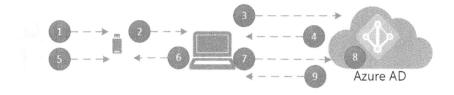

Figure 7.6 – FIDO2 authentication sequence

The steps are as follows:

1. The user plugs in a FIDO2 security key.

2. Windows detects the security key.

3. Windows sends an authentication request to Azure AD.

4. Azure AD responds by sending a nonce back to the login device.

5. The user authenticates to the FIDO2 key, unlocking the secure storage area containing the private key.

6. The FIDO2 key signs the nonce with the private key and sends it to Windows.

7. Windows generates a PRT request and sends it with the signed nonce to Azure AD.

8. Azure AD verifies the signed nonce with the FIDO2 device's public key.

9. Azure AD returns the PRT to the login device.

FIDO2, such as Windows Hello, has specific requirements for supported hardware.

> **Supported FIDO2 security tokens**
>
> You can see an up-to-date list of supported FIDO2 security keys or tokens here: `https://learn.microsoft.com/en-us/azure/active-directory/authentication/concept-authentication-password-less#fido2-security-key-providers`.

As you've seen from the diagrams, each of the password-less options (Windows Hello, Microsoft Authenticator, and FIDO2) follows a similar authentication workflow, based on PKI.

Comparison

Now that you have an understanding of the different password-less options available for Microsoft 365, let's look at some information that will help you choose the appropriate solution. *Table 7.1* describes some basic features and requirements for each authentication scheme:

	Windows Hello for Business	**Authenticator app**	**FIDO2 security keys**
Prerequisite requirement	Device with a built-in TPM and biometric recognition running Windows 10 (1809 or later) or Windows 11; Azure AD	Authenticator app for iOS or Android; device supporting biometric recognition	Windows 10 (1903 or later) or Windows 11; Azure AD
Authentication mode	Platform	Software/soft token	Hardware
User experience	Sign in to supported device using PIN or biometric data	Sign in to supported applications and browsers using PIN or biometric data	Sign in using FIDO2 device with supported PIN or biometric data
Scenarios	Password-less sign-in with Windows device and supported applications	Multi-platform password-less solution for web applications	Password-less sign-in for single- or multi-user scenarios or where soft tokens are not suitable

Table 7.1 – Authentication method comparison table

It's also important to consider the various end user scenarios that your organization utilizes to ensure you're recommending an appropriate mechanism based on your real-world use cases. *Table 7.2* describes a few example scenarios:

Role/persona	Scenario/use case	Platform	Suitable or recommended password-less methods
Administrator	Secure device access for administrative tasks	Assigned Windows 10 or Windows 11 device	Windows Hello for Business; FIDO2
Administrator	Administrative tasks on down-level or non-Windows devices	Mobile, down-level, or non-Windows devices	Microsoft Authenticator app
Information/knowledge worker	Productivity work	Assigned Windows 10 or Windows 11 device	Windows Hello for Business; FIDO2
Information/knowledge worker	Productivity work	Mobile, down-level, or non-Windows devices	Microsoft Authenticator app
Frontline worker	Kiosks, Azure Virtual Desktop (preview)	Shared Windows 10 or Windows 11 devices; Azure Virtual Desktop (Preview)	FIDO2

Table 7.2 – Password-less login scenarios

With that information in hand, it's time to look at the implementation aspects.

Configuring and managing multi-factor authentication

Configuring users for MFA can increase the security posture of your Microsoft 365 environment, in addition to protecting any apps that use Azure AD for identity and authentication.

In this section, we'll look at configuring MFA for your tenant.

Per-user multi-factor authentication

If MFA was configured in your tenant before October 2019, it may have been configured using the legacy MFA scheme. Prior to newer technologies, MFA was enabled on a per-user basis by manually updating each user's account to enforce the use of MFA.

Prior to implementing either Microsoft-managed security defaults or Conditional Access policies, you will need to disable the legacy per-user MFA. Having per-user MFA enabled while configuring a Conditional Access policy that prompts for MFA may cause unintended or unexpected MFA prompts.

To disable per-user MFA, follow these steps:

1. Navigate to the Microsoft 365 admin center (`https://admin.microsoft.com`).

2. Expand **Users** and select **Active users**.

3. Select **Multi-factor authentication**.

Figure 7.7 – The Active users page

4. If your tenant already has Conditional Access policies, you may need to select the **Legacy per-user MFA** link to launch the legacy MFA page.

5. On the **Multi-factor authentication** page, configure the per-user MFA status to **Disabled** for users that have **Enforced** or **Enabled** set. You can select multiple users but can only multi-select users that have the same MFA status type.

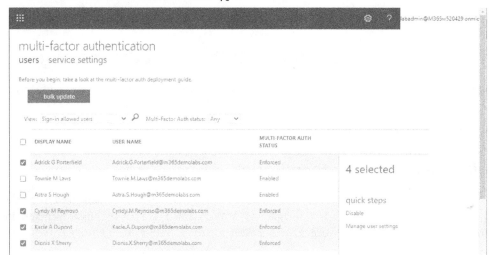

Figure 7.8 – Selecting users

Once per-user MFA is disabled, you can configure the security defaults or the Conditional Aaccess policies.

Security defaults

For most organizations, security defaults are a good choice for configuring broad baseline security policies. Security defaults make the following security changes:

- Requiring all users to register for MFA

- Requiring administrators to perform MFA upon sign-in

- Requiring users to do MFA when necessary

- Blocking basic authentication and other legacy authentication protocols

- Requiring administrators to perform MFA when accessing privileged resources, such as the Azure portal, Azure PowerShell, or the Azure CLI

Security defaults can be modified by users with the Global Administrator, Conditional Access Administrator, or Security Administrator role. Security defaults can be enabled or disabled using the following process:

1. Navigate to the Azure portal (`https://portal.azure.com`).

2. Select **Azure Active Directory**.

3. Under **Manage**, click **Properties**.

4. Scroll to the bottom of the page and click **Manage security defaults**.

5. On the **Security defaults** flyout, select either **Enabled** or **Disabled** and click **Save**.

If you are going to configure Conditional Access policies, you should disable **Security defaults.** If you are not going to configure Conditional Access policies, you should enable **Security defaults**.

> **Further reading**
>
> For more information on the impact of security defaults, see the following: `https://learn.microsoft.com/en-us/azure/active-directory/fundamentals/concept-fundamentals-security-defaults`.

Conditional Access

Conditional access provides the most fine-grained control when managing the MFA requirements for your organization. Conditional access policies can be configured from the Azure portal.

To access the Conditional access configuration page, follow these steps:

1. Navigate to the Azure portal (`https://portal.azure.com`).

2. Select **Azure Active Directory** | **Security** | **Conditional Access**, and then choose **Policies**.

You can create new policies or use one of the 14 Microsoft-provided sample Conditional Access policy templates. Policies created by the template can be modified once they have been deployed to your tenant.

To configure a template-based policy, follow these steps:

1. From the **Conditional Access** | **Policies** page, select **New policy from template (Preview)**.

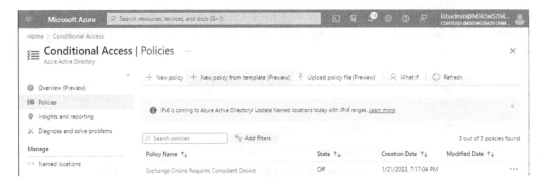

Figure 7.9 – Creating a new Conditional Access policy from a template

2. Select one of the templates, such as **Require multifactor authentication for all users,** and click **Review + create**.

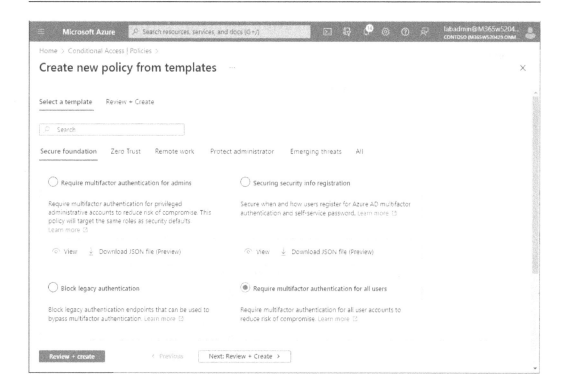

Figure 7.10 – Selecting a template

3.   Review the settings and click **Create**.

Policies created through the templates cannot be modified during creation, with the exception of the enforcement mode. All template-based policies are configured in **Report only mode**, which can be toggled during creation. The user creating the policy is excluded from the policy to prevent accidental lock-out.

After the template policies have been configured, you can edit the scope and conditions for the policy like you would with manually created policies.

> **Further reading**
>
> For more information on Conditional Access templates, see here: https://learn.
> microsoft.com/en-us/azure/active-directory/conditional-access/
> concept-conditional-access-policy-common.

With the exception of Windows Hello, password-less sign-in methods (such as the Microsoft Authenticator app or FIDO2 security keys) will require users to register for MFA.

Additional multi-factor authentication behavior settings

In addition to the core options for the methods and types of MFA, Azure AD also supports a number of settings to further modify the behavior of MFA. These properties are located under **Azure Active Directory | Security | Multi-factor authentication** in the Azure portal.

Area	Description	Setting
Account lockout	Temporarily locks accounts from using MFA if there are too many denied authentication attempts in a row.	**Number of multi-factor authentication denials to trigger lockout** Default: <none>, Valid range: 1-99
		Minutes until lockout counter is reset Default: <none>, Valid range: 1-1440
		Minutes until account is automatically unblocked Default: <none>, Valid range: 1-9999
Block/unblock users	Maintain a list of users to block from receiving MFA requests	Add or remove users from the **Blocked users** list
Fraud alert	Allow users to report fraud if they receive MFA requests that they did not initiate	**Allow users to submit fraud alerts** Default: Off
		Automatically block users who report fraud Default: <grayed out>
		Code to report fraud during initial greeting Default: 0, Valid range: 1-99999
Notifications	Notify this address of MFA requests	**Recipient's Email Address** <none>
OAuth tokens	Upload OAuth token data for end users	Upload OAuth token CSV data

Area	Description	Setting
Phone call settings	Customize the verification phone calls for users that choose an MFA method that supports calling	**Multi-factor authentication caller ID number (US phone number only)** Default: \<none\>, Valid range 1-12 digits
		Operator required to transfer extensions Default: \<grayed out\>
		Add greeting Record a custom voice greeting

Table 7.3 – Additional MFA settings

Implementing and managing authentication methods

After selecting an appropriate authentication mechanism that meets your organization's business requirements and configuring MFA requirements, you can begin deployment.

> **Exam note**
>
> Full deployment and configuration of these methods are outside the scope of the MS-100 exam, but it would be good to spend a little bit of time following the docs for deeper dives into the product documentation.

Let's go through an overview of the configurations necessary to enable password-less authentication methods.

Configuring Windows Hello

WHFB supports cloud-only, hybrid Azure AD, and on-premises deployments. The easiest method to deploy Windows Hello is in a cloud-only model since the Microsoft 365 organization is set up for it automatically. We'll look at that scenario in this section.

During the **out-of-box experience (OOBE)**, users are prompted for credentials. After providing an Azure AD credential, if the Intune enrollment policy has not been configured to block WHFB, the user will be prompted to enroll with their biometric data (such as a facial scan with a compatible camera) and set a PIN.

Devices will be joined to Azure during the initial sign-in process and WHFB will be enabled.

If your subscription supports it, Microsoft recommends creating a WHFB policy to configure settings for your organization:

1. Navigate to the Intune admin center (`https://intune.microsoft.com` or `https://endpoint.microsoft.com`).

2. Expand **Devices**, and under **Device enrollment**, select **Enroll devices**.

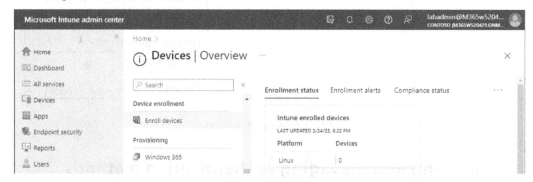

Figure 7.11 – Enroll devices

3. Select **Windows enrollment** and then choose **Windows Hello for Business**.

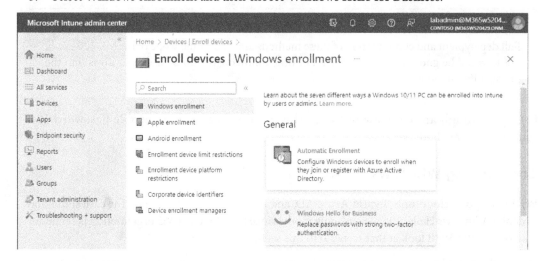

Figure 7.12 – Windows Hello for Business

4. Under **Assigned to**, select a group (if scoping the enrollment policy to a subset of the user).

5. Configure the options for WHFB (bold options are the default settings for the enrollment policy):

- **Configure Windows Hello for Business**: **Enabled**, Disabled, Not Configured
- **Use a Trusted Platform Module (TPM)**: **Required**, Preferred
- **Minimum PIN length**: Configure a numeric value between 4 and 127
- **Maximum PIN length**: Configure a numeric value between 4   and 127
- **Lowercase letters in PIN**: **Not allowed**, Allowed, Required
- **Uppercase letters in PIN**: Not allowed, **Allowed**, **Required**
- **Special characters in PIN**: Not allowed, **Allowed**, **Required**
- **PIN expiration (days)**: **Never**, numeric value between 1 and 730
- **Remember PIN history**: **Never**, numeric value between 1 and 50
- **Allow biometric authentication**: **Yes**, No
- **Use enhanced anti-spoofing, when available**: **Not configured**, Yes, No
- **Allow phone sign-in**: **Yes**, No
- **Use security keys for sign-in**: **Not configured**, Enabled, Disabled

6. Click **Save** to update the enrollment policy.

With the policy configured, new device enrollments (for the configured user group) will receive the WHFB setup prompt to begin enrollment, as shown in *Figure 7.13*:

Figure 7.13 – WHFB enrollment

After completing enrollment, users will be able to unlock and log in to devices using supported biometrics or their PIN.

Users that are already connected to Azure AD can also trigger the Windows Hello setup wizard by either navigating to the **Account protection** blade in the Windows settings app or pressing *Windows + R* and entering ms-cxh://nthaad in the **Run** dialog box.

Next, we'll look at configuring Microsoft Authenticator for password-less sign-in.

Configuring Microsoft Authenticator

The Microsoft Authenticator app provides a convenient way to sign in to any Azure AD account with a supported mobile device. Before users can sign in using the method, however, it will need to be enabled in your tenant through the authentication policy.

Configuring the authentication policy

To enable users to sign in with Microsoft Authenticator, you need to configure the authentication policy. The authentication policy is shared across the tenant, though different authentication methods are scoped for groups of users.

Configuring and managing the policy requires an account with the Global Administrator or Authentication Administrator role.

1. Navigate to the Azure portal (https://portal.azure.com).

2. Select **Azure Active Directory** | **Security** | **Authentication methods** and then select **Policies**.

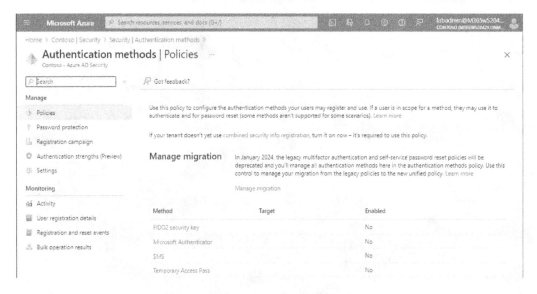

Figure 7.14 – Authentication methods

3.   Select **Microsoft Authenticator**.

4.   On the **Enable and Target** tab of the **Microsoft Authenticator settings** page, slide the **Enable** toggle to **on**.

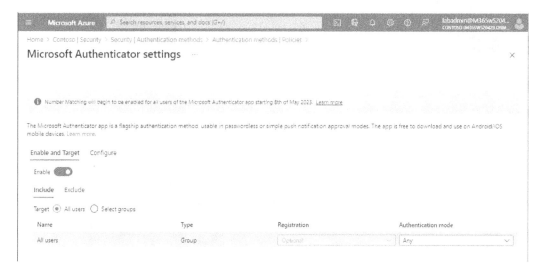

Figure 7.15 – Enabling Microsoft Authenticator

5.   Using the **Include** and **Exclude** tabs, specify which users the policy settings will apply to. Select the **All users** radio button to include all users in the policy or choose the **Select groups** radio button to specify which groups will be included or excluded. Each group can have a separate **Authentication mode** value selected, including **Any** (default), **Passwordless**, or **Push**. Choosing **Push** as the option prevents the use of the password-less phone sign-in credential.

6.   Click **Save** to update the policy configuration.

After configuring the policy, users will need to register any devices to be used for passwordless authentication.

Registering devices

Before users can log in to the service using Microsoft Authenticator, they will need to register their devices. If they've already registered for MFA, nothing else needs to be done.

If a user who has not registered signs in to the Microsoft 365 portal, they are greeted with a **More information required** dialog as part of the sign-in process.

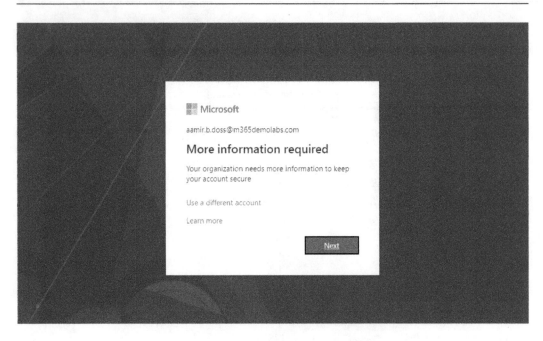

Figure 7.16 – More information required

During the process, they are redirected to download the Microsoft Authenticator app.

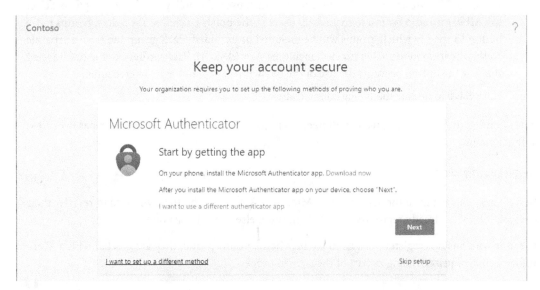

Figure 7.17 – The Keep your account secure page

After they click **Next**, they are prompted to launch the Microsoft Authenticator app and click **Add an account**. Following the directions on the mobile device should launch a new window, which allows them to scan a unique QR code to link their device to their account.

Figure 7.18 – Registering a device

Once the device has been linked, the enrollment process will ask the user to confirm a code between the registration screen and their Microsoft Authenticator app. After completing the challenge, users should be presented with a confirmation screen, similar to the one shown in *Figure 7.19*.

Contoso

Keep your account secure

Your organization requires you to set up the following methods of proving who you are.

Success!

Great job! You have successfully set up your security info. Choose "Done" to continue signing in.

Default sign-in method:

Authenticator app

Done

Figure 7.19 – The authenticator registration screen

The final step for the user for full password-less sign-in from the Microsoft Authenticator app is to configure the device itself. In Microsoft Authenticator, the user can open the app and select **Enable phone sign-in**:

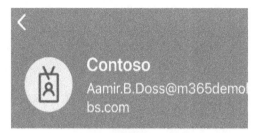

Figure 7.20 – Microsoft Authenticator's phone sign-in box

This will start a process to configure the device for password-less sign-in. After configuration, the user can choose to log in with an app instead, triggering the phone authentication notification on their device. See *Figure 7.21*:

Figure 7.21 – Launching password-less sign-in

The user then completes the login challenge in the Microsoft Authenticator app to finish logging in to Microsoft 365.

Configuring FIDO2

When setting up FIDO2-based authentication, you'll follow a process similar to Microsoft Authenticator – updating the authentication policy to allow the method and then instructing users to self-register their security keys.

Configuring the authentication policy

To enable users to sign in with FIDO2 security keys, you need to configure the authentication policy. Configuring the policy requires an account with the Global Administrator or Authentication Administrator role.

1. Navigate to the Azure portal (`https://portal.azure.com`).

2. Select **Azure Active Directory** | **Security** | **Authentication methods** and then select **Policies**.

3. Select **Microsoft Authenticator**.

4. On the **Enable and Target** tab of the **FIDO2 security key settings** page, slide the **Enable** toggle to **on**.

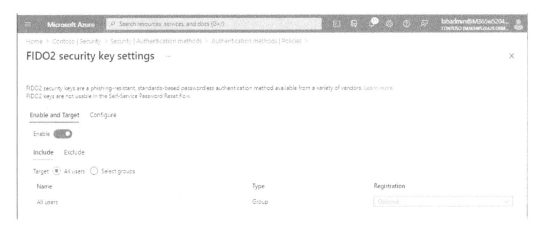

Figure 7.22 – Enabling Microsoft Authenticator

5. Using the **Include** and **Exclude** tabs, specify which users the policy settings will apply to. Select the **All users** radio button to include all users in the policy or choose the **Select groups** radio button to specify which groups will be included or excluded.

6. Click **Save** to update the policy configuration.

The next step is to instruct users to register the security keys.

Registering devices

Like Microsoft Authenticator-based authentication, FIDO2 authentication requires end users to register the compatible device they wish to use for authentication.

> **Note**
>
> In order to register a FIDO2 security key, the user must already have an Azure AD MFA method configured. If they do not have one, they must add one (such as Microsoft Authenticator or SMS). If that is not possible, an administrator can issue a **Temporary Access Pass (TAP)** to allow the user to complete registration. For more information on configuring a TAP, please see the following: `https://learn.microsoft.com/en-us/azure/active-directory/authentication/howto-authentication-temporary-access-pass`.

To register a FIDO2 security key, users must follow these steps:

1. Navigate to `https://myprofile.microsoft.com` or, from the Microsoft 365 portal, expand the profile icon, and select **View account**.

Figure 7.23 – Accessing the user's account

2. Click **Security Info**.
3. Select **Add method** and click **Security key**.
4. Select either **USB device** or **NFC device**.
5. Ensure the key is ready and click **Next**.
6. In the dialog box, create and enter a PIN for the security key and then perform the required gesture (biometric/touch) to confirm.
7. Enter your name for the key in **Name** and click **Next**.
8. Click **Done**.

After the key has been registered, users can sign in to Azure AD using their security key. On the Azure sign-in page, after entering a username, users can select the **Sign in with Windows Hello or a security key** option, which will cause the browser to issue a prompt to insert the key, as shown in *Figure 7.24*:

Figure 7.24 – Sign in with Windows Hello or a security key

Next, we'll look at configuring **self-service password reset** (**SSPR**).

Implementing and managing self-service password reset

SSPR is a feature that allows users to change or reset passwords without administrator or service desk involvement. Self-service passwords can be configured for Azure AD cloud-only environments as well as enabling SSPR of hybrid identity through Azure AD Connect's Password Writeback feature.

Configuring self-service password reset

Enabling SSPR is a straightforward task. Like many other features in Azure AD, it can be scoped to a group of users.

To enable SSPR, follow these steps:

1. Navigate to the Azure portal (`https://portal.azure.com`) and select **Azure Active Directory**.

2. Under **Manage**, select **Password reset**.

3.   On the **Properties** page, click **Selected** if you want to be able to select one or more groups to enable SSPR. Click **All** if you want to enable all users for SSPR.

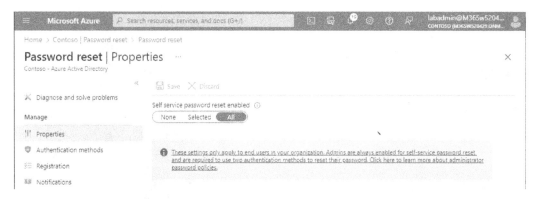

Figure 7.25 – Enabling SSPR

4.   Click **Save**.

Now that password reset has been enabled, you can manage and configure the features.

Managing self-service password reset

SSPR has a number of configuration options, including **Authentication methods**, **Registration** settings, **Notifications** options, portal **Customization** options, and **On-premises integration**. Each of those options can be configured on the **Password reset** configuration blade of the Azure portal.

Authentication methods

Authentication methods are used to define how a user proves their identity, such as MFA or answering security questions. The **Authentication methods** page lets you select which options a user can register, as well as the number of methods needed to perform a reset.

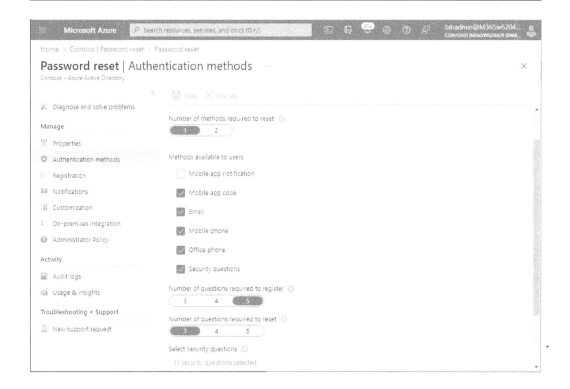

Figure 7.26 – Authentication methods

If you choose security questions, additional options are configurable, including the number of questions a user must supply when they select that option and the number of those security questions they must answer to prove their identity. You can choose up to 20 security questions from a list of pre-defined options or create your own security questions. Administrators are unable to pre-populate or retrieve answers to end user security questions; users must select their own questions.

> **Exam tip**
>
> Using the **Office phone** registration option requires an Azure AD Premium license (either P1 or P2) and can be pre-populated with a phone number in AD under the **telephoneNumber** attribute (if using Azure AD Connect to synchronize data). Other fields that can be pre-populated for SSPR include a user's alternate email address and mobile phone number. An alternate email does not synchronize from the on-premises AD and must be set using `Set-AzureADUser -OtherMails`, `Set-MsolUser -AlternateEmailAddresses`, or `Set-MgUser -OtherMails`.

Registration

The options on this page allow you to configure a workflow to force users to register for SSPR the first time they log in to the Microsoft 365 portal, as well as the interval in days in which users are asked to re-confirm their details.

Notifications

The **Notifications** page allows you to configure options for alerting on password changes. You can select **Notify users on password resets,** which sends users an email when their own password is reset via SSPR. The **Notify all admins when other admins reset their password** setting determines whether all Global Administrators receive a notification when any Global Administrator resets their password via SSPR.

Customization

The **Customization** page allows you to display a custom URL or email address for support-related requests.

On-premises integration

If you have configured Azure AD Connect or Azure AD Connect cloud sync with your organization, you can manage SSPR integration features, as shown in *Figure 7.27*:

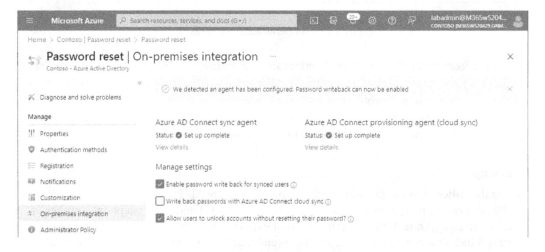

Figure 7.27 – On-premises integration

It's important to note that the **Enable password write back for synced users** option only modifies the behavior of Azure AD sending password reset data back to the on-premises environment, effectively stopping on-premises integration. It *does not* modify the on-premises Azure AD Connect configuration.

Next, we'll look at the features of Azure AD password protection.

Implementing and managing Azure AD password protection

Azure AD password protection is a set of features designed to limit the effects of common password attacks. To view the password protection configuration, navigate to **Azure Active Directory | Security | Authentication methods** and select **Password protection**.

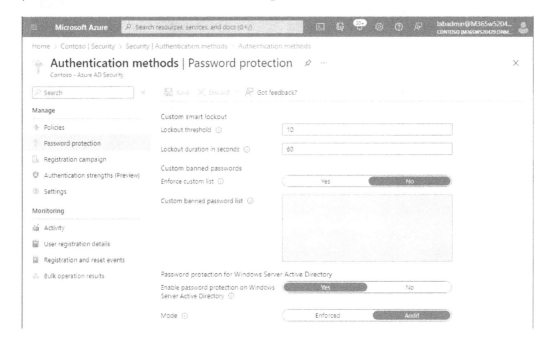

Figure 7.28 – Password protection

There are three groups of settings to configure:

- Custom smart lockout
- Custom banned passwords
- Password protection for Windows Server Active Directory

Let's briefly examine each set of configurations.

Custom smart lockout

The smart lockout settings determine how Azure AD handles failed login attempts. **Lockout threshold** is the number of times in a row a user can enter a bad password before getting locked out. By default, **Lockout threshold** is set to **10** in Azure Worldwide (sometimes referred to as *Commercial* or *Public*) and Azure China 21Vianet tenants, while it is set at **3** for Azure US Government customers.

Figure 7.29 – Account lockout

Lockout duration in seconds only specifies the initial lockout duration after the lockout threshold has been reached. Each subsequent lockout increases the lockout duration. As a security mechanism, Microsoft does not publish the rate at which the duration increases.

Custom banned passwords

While Microsoft recommends moving toward password-less authentication as a primary mechanism, passwords are still required to be configured in a number of scenarios. To help minimize using well-known, weak, or easily guessable passwords, you choose to specify a custom list of words that you want to exclude from being used as passwords. For example, you may wish to include your organization's name or abbreviation, products or services offered by your organization, or local sports teams.

To enable the option, slide the **Enforce custom list** toggle to **Yes**, and then add up to 1,000 banned words in the **Custom banned password list** text area. The list is not case-sensitive. Azure AD automatically performs common substitutions (such as 0 with o),

Password protection for Windows Server Active Directory

This settings area allows you to extend the custom banned password list to your on-premises infrastructure. There are two components:

- **Azure AD Password Protection DC agent**, which must be installed on domain controllers.

- **Azure AD Password Protection proxy**, which must be installed on at least one domain-joined server in the forest. As a security best practice, Microsoft recommends deploying on a member server since it requires internet connectivity.

In this configuration, the Azure AD Password Protection proxy servers periodically retrieve the custom banned password list from Azure AD. The DC agents cache the password policy locally and validate password change requests accordingly.

If **Enable password protection on Windows Server Active Directory** is configured to **Yes**, then you can choose in what mode to process password change requests. They can be processed in **Audit** mode (where changes are logged) or in **Enforced** mode, where password resets are actively evaluated against the banned password list and rejected if they do not meet the requirements.

> **Further reading**
>
> To view detailed steps for deploying password protection on-premises, see here: `https://learn.microsoft.com/en-us/azure/active-directory/authentication/concept-password-ban-bad-on-premises`.

Investigating and resolving authentication issues

Resolving authentication issues in Azure AD can be tricky, due to the number of authentication methods, sign-in methods, and other configurations that may be put in place.

The first step, when attempting to troubleshoot an issue, is to review any available sign-in logs in the Azure portal. To locate the sign-in logs, navigate to the Azure portal (`https://portal.azure.com`) and then select **Azure Active Directory** | **Sign-in logs**:

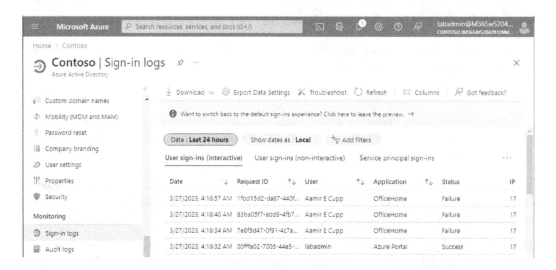

Figure 7.30 – Sign-in logs

Each authentication failure generates an individual entry. You can select an entry to see expanded details, as shown in *Figure 7.31*:

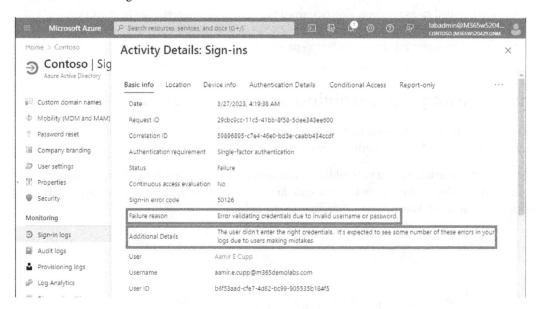

Figure 7.31 – Activity details

The **Basic info** tab displays high-level information about this particular event. The critical piece of information will typically be listed next to **Failure reason**, and some expanded explanation may be available in the **Additional Details** property. In the example shown in *Figure 7.31*, it's easy to determine that the user entered an incorrect password. If the user has entered an incorrect password multiple times in a row, it may be a sign of a forgotten password or an attempted identity breach. *Figure 7.32* shows the same account after it has met the smart lockout threshold:

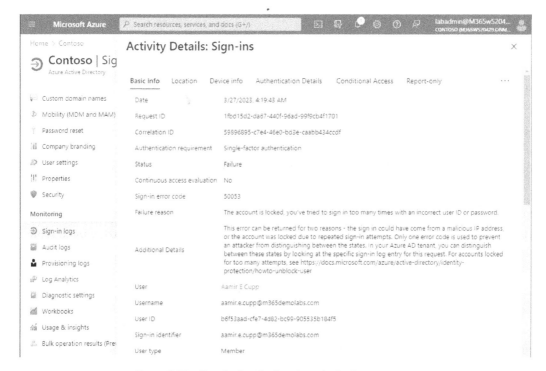

Figure 7.32 – Sign-in details showing a locked-out account

The **Location** tab will show detailed information regarding the source IP address, and, if possible, resolution to a particular geographic location.

The **Device info** tab displays information regarding the device that was attempting a login, such as a Windows 10 device with the Edge browser.

The **Authentication Details** tab provides additional information regarding the authentication method, including whether the user is configured for **Password Hash Sync**, **Federation**, or **Pass-through Authentication**, or whether they're using a cloud-managed identity.

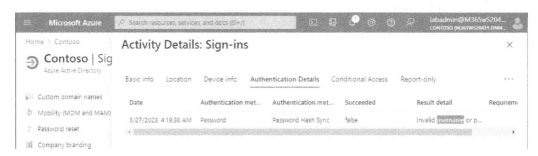

Figure 7.33 – Authentication details

Finally, the last two tabs, **Conditional Access** and **Report-only**, show what policies took effect during the sign-in process.

Resolving an authentication issue sometimes requires examining several logs to determine the source of the error. In many cases, however, the detailed data provided on each of the tabs of an event's activity details should provide adequate information to pinpoint the source of the error.

Summary

In this chapter, you learned how to evaluate password-less sign-in options for your organization and deploy the ones that best suit your needs. Some password-less options, such as Windows Hello or FIDO2 keys, may require specialized hardware such as cameras, USB devices, or fingerprint readers, while the Microsoft Authenticator app method requires only the Microsoft Authenticator app on any supported Android or iOS-based device.

You also learned about deploying features such as SSPR and Azure AD Password Protection to further reduce administrative overhead and help your organization comply with security policies.

In the next chapter, we'll learn about implementing secure access in the context of Microsoft 365.

Knowledge check

In this section, we'll test your knowledge of some key elements from this chapter.

Questions

1. Which password-less option supports the broadest array of devices?

    A. FIDO2 security token

    B. OATH token

    C. Microsoft Authenticator app

    D. Windows Hello for Business

2. The _____ is used to enable the Microsoft Authenticator app as an authentication method.

   A. Authentication context

   B. Authentication method

   C. Authentication policy

   D. Authentication registration

3. Identify the password-less options based on public key cryptography principles.

   A. Microsoft Authenticator app

   B. Windows Hello for Business

   C. FIDO2 security key

   D. Federation

4. Generally, before a user can register a FIDO2 security token for password-less authentication, what must they do?

   A. Establish a PIN

   B. Establish a second factor of authentication

   C. Answer a security question

   D. Restart their device

5. You have been instructed to deploy a platform-based password-less solution. Which option meets the criteria?

   A. Microsoft Authenticator app

   B. FIDO2 security token

   C. OATH token

   D. Windows Hello for Business

Answers

1. C: Microsoft Authenticator

2. C: Authentication policy

3. A: Microsoft Authenticator app; B: Windows Hello for Business; C: FIDO2 security key

4. B: Establish a second factor of authentication

5. D: Windows Hello for Business

8
Planning and Implementing Secure Access

Security and identity are some of the most important parts of managing a Microsoft 365 tenant.

As an administrator, you may need to provide a mechanism that allows users to share information with others outside your Microsoft 365 tenant. Planning an access strategy for both internal and external users is critical to maintaining a secure operating environment.

There are a lot of areas that touch on access, specifically around governance and access policies. In this chapter, we'll look at the following areas:

- Planning and implementing access reviews in Azure AD Identity Governance
- Planning and implementing entitlement packages in Azure AD Identity Governance
- Planning for identity protection
- Implementing and managing Azure AD Identity Protection
- Planning Conditional Access policies
- Implementing and managing Conditional Access policies

By the end of this chapter, you should be able to describe the various authentication methods and supporting tools, as well as have an understanding of where to go to troubleshoot authentication issues.

The following main topics will be covered:

- Overview of Identity Governance
- Planning and implementing Identity Governance
- Working with secure access

Let's go!

Overview of Identity Governance

Microsoft Entra **Identity Governance** is a set of policy-based tools for managing the identity and access life cycle across an organization. Identity Governance helps organizations identify which users should have access to which resources under which circumstances while providing audit data to support the access controls.

From the perspective of the MS-100 exam, you'll need to understand three Identity Governance areas:

- Identity life cycle
- Access life cycle
- Privileged access life cycle

Let's review each of these areas.

What is the identity life cycle?

The identity life cycle encompasses everything from the moment an identity is provisioned into your organization until that identity is no longer needed. While the identity life cycle frequently focuses on employees and contractors, it can (and should) also include identities for vendors, partners, or other individuals to whom you grant access to your applications and data.

The diagram in *Figure 8.1* shows a general process flow, starting with someone who has no access. Upon being assigned their first job role, an identity is provisioned. As they move throughout the organization, this identity is updated to reflect their job role until, at some point, they leave the organization:

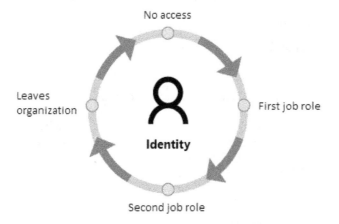

Figure 8.1 – Identity life cycle overview

Identities, from an employee or contractor perspective, are frequently managed through the use of a **human resources information system** (**HRIS**), which is used to track information about the individual's personal and employment information (name, address, dependents, start date, job role, pay rate, and so forth). Platforms such as Workday and SuccessFactors can be integrated with Azure AD and Active Directory to facilitate tracking an individual's data throughout their tenure.

In addition to individuals whose source of identity is managed in your directory, the identity life cycle can also include users in **business-to-business** (**B2B**) scenarios – users from other directories, tenants, or environments that have been granted access to your organization's resources.

What is the access life cycle?

While the identity life cycle represents an identity as it moves throughout the organization, an access life cycle is used to manage how identities have permissions granted or revoked throughout their lifetime:

Figure 8.2 – Access life cycle overview

As users take on new roles, transfer to new departments, and shift responsibilities, the applications and resources they need to access change. The access life cycle is responsible for evaluating what users need to access to perform their duties.

What is the privileged access life cycle?

The privileged access life cycle is similar to the access life cycle, except that it is responsible for governing administrative access to resources such as Exchange or Azure Active Directory. Microsoft recommends a least privilege access model, where people only have access to perform their necessary duties – ideally, only during the time they need to perform those activities. This access model is commonly described as **Just in Time** (**JIT**) and **Just Enough Administration** (**JEA**) access.

Depending on the context, the privileged access life cycle can be implemented through a policy that tracks users' standing (permanent) access roles as they move throughout an organization, or by managing access requests via JIT and JEA to allow individuals to perform the tasks they need to do. Azure AD's Identity Governance features, such as **Privileged Identity Management** (**PIM**), allow organizations to manage how they grant and revoke administrative rights as the individual access needs change:

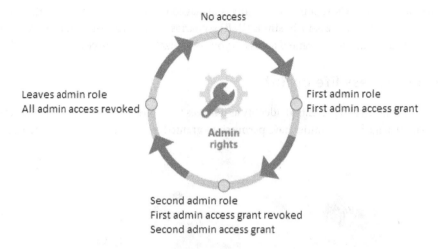

Figure 8.3 – Privileged access life cycle overview

Privileged identity management can be used for dedicated administrators, as well as normal users. The privileged access life cycle can help organizations ensure administrative functions are only accessed by those who need to perform administrative functions during specified times.

Planning and implementing Identity Governance

Identity Governance can be thought of as a method that's used to manage the identity, access, and privileged access life cycles of an organization. In the context of Azure AD, Identity Governance can include managing access to teams, groups, applications, and roles.

> **Note**
>
> Identity Governance features in Azure AD require Azure AD Premium P2, either as a standalone service or included in a bundled SKU such as Enterprise Mobility and Security E5.

Before we explore how to configure the features of Identity Governance, let's review some of its terminology and components:

- **Access reviews**: An access review is a process that is used to validate an entity's compliance or access to resources – whether it's a group, team, application, or other resource.

- **Entitlements**: Entitlements represent resources or roles that an entity (such as a user or guest) can access. Common entitlements include membership in Azure AD security groups, membership of SharePoint Online sites, membership in Microsoft 365 Groups and Teams, or assignments to enterprise applications.

- **Entitlement management**: Entitlement management is the overall term that describes the process of assigning resources.

- **Access packages**: Access packages are bundles or groups of resources (entitlements) that are assigned to a user to complete a role or task.

- **Life cycle workflows**: These are automated workflows that can be configured and extended to automate user onboarding, moves, and offboarding (sometimes referred to as move/add/change or joiner/mover/leaver processes).

- **Connected organization**: An external organization or tenant with which your tenant has a close working relationship.

With that common understanding covered, let's look at working with entitlement packages or access packages.

Working with access packages

In this section, we'll cover how to plan and implement an access package in Azure AD.

An access package, as previously stated, is a collection of resources and policies that can be assigned to users as a whole. Resources (groups, teams, sites, roles, and applications) are stored in a catalog. Someone who has been granted the **access package manager** role can create and administer packages with resources that already exist in the catalog. See *Figure 8.4* for details:

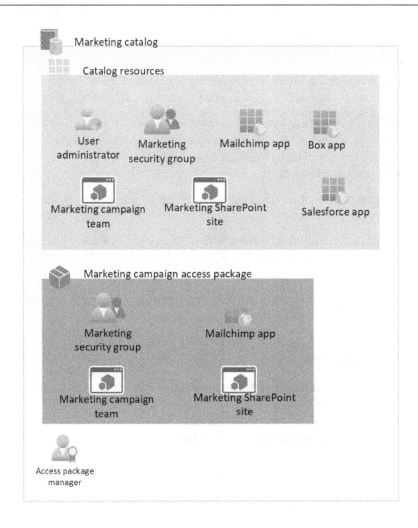

Figure 8.4 – Access package hierarchy

Before we begin the access package planning process, let's look at some configuration settings around Identity Governance.

Configuring Identity Governance settings

Identity Governance has various settings and support options in a few areas that can be managed.

To launch Identity Governance, navigate to the Azure portal (`https://portal.azure.com`), select **Azure Active Directory**, and then choose **Identity Governance** under the **Manage** section.

1. You'll notice that Identity Governance has five nodes under **Entitlement management**:

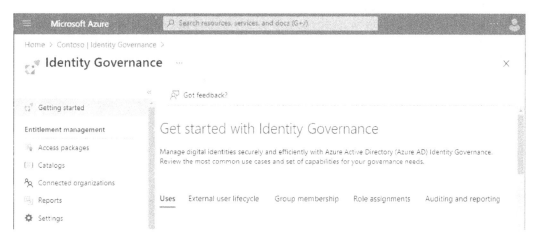

Figure 8.5 – The Identity Governance blade

2.   The main feature areas we're going to look at are **Catalogs**, **Connected organizations**, and **Settings**.

Catalogs

The **Catalogs** page contains a list of available catalogs in your organization. By default, every organization has a built-in catalog called **General**. You can use this catalog to manage your resources and access packages or create others as needed:

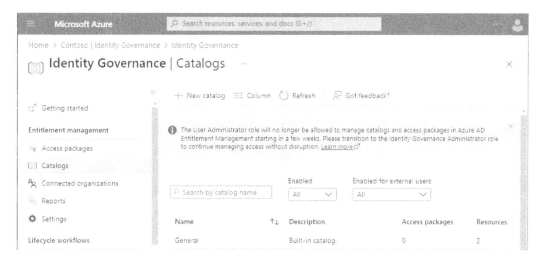

Figure 8.6 – Identity Governance – the Catalogs page

By selecting an existing catalog, you can view what **Resources**, **Access packages**, and **Custom extensions** (Logic Apps) are associated with the catalog. You can also view and assign delegated administrative **Roles** for the catalog and view **Reports** that include information on who has requested or been assigned access packages.

Connected organizations

Connected organizations are those Microsoft 365 or Azure AD tenants with which your organization works closely together. Similar in concept to an Active Directory trust relationship, connected organizations allow external users to access resources located in your tenant:

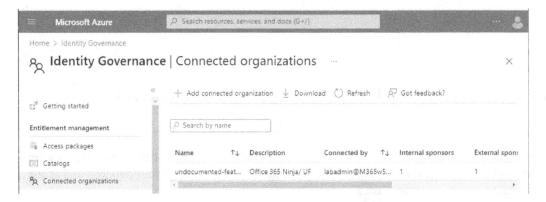

Figure 8.7 – Identity Governance – the Connected organizations page

When configuring a connected organization, you simply enter the name of the organization and one of the verified domains. Once you have added a connected organization, users from all verified domains in the external directory are recognized as part of the relationship.

Settings

The **Settings** page allows you to configure how certain tenant-wide Identity Governance features work, including how to manage the life cycle of external users and delegate entitlement management capabilities. This can be seen in *Figure 8.8*:

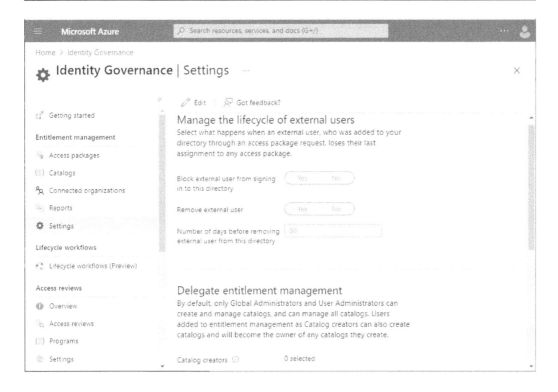

Figure 8.8 – Identity Governance – the Settings page

Periodically, as new Identity Governance preview features are released, they may show up on this page so that you can adopt them in preview mode before they are broadly distributed.

Next, we'll look at planning an access package.

Planning access packages

Your organization can have multiple catalogs, and each catalog can have multiple access packages. You may wish to create catalogs per organization, per business unit, per project, or any other criteria that you select. Generally, catalogs create resources that are related in some way.

If you have delegated the access package manager role to another individual, that individual can only add resources to an access package that already exists in the corresponding catalog. Administrators, however, can add resources that don't exist in the current catalog.

> **Note**
> When an administrator adds an unlisted resource to an access package, the resource is automatically added to the catalog where the access package is being created.

When planning for an access package, be sure to identify the following components. These should be included as they help you decide on configuration options:

- **Resource roles**:

  - Groups and Teams

  - Applications

  - SharePoint sites

- **Requests**:

  - Who can request access?

    - Users in the directory

    - External users in connected organizations

    - None (only assigned by administrators)

  - Whether new requests are allowed (enabled) or not (disabled)

  - Whether Entra Verified IDs will be used

- **Requestor information**:

  - Ability to request custom information from the access package requestor, such as justifications or additional business purposes

- **Life cycle**:

  - Whether access package assignments will expire

  - Whether the access package will require access reviews

- **Custom extensions**:

  - Whether any customized Logic Apps workflows are triggered through various stages of the access package life cycle

Once you have identified the resources that are required for the access package, you can begin creating one.

Implementing access packages

You can create access packages through the **Identity Governance** blade of the Azure portal. To configure a new access package, follow these steps:

1. From the **Identity Governance** blade of the Azure portal, select **Access packages** under **Entitlement management**. Then, click **New access package**:

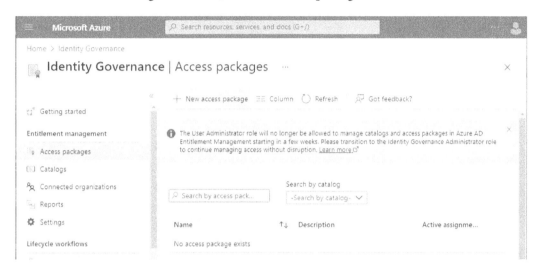

Figure 8.9 – Identity Governance – the Access packages page

2. From the **Basics** tab, enter **Name** and **Description details**, and select which **Catalog** the access package will be created in (or select **Create new catalog** to create a new catalog that will contain this access package). Click **Next**:

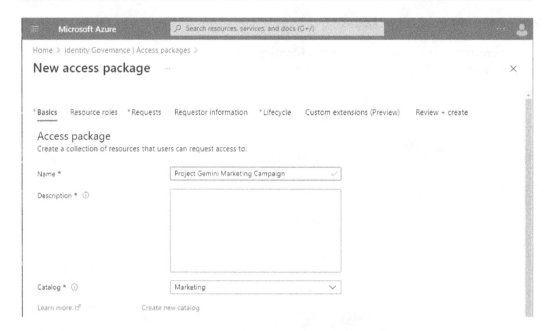

Figure 8.10 – New access package – Basics

3. From the **Resource roles** tab, click **Groups and Teams** to add Microsoft 365 Groups or Teams. Click **Applications** to add enterprise applications configured in your directory, and click **SharePoint sites** to add sites to be associated with this package. For each resource, select a **Role**. Click **Next**:

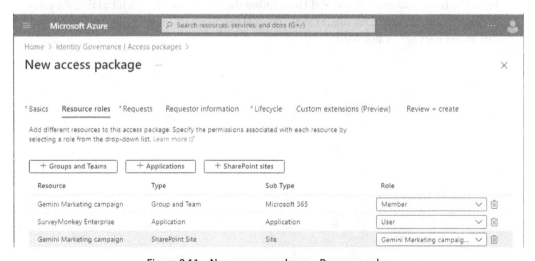

Figure 8.11 – New access package – Resource roles

4. From the **Requests** tab, select who can request access to this access package. You can select **For users in your directory**, **For users not in your directory**, or **None**. Depending on your selection, you may have additional options for managing the scope (users, groups, and guests, as well as connected organizations).

5. Also from the **Requests** tab, you can configure **Approval** options. You can choose to **Require approval** or **Enable new requests**, as well as choose whether you require Entra **Verified IDs**. Click **Next**:

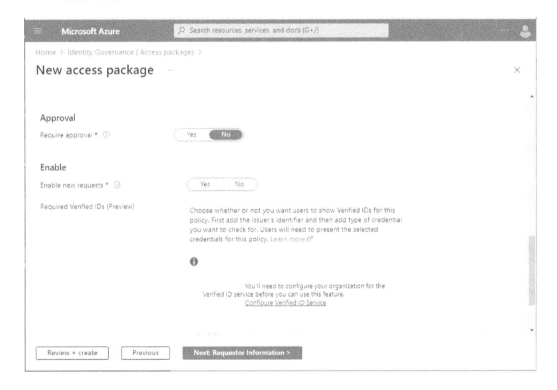

Figure 8.12 – New access package – Requests

6.   From the **Requestor information** tab, you can enter additional questions for the requestor to answer, as shown in *Figure 8.13*:

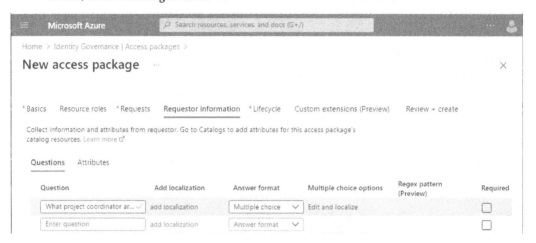

Figure 8.13 – New access package – Requestor information

7.   Click **Next** to proceed.

8.   From the **Lifecycle** tab, you can configure an **Expiration date** for the assignment, as well as whether **Access Reviews** will be required (and their frequency). Click **Next**:

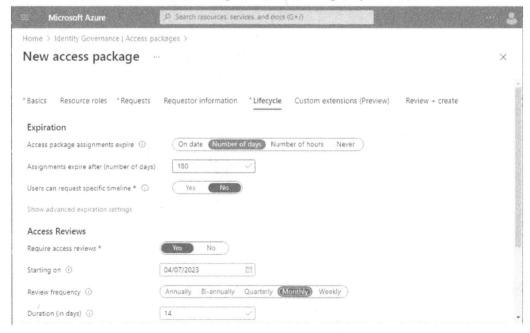

Figure 8.14 – New access package – Lifecycle

9. From the **Custom extensions (Preview)** tab, if desired, choose a **Stage option** (such as **Request is approved**) and a workflow under **Custom Extension**. You must have configured a logic app as a custom extension ahead of time to use this feature:

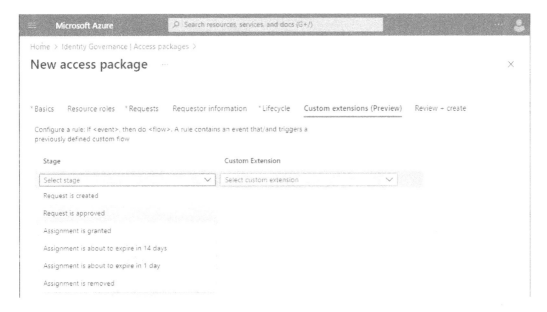

Figure 8.15 – New access package – Custom extensions (Preview)

10. Click **Next**.

11. Review the settings and click **Create**.

Once an access package has been created, depending on your package settings, users may be able to request it (or it may be assigned by an administrator).

To manually add an assignment, follow these steps:

1. From the **Identity Governance** blade, select **Access packages** and then choose the access package to assign.

2. Under **Manage**, select **Assignments**.

3. Click **New assignment**:

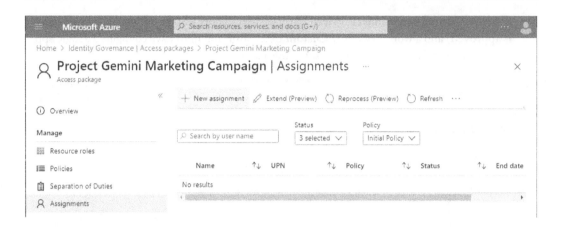

Figure 8.16 – Assigning an access package

4.   Select a policy, select a target (either **User already in my directory** or **Any user**), set start and end dates, and click **Add**.

5.   After the assignment is complete, the status will be **Delivered**. See *Figure 8.17*:

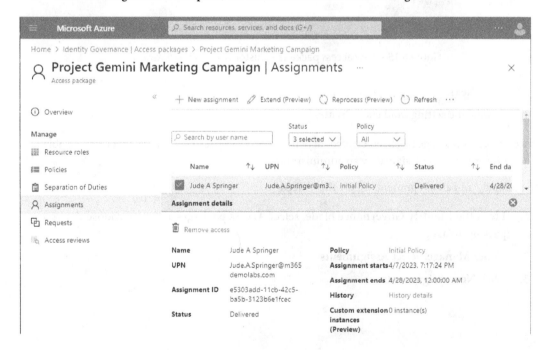

Figure 8.17 – Verifying access package assignment

> **Further reading**
>
> You can learn more about common entitlement management scenarios and processes here: https://learn.microsoft.com/en-us/azure/active-directory/ governance/entitlement-management-scenarios.

Working with access reviews

Access reviews are tools that help organizations track the resource access life cycle. Some of the features of access reviews include the following:

- Performing ad hoc or scheduled reviews to evaluate who has access to resources (such as applications, teams, or groups)

- Tracking reviews

- Delegating reviews to other individuals, including end users who can self-attest that they still need access

- Automate review outcomes, such as removing users from groups or teams

- Access reviews operate in a cycle, as shown in *Figure 8.18*:

Figure 8.18 – The access reviews cycle

As you've already seen, access reviews can be built into an access package. They can also be used as standalone tools.

Let's take a look at how we can plan an access review.

Planning access reviews

When planning out your access review strategy, you need to decide what it is you're going to review – such as Microsoft 365 Groups, Teams, or applications.

> **Exam tip**
> There are some caveats when selecting groups to review: you can't choose dynamic groups or role-assignable groups as targets of an access review.

Depending on the type of review (teams, groups, or applications), you'll need to also understand who the reviewers will be.

For groups, the potential options are as follows:

- **Group owner(s)**
- **Selected user(s) or group(s)**
- **Users review their own access**
- **Managers of users**

Applications have similar options for reviewing:

- **Selected user(s) or group(s)**
- **Users review their own access**
- **Managers of users**

You can choose to configure single or multi-stage reviews to help ensure individuals with the appropriate level of responsibility or authority are signing off on an access decision.

Another important factor when designing an access review strategy is specifying the recurrence. Your organization may have security or regulatory compliance requirements, or other business needs that necessitate how often reviews should occur. You can specify a recurrence of **One time**, **Weekly**, **Monthly**, **Quarterly**, **Semi-annually**, or **Annually**, as well as start dates and ending parameters (**Never**, **End on a specific date**, or **End after a number of occurrences**).

Finally, you need to plan for how you will handle exceptions, default actions, and notifications:

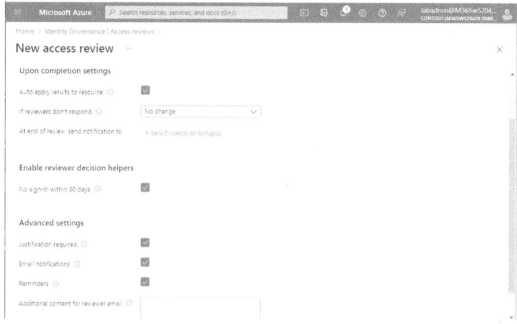

Figure 8.19 – New access review settings

With those settings in mind, let's create an access review!

Implementing access reviews

Creating an access review is straightforward. To create an access review, follow these steps:

1. From the **Identity Governance** blade in the Azure portal (`https://portal.azure.com`), select **Access reviews** and then choose **New access review**:

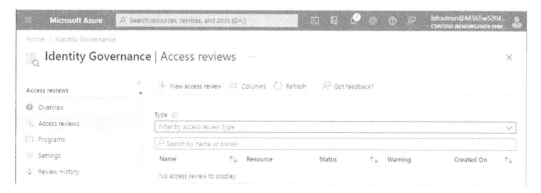

Figure 8.20 – The Access reviews page

2. On the **Review type** page, select the type of review to perform from the dropdown:

    - If you select **Teams + Groups**, you can choose **All Microsoft 365 groups with guest users** or **Select Teams + groups**. If you specify **All Microsoft 365 groups with guest users**, you have no scope options to select, as the scope is automatically configured for **Guest users only**. If you choose **Select Teams + groups**, then you can select a scope of either **Guest users only** or **All users**. In either group scenario, you can choose **Inactive users only**, along with a time for inactivity (measured in days).

    - For **Applications**, you must select one or more enterprise applications that are currently configured in Azure AD:

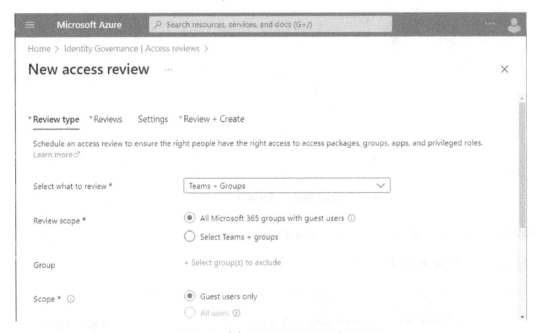

Figure 8.21 – Selecting an access review type

3. From the **Reviews** tab, select whether you will be performing a single or multi-stage review. For each review (or review stage), select who will be performing the review. Depending on the reviewer option selected, you may need to specify individual users or groups. You may also have the option to specify a dedicated **Fallback reviewer**, who will be contacted if the primary user no longer exists for some reason.

4. From the **Reviews** tab, configure a recurrence. Click **Next** when you're finished:

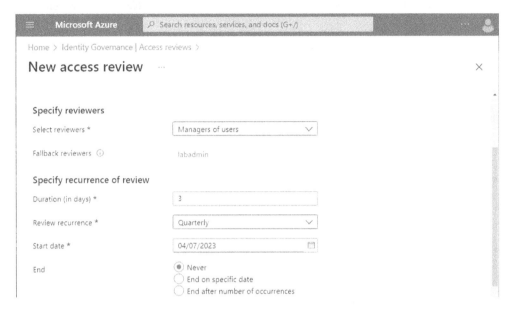

Figure 8.22 – Configuring reviewers and their frequency

5. From the **Settings** tab, you can choose to **Auto apply results to resource**, as well as perform a default action called **If reviewers don't respond**, as shown in *Figure 8.23*:

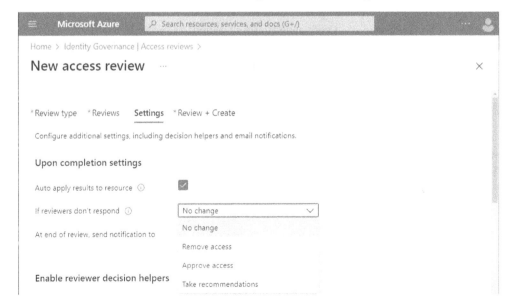

Figure 8.23 – New access review – Upon completion settings

6. Also from the **Settings** tab, you can configure additional notification options, reminders, and a decision helper that displays the review targets' last sign-in. Click **Next: Review + create**:

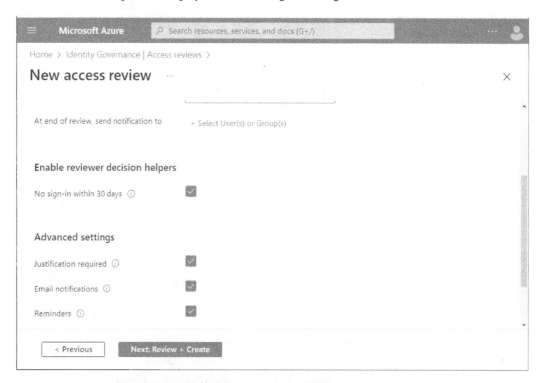

Figure 8.24 – Configuring advanced settings for review

7. Enter a name and description for the review and click **Create**.

Once an access review has been created, it will adhere to the schedule you configured. Users will be notified via email when they have pending actions to review.

You can also view the history of performed access reviews by selecting **Review History** under **Access reviews**, as shown in *Figure 8.25*. You can create a new report of access reviews by selecting **New report** and choosing the date range and types of reviews and outcomes you want to inventory:

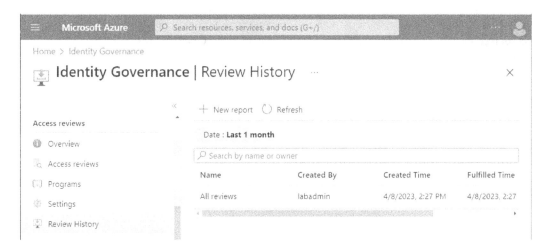

Figure 8.25 – Review History

Next, we'll look at some of the Azure Identity Protection features.

Working with Identity Protection

Azure Identity Protection is an Azure AD Premium P2 feature (with a few limited features available in P1) that allows organizations to identify several types of risks in the Azure AD environment based on signals received and processed, including the following:

- Impossible or atypical travel (logging in from two geographically distant areas in a very short amount of time)

- Usage of anonymous IP address ranges

- Usage of malware-linked IP addresses

- Leaked credentials, such as end user or workload identity client IDs or secret values

- Password spray attempts

These risks are categorized into three tiers: low, medium, and high. While Microsoft doesn't provide exact details on what signals or combinations of signals are used as the basis of categorization, it does provide reporting and workflows that can mitigate the risks.

When these types of activities or events are detected, notifications are generated for administrators. For example, users attempting to log in when impossible travel is detected may be presented with a dialog to re-confirm their identity using an already established multi-factor authentication method.

Depending on how your security organization is structured, you may be able to delegate certain levels of responsibility. The following table describes the roles and types of access available to Identity Protection users:

Role	Actions Allowed	Actions Prohibited
Global Administrator	All	
Security Administrator	All	Reset user passwords
Security Operator	View all Identity Protection reports Dismiss user risk, confirm safe sign-in, confirm compromise	Configure policies Reset user passwords Configure alerts
Security Reader	View all Identity Protection reports	Configure policies Reset user passwords Configure alerts Give feedback on detections
Global Reader	Read-only access to Identity Protection	
Conditional Access Administrator	Create Conditional Access policies that use risk as a sign-in condition	All Identity Protection actions

Table 8.1 – Identity Protection roles

Identity Protection data is contained in four reports:

- Risky users
- Risky workload identities
- Risky sign-ins
- Risk detections

Figure 8.26 shows examples of risk items:

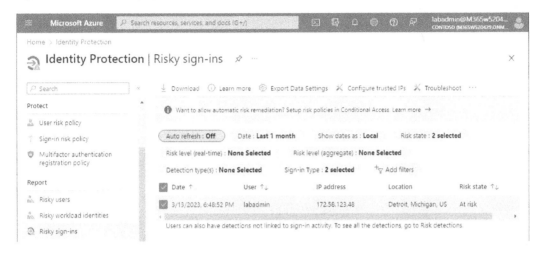

Figure 8.26 – Identity protection reports

Using the data in these reports, you can review details of risk events in the tenant.

Planning for Identity Protection

Azure AD Identity Protection detects identity-based risks in your organization and reports and allows administrators to perform remediations. Before implementing Identity Protection policies, you should review the existing reports.

Investigating risks

You can review risks by reviewing the various risk detection reports on the **Identity Protection** blade (`https://aka.ms/identityprotection`). For example, you can expand the **Risky users** report and select an individual user, as shown in *Figure 8.27*:

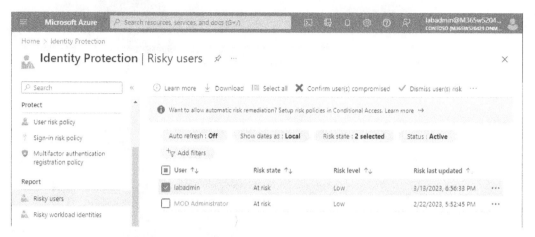

Figure 8.27 – Risky users report

By clicking on the user, you can view details regarding the items contributing to the risk level for the user, as well as historical data for risk-related events. You can perform additional actions for a user, such as confirming that a user has been compromised, dismissing risk, blocking the user from login, or opening the corresponding events in Microsoft 365 Defender:

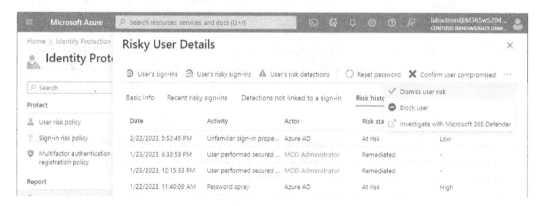

Figure 8.28 – The Risky User Details pane

The **Risk info** area of the **Risky Sign-in Details** page allows you to further understand the types of risks associated with the user, as shown in *Figure 8.29*:

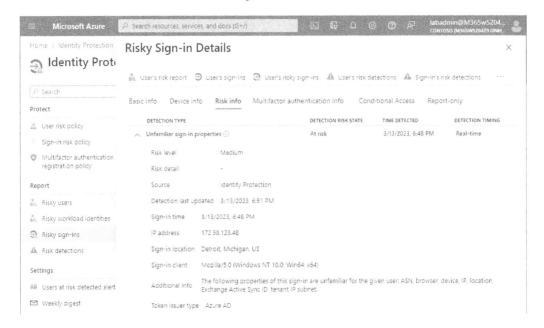

Figure 8.29 – The Risky Sign-in Details page

After reviewing risky sign-in data and confirming safe or compromised logins, you can move on to remediating risks.

Remediating risks

All active, non-dismissed risks contribute to an individual user's risk level, which equates to the probability that a user has been compromised. Risk remediation involves reviewing the logs and reports available and then making decisions on how to proceed: reset passwords, block accounts from logging in, disable the users' devices, revoke any sign-in tokens, or confirm that the account is safe.

Implementing and managing Identity Protection

Identity Protection has three policy configuration nodes in the **Identity Protection** blade:

- **User risk policy**
- **Sign-in risk policy**
- **Multifactor authentication registration policy**

The Identity Protection **User risk policy** area is used to scope various Identity Protection features and enable the settings to control access enforcement:

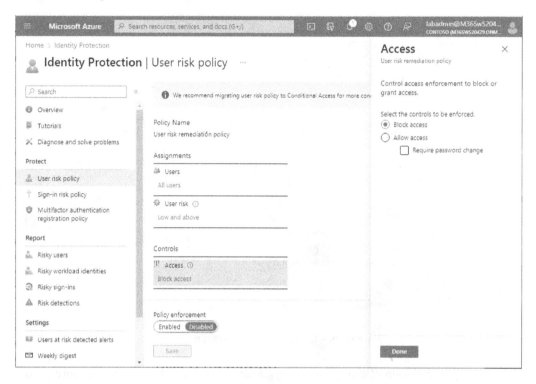

Figure 8.30 – User risk policy

The **Sign-in risk policy** area features similar scoping and control policy settings, as shown in *Figure 8.31*:

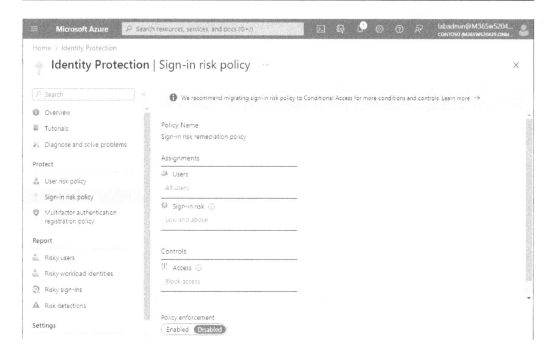

Figure 8.31 – Sign-in risk policy

Finally, the **Multifactor authentication registration policy** area's controls can be used to configure Azure AD multi-factor authentication as part of self-remediation for at-risk users:

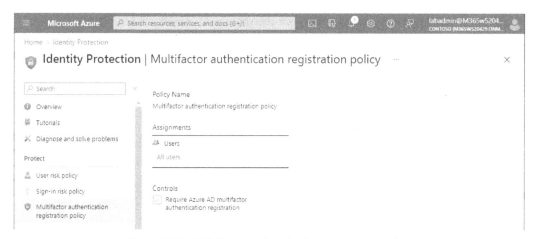

Figure 8.32 – Multifactor authentication registration policy

Microsoft recommends migrating the native Identity Protection policies to Conditional Access policies, as shown in *Figure 8.33*:

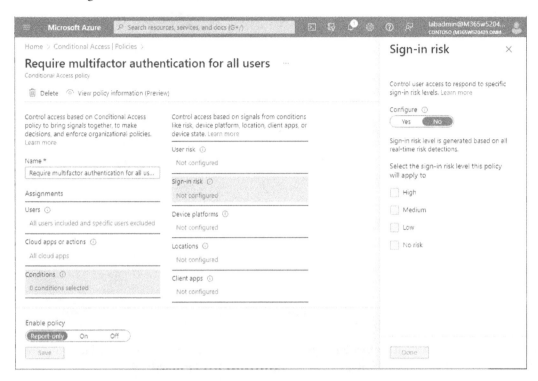

Figure 8.33 – Migrating Identity Protection policies to Conditional Access

Next, we'll look at securing access with Conditional Access policies.

Working with secure access

With the increase in hybrid and remote work, ensuring users can securely access organization resources is more important than ever. Conditional Access policies, part of Azure AD Premium Plans P1 and P2, Enterprise Mobility + Security E3 and E5, and Microsoft 365 F1, E3, and E5, are Microsoft's recommended way to provide identity security for Microsoft 365 users.

In this section, we'll look at planning and configuring Conditional Access to secure identity and resources.

Planning Conditional Access policies

Conditional Access policies can be used to secure Microsoft 365 workloads and applications that are federated with Azure AD:

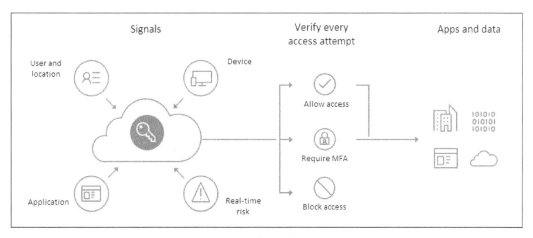

Figure 8.34 – Conditional access signals

Conditional Access requires Azure AD Premium Plan P1 for all features, except for risk-based Conditional Access, which requires Azure AD Premium Plan P2. Administering and configuring Conditional Access requires either the Global Administrator, Conditional Access Administrator, or Security Administrator role.

A Conditional Access policy is made up of the following components:

- Assignments
- Conditions
- Access controls

Let's explore each of these areas.

Assignments

Assignments are used to control the scoping of a policy. The **Users** assignment control includes users, groups, and directory roles.

The **Cloud apps or actions** assignment is used to select which cloud apps, user actions, or authentication contexts are included or excluded. If you're selecting cloud apps, you can choose any enterprise application that is connected to Azure AD. If you're selecting user actions, you can include the **Register security information** and **Register or join devices** actions. You can also select an authentication context – a configuration object that is used to identify and secure content inside SharePoint.

> **Further reading**
>
> For more information on authentication contexts, see `https://aka.ms/authentication-context`.

Conditions

Conditions are the scenarios under which access will be granted or blocked. Conditions include **User risk**, **Sign-in risk**, **Device platforms**, **Locations**, **Client apps**, and **Filter for devices**. You can configure one or more conditions as part of a policy.

Access controls

Access controls are used to specify how access is granted and what experiences are allowed. Access controls are divided between **Grant** and **Session**.

The **Grant** configuration node is used to either block access if the conditions are met or grant access with certain stipulations: **Require multifactor authentication**, **Require authentication strength**, **Require device to be marked as compliant**, **Require Hybrid Azure AD joined device**, **Require approved client app**, **Require app protection policy**, or **Require password change**. You can choose to require only a single control or require all of the selected controls.

The **Session** configuration node controls are used to enable or manage limited experiences in supported cloud applications. You can choose to **Use app enforced restrictions** (only available in Office 365, Exchange Online, and SharePoint Online), **Use Conditional Access App control**, **Sign-in frequency**, **Persistent browser session**, **Customize continuous access evaluation**, **Disable resilience defaults**, or **Require token protection for sign-in sessions**.

You can configure both Grant and Session controls.

> **Further reading**
>
> For more information on session controls, see `https://aka.ms/caapprestrictions`.

Finally, as part of the planning process, you can choose to enable a policy in **Report-only** mode. That way, you can configure the settings and then review the sign-in logs to see whether the policy would have been applied during a particular sign-in or access attempt.

Implementing and managing Conditional Access policies

Conditional Access provides the most fine-grained control when you're managing the multi-factor authentication requirements for your organization. Conditional Access policies can be configured from the Azure portal.

To access the Conditional Access configuration page, follow these steps:

1. Navigate to the Azure portal (`https://portal.azure.com`).

2. Select **Azure Active Directory | Security | Conditional Access**, and then choose **Policies**.

You can create new policies or use one of the Microsoft-provided sample Conditional Access policy templates (14 in total). Policies created via templates can be modified once they have been deployed to your tenant.

To configure a template-based policy, follow these steps:

1. From the **Conditional Access | Policies** page, select **New policy from template (Preview)**:

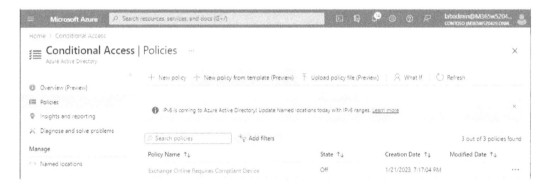

Figure 8.35 – Creating a new Conditional Access policy from a template

2. Select one of the templates, such as **Require multifactor authentication for all users**, and click **Next: Review + create**:

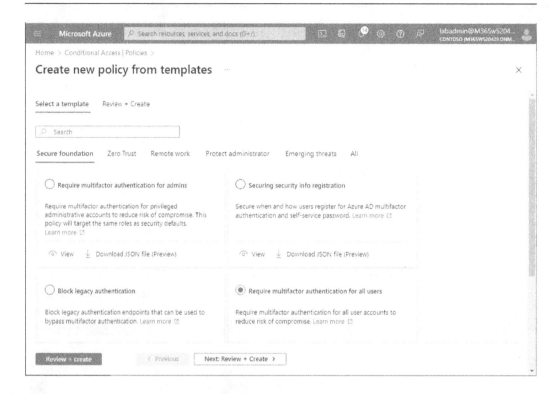

Figure 8.36 – Selecting a template

3. Review the settings and click **Create**.

Policies created through templates cannot be modified during creation, except via enforcement mode. All template-based policies are configured in **Report only** mode, which can be toggled during creation. The user creating the policy is excluded from the policy to prevent accidental lock-out.

Once the template policies have been configured, you can edit the scope and conditions for the policy – for example, a manually-created policy.

> **Further reading**
>
> For more information on Conditional Access templates, see https://learn.microsoft. com/en-us/azure/active-directory/conditional-access/concept- conditional-access-policy-common.

Summary

In this chapter, you learned about Azure AD Identity Governance and Identity Protection features. Access packages can be used as part of Identity Governance to help you manage the life cycle of resource access, including granting roles and access to SharePoint sites, Teams, and Groups. You can also use access reviews to periodically audit things such as application access or group membership. You also learned about Identity Protection features, such as risk-based access policies, and how to investigate and remediate risks.

In the next chapter, we'll learn how to configure application access.

Knowledge check

In this section, we'll test your knowledge of some key elements from this chapter.

Questions

Answer the following questions:

1. Which feature of Identity Governance is responsible for auditing group membership?

    A. Access packages

    B. Privileged access management

    C. Access reviews

    D. Conditional Access

2. When configuring an access package, which component is used to store resources?

    A. Catalog

    B. Connected organization

    C. Access package definition

    D. Access review

3. An access review can be configured as part of an access package.

    A. True

    B. False

4. When configuring a Conditional Access policy, which of the following are Grant controls?

   A. Require multi-factor authentication

   B. Require a Hybrid Azure AD joined device

   C. Locations

   D. Sign-in risk

5. You can mark identity risks as safe through which interface?

   A. Access reviews

   B. Conditional Access

   C. Identity Governance

   D. Identity Protection

Answers

The following are the answers to this chapter's questions:

1. C: Access reviews

2. A: Catalog

3. A: True

4. A: Require multi-factor authentication; B: Require Hybrid Azure AD joined device

5. D: Identity Protection

9

Planning and Implementing Application Access

So far, you've learned about configuring a Microsoft 365 tenant and configuring access, roles, and security pertaining to resources primarily located in the Microsoft 365 environment. In this chapter, we're going to expand into managing access to additional applications—whether they're on-premises or other cloud-based SaaS applications.

This chapter covers the following exam objectives:

- Planning access and authentication
- Configuring application registration
- Managing user permissions for application registrations
- Managing OAuth application requests
- Configuring Azure AD Application Proxy
- Publishing enterprise applications in Azure AD

That's a number of objectives, so let's dive in!

Planning access and authentication

Prior to the explosion of cloud-based SaaS applications, organizations that purchased applications or connected to partner organizations would commonly configure identity federation with the entity hosting an application. One of the most common methods was through **Active Directory Federation Services** (**AD FS**).

With the advent of cloud-based applications and widespread adoption of the **Security Assertion Markup Language** (**SAML**) and **OpenID Connect** standards, it's easier than ever to connect your organization's users to third-party applications.

> **Authentication frameworks**
>
> Both **Security Assertion Markup Language** and **OpenID Connect** are standard frameworks for **authentication (AuthN)** and **authorization (AuthZ)**. Both frameworks allow developers to create applications that obtain and exchange identity information from an external or trusted directory instead of having to maintain an identity store in the application. This helps consumers of these applications manage a single identity store connected to all of their applications instead of having to manage identity separately for each application or service they use.

As a Microsoft 365 administrator, you're likely responsible for deploying, implementing, or otherwise integrating applications into your organization's Azure AD environment.

Configuring application registration

When you want to use Azure AD as the **identity provider** (**IdP**) for an application, you need to register the application with Azure AD. Registering an application with Azure AD establishes a trust relationship between the application (trusting) and the Microsoft Azure AD identity platform (trustee).

Understanding application registration

The registration process allows Azure AD to understand the details of the application, such as the URL of the service, and where to send authentication replies. Applications can request access to Azure resources, so be sure to carefully examine what permissions are needed.

In addition to providing the basic details of the application, registration also grants the following benefits:

- Allows for branding customization of the sign-in dialog box
- Allows you to limit the scope of sign-in: **single-tenant**, for applications that are only accessible to your own organization's users or **multi-tenant**, for applications that are available to users whose identities are managed outside your Azure AD boundary (such as LinkedIn, Google, and other Microsoft identity platforms)
- Allows you to request scope permissions, such as `user.read` or `directory.read`
- Allows you to define scopes that the application is allowed to access
- Allows you to share client secrets for secure data applications

Let's see it in action!

Registering a new application

Application registration is performed in the Azure portal. To configure a new application registration, follow these steps:

1. Log in to the Azure portal (`https://portal.azure.com`) and navigate to Azure Active Directory.

2. Under the **Manage** section, select **App registrations** and then select **New registration**.

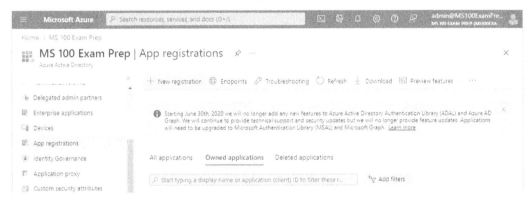

Figure 9.1 – App registrations page

3. On the **Register an application** page, enter a name. This name will be displayed on the sign-in page as well as in other places, such as **My Apps**.

4. Under **Supported account types**, select the scope of users that will be able to access this application.

Figure 9.2 – Configuring a new app registration

5. Click **Register**.

6. On the app's **Overview** page, take note of the available options. Select **Add a Redirect URI**, and then select **Add a platform**.

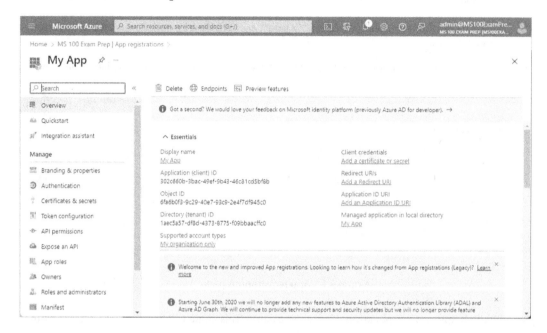

Figure 9.3 – New app overview page

7. On the **Configure platforms** flyout, select which type of platform you wish to configure for your application. You can configure multiple platforms.

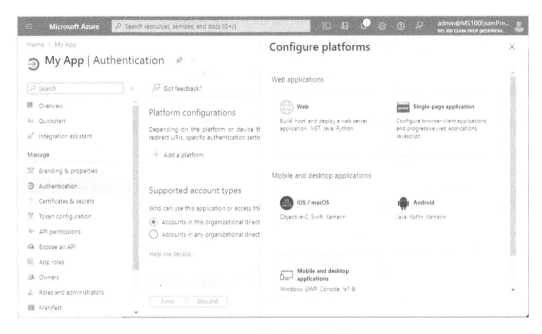

Figure 9.4 – Configure platforms flyout

8. Enter values for the **Redirect URIs** and **Front-channel logout URL** inputs (if **Web** was selected). If you selected another platform type, configure the appropriate values.

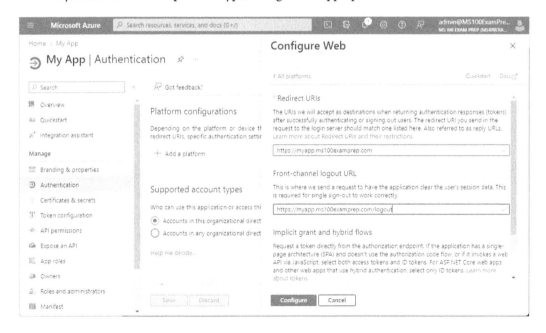

Figure 9.5 – Configure a platform flyout

9.   Select the tokens you wish to issue during the authorization request.

10. When finished, click **Configure**.

When developing the application and configuring its parameters, you will connect it to Azure AD using the information contained in the application registration.

Managing user permissions for application registrations

All applications that interact with a user's device or content require some sort of access to be granted. When working with Azure AD, applications will request access to perform certain functions, such as reading a user's calendar, looking up a contact in the global address list, or sending mail on the user's behalf.

In the context of OAuth 2.0 and the Microsoft identity platform, these permission definitions are called **scopes**. When a user or application makes a request to access a particular type of data, the requested scope is appended to the request. For example, if an application sends the request string `https://graph.microsoft.com/Calendars.ReadWrite`, the application is asking for the ability to read and write calendar items for the user through Microsoft Graph.

Many applications simply request the permissions they need when they need them, prompting the user to approve them. Frequently, in this scenario, an application is asking for **delegated permissions**—or the ability to act on behalf of the user. The app's access is limited to what the user has the ability to access.

Another example may be configuring a service principal to monitor a mailbox and start a workflow. In this case, you may be granting **application permissions**, since the application is acting on its own without a signed-in user performing tasks.

Consent is the process of approving application access. Users can typically consent on their own behalf, though application permissions must be granted consent by an administrator (aptly called **administrator consent**). For example, when someone attempts to access an app, they may be presented with a consent screen similar to the one shown in *Figure 9.6*:

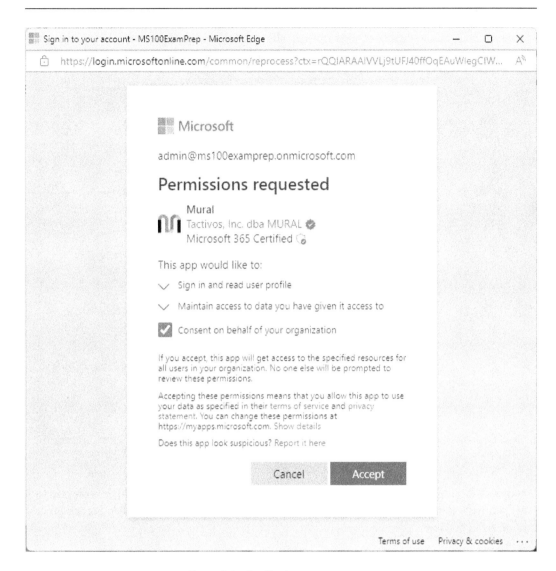

Figure 9.6 – Application consent screen

Administrators may also pre-authorize applications and permissions in the environment, granting consent ahead of time so that users are not prompted.

The Azure portal provides several built-in options, allowing for a range of autonomy for users when it comes to consenting to application permission requests, as shown in *Figure 9.7*:

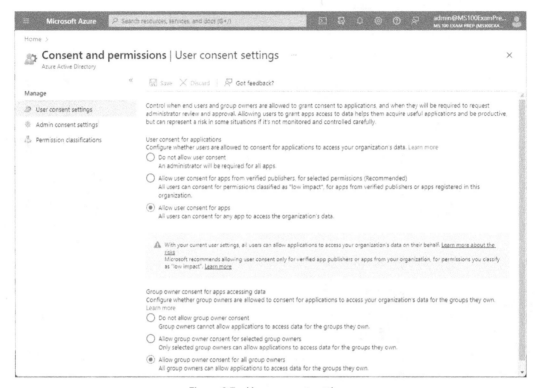

Figure 9.7 – User consent settings

If you choose to allow users to consent for permitted apps and permissions, you will be prompted to classify permissions into *Low*, *Medium*, and *High* risk categories. The *Medium* and *High* risk categories are currently in preview.

Similarly, **Admin consent settings** shown in *Figure 9.8* provides controls over how to configure consent workflows.

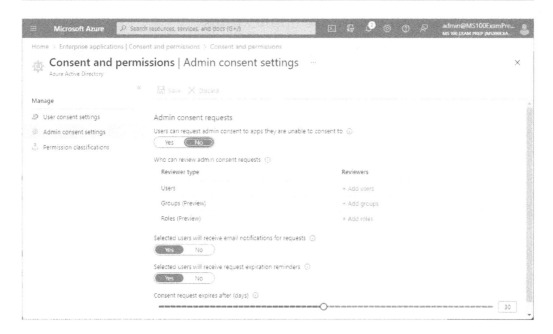

Figure 9.8 – Admin consent settings

The **admin consent workflow**, enabled through the **Users can request admin consent to apps they are unable to consent to** slider, enables users to request consent. The user is presented with an approval dialog box. After confirming the request, an admin who has been delegated as a reviewer can grant or deny the consent request.

Managing OAuth application requests

As an administrative best practice, you should periodically review OAuth application requests to ensure the applications listed are still required and that the permissions granted conform to your organization's policies.

OAuth access and permissions can be reviewed in two places on the Microsoft 365 platform:

- Azure AD Enterprise applications
- The Microsoft 365 Defender portal

Let's quickly take a look at each of these.

Reviewing Azure AD Enterprise applications

The easiest place to get the broadest view of all of your applications and permissions is in the Azure AD portal. You've already seen how to create applications and manage permissions, so this process will be very familiar:

1. Navigate to the Azure portal (`https://portal.azure.com`) and navigate to **Azure Active Directory | Enterprise applications**.

2. Under **Manage**, select **All applications**.

3. Select an application to examine the permissions and consent information.

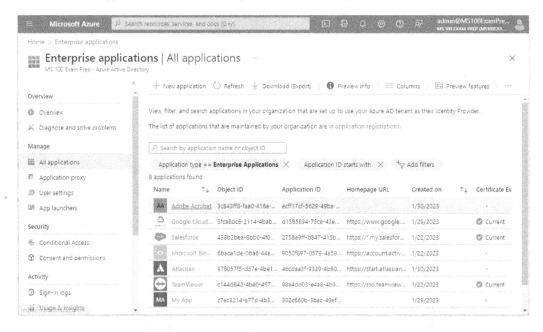

Figure 9.9 – Enterprise applications page

4. Under **Security**, select **Permissions**.

5. Click an individual permission to review the details, as shown in *Figure 9.10*.

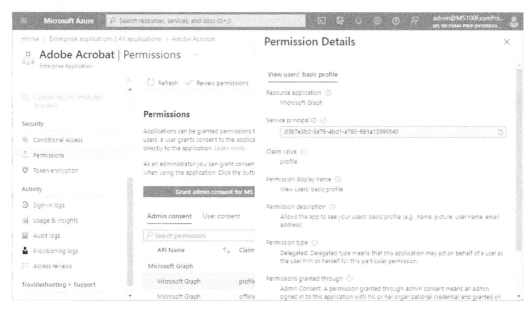

Figure 9.10 – Reviewing an individual application permission

You can also click the **Review permissions** button at the top of the application's **Permissions** page to get helpful tips for reviewing an application's permissions.

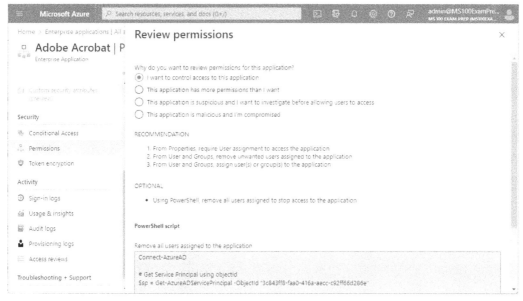

Figure 9.11 – Reviewing permissions

Next, we'll look at Microsoft 365 Defender.

Reviewing the Microsoft 365 Defender portal

You can start reviewing OAuth application information in the Microsoft 365 Defender portal (`https://security.microsoft.com`) under **Cloud apps | OAuth apps**, as shown in *Figure 9.12*:

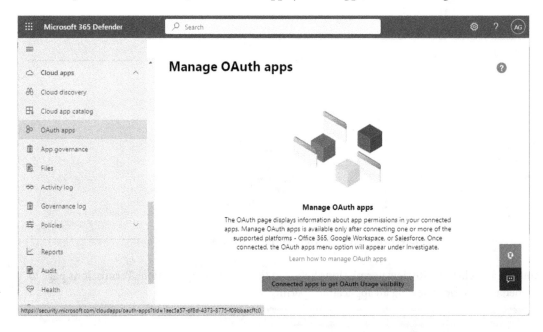

Figure 9.12 – Viewing OAuth apps in Microsoft 365 Defender Security Center

If your organization has not yet configured any apps, you can use the interface to connect to your existing SaaS app deployments and review the alerts and logs that are generated.

If you have connected your applications, you will see data show up as access and authorization requests are retrieved from the Azure AD logs.

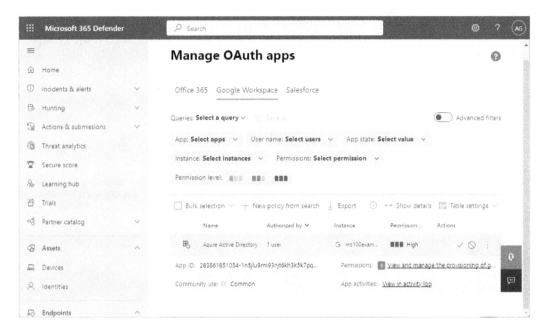

Figure 9.13 – Manage OAuth apps in the Microsoft 365 Defender portal

Microsoft Defender for Cloud Apps provides a number of additional features, such as being able to identify and filter logs, review the security profile of connected applications, and even create alerts and remediation rules.

Next, we'll shift gears and look at the features of Azure AD Application Proxy.

Configuring Azure AD Application Proxy

In addition to providing identity services, Azure AD also has features to help connect your on-premises applications and make them available as endpoints on the internet. The feature, known as **Azure AD Application Proxy** (sometimes referenced as **Azure AD App Proxy** or **Azure App Proxy**), provides a sort of gateway or conduit between your on-premises applications and Azure AD.

> **Important**
>
> For an on-premises application to be compatible with the Azure AD App Proxy connector service, it must have a web frontend, use Remote Desktop Gateway, or rich client apps that are integrated with the Microsoft Authentication Library. Azure AD App Proxy cannot publish standard Windows desktop applications.

After one or more Azure AD App Proxy **Connectors** are deployed, applications can be registered in Azure AD to use the connectors. When a user accesses the application, their request is relayed via the connector to the on-premises app. See *Figure 9.14*.

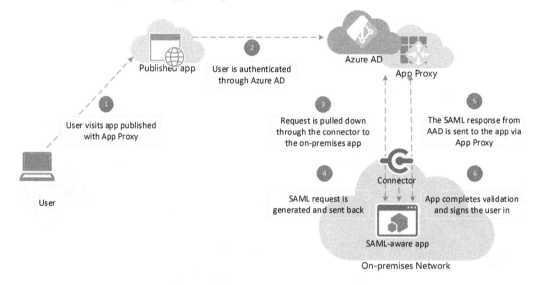

Figure 9.14 – Overview of authentication for a published app

Now that you have an understanding of the workflow, let's start working with an app!

Configuring prerequisites

Azure AD Application Proxy has a few prerequisites that must be achieved before performing a deployment:

- An Azure AD Premium P1 or P2 license.

- At least one server running Windows Server 2012 R2 or 2016. Windows Server is also supported but requires the deployment of an additional registry key to enable communication.

- If **Kerberos Constrained Delegation** (**KCD**) is required, the machine must be domain-joined to the same directory where the applications are being published. Apps to be published must be configured to use Kerberos and have service principal names. For more information on configuring KCD, see https://learn.microsoft.com/en-us/azure/active-directory/app-proxy/application-proxy-configure-single-sign-on-with-kcd.

- Outbound connectivity on port 80 for **certificate revocation list** (**CRL**) checking.

- Outbound connectivity on port 443 to *.msappproxy.net, *.servicebus.windows. net, login.windows.net, and login.microsoftonline.com.

Versions of the Azure AD App Proxy connector prior to 1.5.132.0 required many additional ports for communication. It is recommended that organizations deploy or update to the latest version of the connector.

Deploying Azure App Proxy

To deploy Azure App Proxy, follow these steps:

1. Log in to the Azure portal (https://portal.azure.com).
2. In the **Search** bar, enter app proxy and select **App Proxy** from the application list.
3. Click **Download connector service**.

Figure 9.15 – Downloading the Azure App Proxy connector

4. Review the system requirements and installation instructions on the flyout.
5. Click **Accept terms & Download**.
6. After the file has downloaded, launch it.
7. Select **I agree to the license terms and conditions** and click **Install**.

Figure 9.16 – Azure AD App Proxy launch screen

8.   Enter your account credentials to begin registering the Azure AD App Proxy connector with Azure AD.

Figure 9.17 – Entering sign-in credentials for Azure AD App Proxy

9.   When the installation and registration have been completed, click **Close**.

10. Refresh the Application proxy page in the Azure portal and verify that the newly-installed app proxy is working.

Azure AD Application Connectors can be grouped together to form load-balancing and redundancy configurations. You can configure multiple groups to reduce single points of failure and publish applications from a variety of network locations.

For high availability and load balancing, Microsoft recommends installing a minimum of two Azure AD App Proxy connectors in your environment (but preferably three).

Publishing enterprise applications in Azure AD

As you've seen throughout this chapter, Azure AD's capability as an identity provider opens up the ability to use your organization's identity store to access innumerable resources.

In this section, we'll dive into features of Azure Active Directory that help you connect your users to applications. We'll look at two similar features for making applications available:

- Publishing on-premises applications for remote access
- Publishing applications from the app gallery

Let's go!

Configuring a group

Microsoft recommends, as a best practice, managing application access with a group. By integrating access directly with a group, you can enable features such as access reviews to manage access to the application.

To configure a group, simply log in to either the Microsoft 365 Admin center (`https://admin.microsoft.com`), expand **Teams & groups**, and select **Active teams and groups**. Select the **Add a group** button and fill in the details accordingly.

You can also do it from the Azure AD portal (`https://portal.azure.com`) by entering `Groups` in the search bar and then selecting **New group**. You can use either security groups or Microsoft 365 groups. In this example, we've created two standard security groups: *HP Jet Admin Users* and one called *Salesforce Users*. These security groups will be used to manage access to the applications.

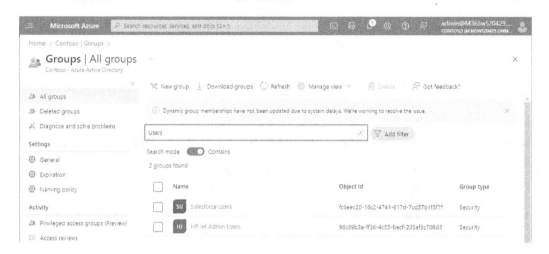

Figure 9.18 – Security groups

Once you have a group created to manage access, you can proceed with configuring the applications.

Publishing on-premises applications for remote access

You can make any on-premises web application available via Azure AD App Proxy. The apps can run on any platform (not just Microsoft Windows and Internet Information Server).

> **Important**
>
> Azure AD App Proxy requires Azure AD Premium P1 or Azure AD Premium P2.

Configuring an app

You've already learned about Azure App Proxy's capabilities and have installed the connector. In this section, we'll use it to configure an on-premises application:

1. Navigate to the Azure portal (`https://portal.azure.com`).

2. Enter `app proxy` in the search bar and select **Application Proxy** from the results or navigate to it via **Azure Active Directory | Enterprise applications | Application proxy**.

3. Select **Configure an app**.

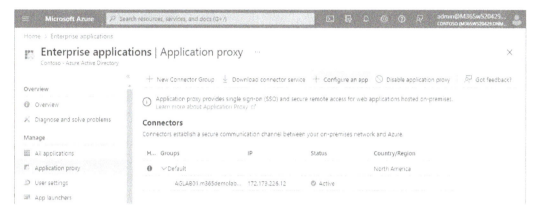

Figure 9.19 – App proxy Configure an app

4. On the **Basic** tab, enter a name for the application (as it will be displayed in **Enterprise Apps** and on the **My Apps** page).

5. Enter a value for **Internal Url**. This value must be resolvable and accessible from the server where the Azure AD App Proxy connector is installed.

6. Enter a value for **External Url**. This value, though not mandatory, will allow the application to be accessible directly (instead of requiring users to log in to Microsoft 365 or **My Apps** first to see it).

> **Note**
>
> By default, the domain portion is linked to an Azure AD App Proxy domain name (msappproxy. net), though you can choose any domain registered in your tenant. If you select a public domain you own, you'll need to configure a DNS CNAME record in your organization's external DNS to point to the default Azure AD App Proxy value.
>
> While the onmicrosoft.com initial domains *do* appear in the domain list, Microsoft recommends that you *do not* choose them.

7. Select a **Pre Authentication** method (either **Passthrough** or **Azure Active Directory**).

> **Pre authentication settings**
>
> Pre-authentication determines whether users are verified against Azure AD prior to gaining access to the application. Setting this option to **Azure Active Directory** means that users are validated against Azure AD first, while setting it to **Passthrough** means they are not. Only apps configured for Azure AD pre-authentication are eligible to be configured for MFA and conditional access.

8. Select a **Connector Group** option.

9. When you've finished, click **Create**.

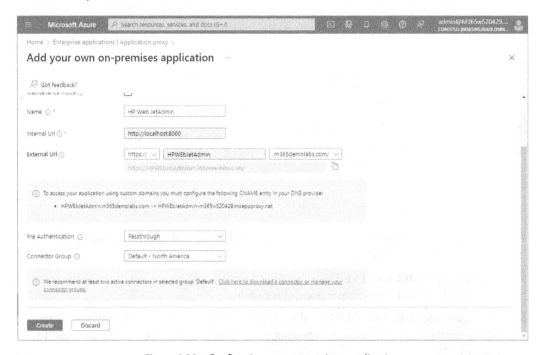

Figure 9.20 – Configuring an on-premises application

After a few moments, the Azure AD App Proxy configuration has been created.

Configuring access

By default, no security controls have been configured for this application, so all users can launch it. To make it available to only appropriate users, you will want to configure the app's security.

You can provision access following these steps:

1. From the Azure AD portal, navigate to **Azure Active Directory | Enterprise applications** and select the newly configured application.

2. Under **Manage**, select **Users and groups**.

3. Click **Add user/group**.

4. On the **Add Assignment** page, under **Users and groups**, click **None Selected**.

5. On the flyout, choose the users and groups you want to have access to this application.

6. Click **Assign**.

After a few minutes, the newly configured app should show up for users on both the Microsoft **My Apps** page (`https://myapps.microsoft.com`) as well as the Microsoft 365 app launcher.

Testing the app

After you have completed the configuration of your application, you may begin working with it. You can test it using the **Test Application** function in the Azure AD App Proxy configuration:

1. Navigate to **Enterprise applications** in the Azure portal (**Azure Active Directory | Enterprise applications**) and select the app to test.

2. Under **Manage**, select **Application proxy**.

3. In the details pane, select **Test Application**.

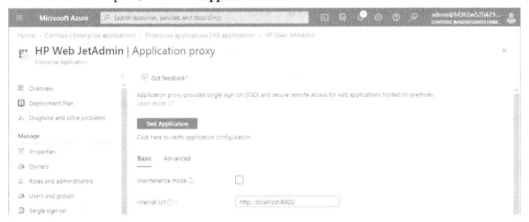

Figure 9.21 – Newly configured application

4. On the **Test Application Proxy configuration** flyout, click **Open application**.

5. Verify that the application can be reached.

Figure 9.22 – Testing configured web application

6. Close the browser window.

Congratulations! You've published an on-premises app to Azure AD!

Further reading

Depending on the on-premises application's design, you may be able to (or need to) choose from a variety of authentication protocols or designs. You can use a variety of **Single Sign-on (SSO)** authentication methods, such as SAML, Kerberos, header, and password. To learn more about Azure AD App Proxy, head to `https://learn.microsoft.com/en-us/azure/active-directory/app-proxy/application-proxy`.

Publishing applications from the application gallery

In addition to publishing custom applications, you can also use the **Application Gallery** (sometimes referred to as the app gallery), a large database containing configuration templates for thousands of SaaS applications. Configuring an application requires a couple of prerequisites:

- An Azure AD account that is a member of one of the following roles: Global Administrator, Cloud Application Administrator, or Application Administrator
- A third-party application that is already present in the Azure app gallery (`https://learn.microsoft.com/en-us/azure/active-directory/saas-apps`) or a custom-built application that supports SAML or OpenID Connect authentication

In the following example, we'll configure the Salesforce app to integrate with Azure AD. While each application may have its own unique configuration properties, the general process for publishing an application and making it available to users is the same.

Adding the application from the gallery

As previously mentioned, each application may have unique settings or input screens for which you need specific data. Some applications, such as the Salesforce app, have additional browser helper extensions that will allow you to import current session information to help speed up the configuration. Review both the individual application's setup steps as well as the corresponding documentation in the app gallery for the most complete information.

To configure an enterprise application, follow these steps:

1. Using an identity with appropriate permissions, log in to the Azure portal (`https://portal.azure.com`) and enter `Enterprise Applications` in the search bar.
2. On the navigation menu, select **All applications** under **Manage** and then click **New application**.

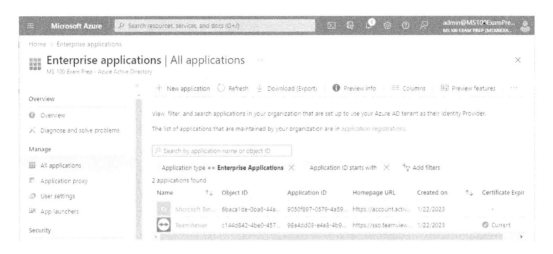

Figure 9.23 – Configuring a new enterprise application

3. In the search box, enter the name of the application you wish to configure and press *Enter*.

4. Select the application from the list.

5. Click **Create**.

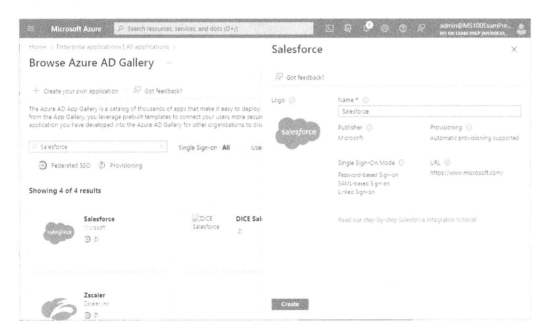

Figure 9.24 – Creating the new enterprise application

6. Under **Getting Started**, select **Assign users and groups**.

7. Click **Add user/group** and then locate the group you created in the *Configuring a group* section. When the group is located, click **Select** to add it.

8. Some applications may prompt you to select a role. To do that, under **Select a role**, click **None Selected** and then select a role in the application that the users will have. When you've finished, click **Assign**. All users who are members of this group will be assigned the corresponding role in the application.

9. Click the **Overview** item from the navigation menu to go back to the enterprise application overview. Under **Set up single sign-on**, select **Get started** to configure the single sign-on parameters for the application.

10. Choose the type of single sign-on method that you will configure for your application. An application may support one or more sign-on methods. If you are following along using the Salesforce app, choose **SAML**.

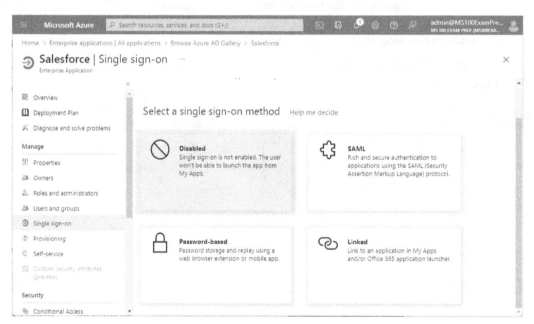

Figure 9.25 – Choosing a sign-on method

11. In the **Basic SAML Configuration** section, click the **Edit** button to fill in the necessary fields.

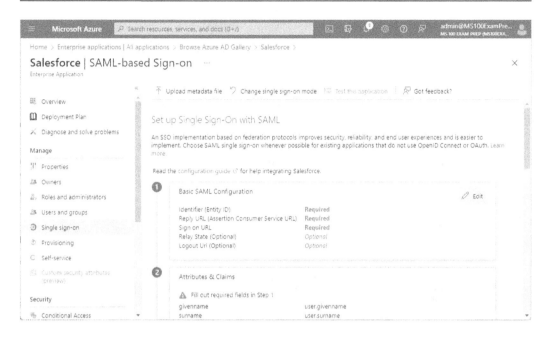

Figure 9.26 – Setting up SAML configuration

12. Fill in the fields per the application vendor's requirements. For this example, we're using the Salesforce app and the corresponding documentation from the Azure app gallery setup.

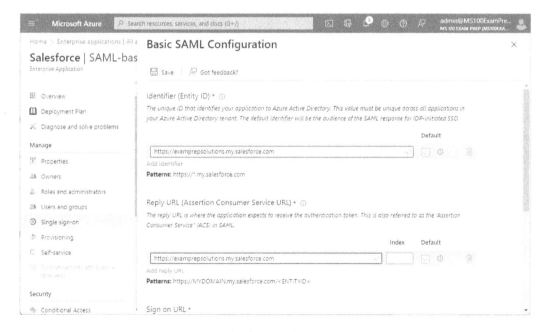

Figure 9.27 – Configuring the SAML properties

13. Click **Save** when finished.

14. On the **Single sign-on** page, scroll down to the **SAML Certificates** section and click **Download** next to **Federation Metadata XML**.

15. Click the **Install the extension** button to install and configure the **My Apps Secure Sign-in** browser extension if offered. This will help speed up the application configuration process. After it has been installed, refresh the **Single sign-on** page.

16. Click **Set up <application name>**. In this case, select **Set up Salesforce**. The browser helper extension will automatically redirect you to the application setup page.

17. Click **Yes** to proceed with the automatic configuration.

Figure 9.28 – Allowing the Azure AD SAML browser extension to run

18. Select **Yes** when prompted to upload the SAML signing certificate. Browse to the downloaded file, select it, and click **Open**.

19. Click **Yes** to save the configuration.

The application has been configured and published for those users who are members of the corresponding user group.

Testing the app integration

Once the application has been configured and published, it's time to test it. You can view the application on the Microsoft **My Apps** page (`https://myapps.microsoft.com`).

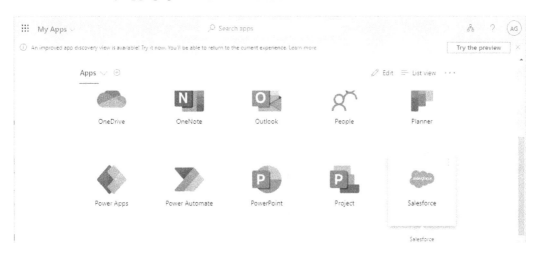

Figure 9.29 – Viewing the My Apps page

During the single sign-on configuration process, the SAML application is looking for user identity data to be provided. The application attempts to match the sign-on name presented by Azure AD, the IdP, to an account located in the application's account database.

If the application and parameters have been configured correctly and a user with the same sign-in name exists in the application, users can now be signed in. Some applications may require the user to select an Azure AD SSO option the first time they log in, as shown in the following figure:

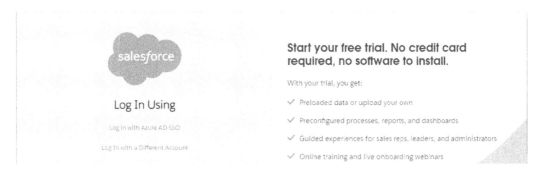

Figure 9.30 – Logging in to an application via Azure AD single sign-on

Configured applications may allow additional provisioning integration as well to enable a fully-automated solution. Provisioning solutions ensure that users created in Azure AD and added to the application security group are automatically configured in the corresponding SaaS application. Be sure to review the individual documentation for each app you configure for additional configuration features.

Summary

In this chapter, you learned about using the capabilities of integrating Azure AD with both on-premises applications (via Azure AD App Proxy) as well as external SaaS applications. These two features allow you to provide your organization with a single interface for accessing applications, regardless of where the users or applications are located.

As an administrator, it's important to be aware of how applications are accessing your data. As a best practice, you should plan on reviewing application permissions in the Azure AD and Microsoft 365 Defender portals on a regular basis.

In the next chapter, we will learn about configuring and deploying Microsoft 365 apps.

Knowledge check

In this section, we'll test your knowledge of some key elements from this chapter.

Questions

1. Which software component needs to be installed to facilitate publishing apps via Azure AD Application Proxy?

    A. Azure AD App Proxy connector

    B. Azure AD Premium connector

    C. Hybrid authentication agent

    D. Microsoft Proxy Agent

2. When publishing an on-premises application, which two pre-authentication methods are available?

    A. NTLM

    B. Password hash

    C. Passthrough

    D. Azure Active Directory

3. Microsoft recommends managing end user application access with which method?

    A. Certificate

    B. Group

    C. Conditional Access

    D. Multifactor authentication

4. The _____ provides pre-configured templates for configuring third-party applications to integrate with Azure AD.

    A. Azure app repository

    B. Azure app template

    C. Azure app gallery

    D. Azure app store

5. SAML stands for:

    A. Secure Application Markup Language

    B. Security Assertion Markup Language

    C. Session Access Management Layer

    D. Session Authentication Management Layer

Answers

1. A: Azure AD App Proxy connector

2. C: Passthrough; D: Azure Active Directory

3. B: Group

4. C: Azure App Gallery

5. B: Security Assertion Markup Language

Part 4:
Planning Microsoft 365
Workloads and Applications

In this part, you'll learn how to plan and deploy Microsoft 365 Apps. You'll also learn about the hybrid technologies and integration that are part of Exchange Online, SharePoint Online, OneDrive for Business, and Microsoft Teams. You'll also learn about the core Microsoft Teams Phone System features.

This part has the following chapters:

- *Chapter 10, Planning and Implementing Microsoft 365 Apps Deployment*
- *Chapter 11, Planning and Implementing Exchange Online Deployments*
- *Chapter 12, Planning and Implementing Microsoft SharePoint Online, OneDrive, and Microsoft Teams*

10

Planning and Implementing Microsoft 365 Apps Deployment

You're probably familiar with the Microsoft Office suite of applications, including Word, Outlook, PowerPoint, and Excel. Microsoft rebranded the subscription-based Office suite as **Microsoft 365 Apps for Enterprise** (although it's frequently called just **Microsoft 365 Apps**). For those who are relatively new to the Microsoft 365 platform, the desktop product suite has most recently been called Microsoft Office 365 ProPlus. Not all of the Microsoft products have been refreshed to reflect the current naming, so you still may see legacy references to Microsoft Office or Microsoft Office 365 ProPlus when working with certain interfaces.

Regardless of the name, though, the Microsoft 365 Apps product bundle has always differentiated itself from the standard Office software you purchase through retail outlets. The differentiators are primarily its subscription-based licensing model (as opposed to perpetual licensing), as well as integration with advanced Microsoft 365 features such as Defender for Office and Safe Links.

This chapter covers the following exam objective areas:

- Planning for client connectivity and device capability
- Planning Microsoft 365 Apps compatibility
- Planning for Microsoft 365 Apps updates
- Configuring Microsoft 365 Apps with the admin center
- Implementing Microsoft 365 Apps deployment

Let's get started!

Planning for client connectivity and device capability

Since Microsoft 365 Apps is primarily delivered via the cloud, it's important to make sure client endpoints are able to communicate with the service platform.

In order to successfully deploy them, you'll need to make sure that both your endpoint devices and network can support the transfer, storage, and processing requirements of the Microsoft 365 Apps suite.

Microsoft lists these core requirements for Microsoft 365 Apps:

- 4 GB RAM (64-bit machines) or 2 GB RAM (32-bit machines)
- 4 GB of available hard disk space (Windows) or 10 GB of available hard disk space (macOS)
- Windows 8.1 or later or the macOS current version, in addition to two previous versions
- Network connectivity for the appropriate services (under *Microsoft 365 Common and Office Online*), as noted at `https://aka.ms/o365endpoints`
- The Microsoft 365 apps are licensed per user and require internet access to be activated, as well as internet access every 30 days to verify that the user's license subscription has not expired, and is otherwise revoked

> **Client readiness**
>
> For organizations that migrate to Microsoft 365 Apps from either previous versions of the perpetual license products or from competing product suites, device compatibility is the most difficult hurdle to overcome. Microsoft recommends that all devices be updated to the most current version of the operating systems and browsers that the organization uses to ensure the most successful deployment or migration.

Planning Microsoft 365 Apps compatibility

Most organizations have deployed a previous version of the Microsoft Office suite. Power users and developers alike have used the power of the Microsoft platform to extend the capabilities of the applications through add-ins and macros.

As part of any upgrade, migration, or deployment exercise, organizations should invest time in validating compatibility with existing products. To that end, Microsoft has provided the Readiness Toolkit to help organizations identify potential compatibility issues with macros and other add-ins.

The Readiness Toolkit can analyze documents and installed add-ins on the local computer or documents stored in a folder and share results from previous reports, or data from **Office Telemetry Dashboard (OTD)**.

> **Note**
>
> OTD is an application that collects data about Office documents and add-ins used throughout your organization. OTD has been deprecated, starting from Microsoft 365 Apps version 2208, and will be removed starting with version 2301. The primary goal of OTD is to assist in migration planning and compatibility testing. The application consists of a dashboard, a SQL server database, one or more **processors** (machines responsible for performing the analysis of the inventory, usage, and health data), a shared folder, and agents built into the Microsoft Office suite.
>
> While OTD is not a primary focus area for this exam, you may want to briefly read the support information regarding it since it may be mentioned until the next exam refresh cycle in 2024: `https://learn.microsoft.com/en-us/deployoffice/compat/deploy-telemetry-dashboard`. OTD will eventually be removed from the MS-100 exam altogether.

To use the Readiness Toolkit, follow these steps:

1. Download and install the Readiness Toolkit from `https://www.microsoft.com/download/details.aspx?id=55983`.

2. Select an option for documents. Choosing **Office documents in a local folder or network share.** does not review the data for installed add-ins.

Figure 10.1 – Readiness Toolkit

3. Click **Next**.

4. Select a path for the Excel report and click **Next**.

5. Select either an **Advanced** or a **Basic** report and click **Next**.

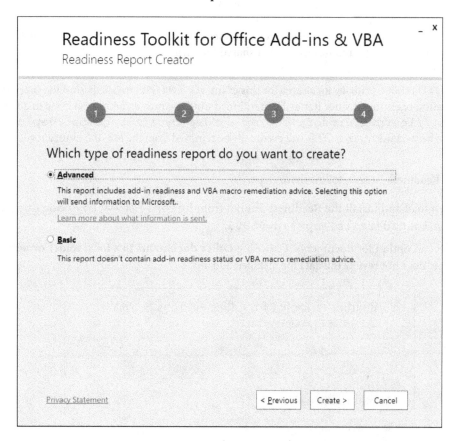

Figure 10.2 – Choosing a report type

6. Click **Open in Excel** to examine the report.

7. Review the report's findings.

The report, shown in *Figure 10.3*, features several tabs and charts with data detailing how **Visual Basic for Applications** (**VBA**) is used in the analyzed documents and any code or function compatibility issues discovered (and corresponding recommendations for fixing), as well as providing detailed information about add-ins that have been deployed across the suite.

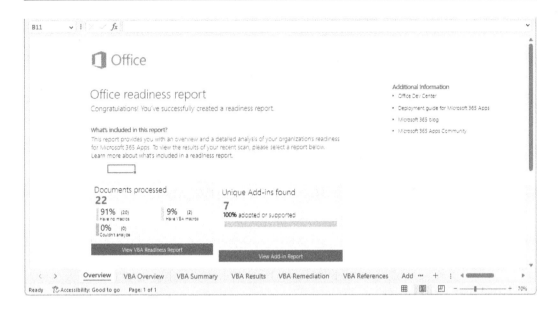

Figure 10.3 – Reviewing the readiness report

Reviewing the report may reveal updates that need to be made to documents, macros, or add-ins to ensure compatibility with the new Microsoft 365 Apps deployment.

Planning for Microsoft 365 Apps updates

Like Windows Enterprise, Microsoft 365 Apps makes use of the concept of **update channels**. Update channels determine the update schedule for endpoints. There are currently three update channels:

- **Current Channel**: Current Channel receives updates at a monthly cadence, including both feature, performance, and security updates. Microsoft recommends configuring a very small percentage of your user base to subscribe to Current Channel to test upcoming features. Current Channel is *not* recommended for business users who have a heavy reliance on macros, app integrations, or third-party add-ins as part of their daily work. Current Channel builds are supported until the next release. While Current Channel is typically updated once a month, the deployment date varies.

- **Monthly Enterprise Channel**: Monthly Enterprise Channel is recommended for users that want the newest features and are willing to provide feedback to Microsoft regarding new features. Like Current Channel, Monthly Enterprise Channel is not intended for broad deployment and should be limited to a very small percentage of your user base. Monthly Enterprise Channel builds are released on the second Tuesday of the month. Unlike Current Channel, however, they are supported for two release cycles.

- **Semi-Annual Enterprise Channel**: Semi-Annual Enterprise Channel is the default and recommended channel for Microsoft 365 updates. Users in this channel will receive feature updates twice a year (in January and July). These updates will include new feature updates that have been made available in Monthly Enterprise Channel. Critical security updates are deployed during the normal monthly security update release cycle, however. Microsoft recommends configuring most of your users for this channel, including users that rely on plugins and complex macros. Semi-annual releases are supported for 14 months.

Now that you understand some of the deployment options, let's look at some deployment options.

Implementing Microsoft 365 Apps deployment

So far, you've learned about the requirements for Microsoft 365 Apps, as well as the servicing and configuration options. In this next section, we'll talk about deployment methodologies and then work through a sample deployment.

Deployment methods

Microsoft 365 Apps uses **Click-to-Run (C2R)** packaging. There are five deployment options available, each with advantages and requirements:

- **Self-install**: With this option, users can self-deploy Microsoft 365 Apps on their workstations by using the **Download** link on the Microsoft 365 portal (`https://portal.office.com`).

- **Deploy from the cloud with the Office Deployment Tool (ODT)**: Administrators can use Microsoft's ODT to deploy Office from the Office CDN. In this scenario, administrators already have management of end user devices. An administrator can connect the client devices to the Office CDN using the ODT for distributing media. The ODT will allow IT administrators to manage Microsoft 365 App options such as languages, update channels, and selected products (for example, excluding Word or including PowerPoint).

- **Deploy from a local source using the ODT**: Using a local source for installation media, administrators can use their infrastructure to create a local source repository to store the latest Office updates and services. This reduces the need for managed endpoints to individually download files over the internet. The ODT is used to manage which configurations are delivered to endpoints.

- **Deploy from a local source with Configuration Manager**: Finally, if organizations have a current version of Microsoft Endpoint Configuration Manager (formerly System Center Configuration Manager), they can use it to deploy and update Microsoft 365 Apps.

- **Deploy from the cloud using Microsoft Intune**: Microsoft's recommended solution is to use Intune inside of Microsoft Endpoint Manager to deploy and manage Microsoft 365 Apps.

Once you have selected an update and servicing cadence for Microsoft 365 Apps, you'll need to decide on how to deploy the software to endpoints, as well as any customization.

Deploying to endpoints

The MS-100 exam emphasizes deployment through the Microsoft 365 Apps admin center, **Microsoft Intune** (formerly **Microsoft Endpoint Manager**), and **Microsoft Configuration Manager**. While other deployment options exist (such as through Group Policy or self-install), they're not the primary focus of the exam.

The Microsoft 365 Apps admin center

The Microsoft 365 Apps admin center is a new tool that combines customization, policy management, deployment, and health monitoring for Microsoft 365 Apps deployments.

The Office Customization Tool

The **Office Customization Tool (OCT)** has been integrated into the **Microsoft 365 Apps admin center**. The tool can be used to build custom configurations for Microsoft 365 Apps. The OCT is a standalone web-based product that can be used to save an XML file, which can be imported into Intune or Configuration Manager. The OCT is also integrated directly into Configuration Manager.

To use the OCT, follow these steps:

1. Navigate to the Microsoft 365 Apps admin center (`https://config.office.com`) and sign in.

2. Expand **Customization** and select **Device Configuration**.

Figure 10.4 – Landing page for the OCT

3. Click **Create** to start a new configuration file.

4. Enter the name of the configuration XML file.

5. Select the options that match your deployment requirements, including the following:

    - **Architecture**: 64-bit is the default and 32-bit is also available.

    - **Office Suites**: None is selected by default; the options include Microsoft 365 Apps for enterprise, Microsoft 365 Apps for business, Office LTSC Professional Plus 2021 Volume License, Office LTSC Professional Plus 2021 (SPLA) Volume License, Office LTSC Standard 2021 Volume License, Office LTSC Standard 2021 (SPLA) Volume License, Office Professional Plus 2019 Volume License, and Office Standard 2019 Volume License.

    - **Visio**: None is selected by default; the options include Visio Plan 2, Visio LTSC Professional 2021 Volume License, Visio LTSC Standard 2021 Volume License, Visio Professional 2019 Volume License, Visio Standard 2019 Volume License, Visio Professional 2016 Volume License, and Visio Standard 2016 Volume License.

    - **Project**: None is selected by default; the options include Project Online Desktop Client, Project Professional 2021 Volume License, Project Standard 2021 Volume License, Project Professional 2019 Volume License, Project Standard 2019 Volume License, Project Professional 2016 Volume License, and Project Standard 2016 Volume License.

    - **Additional products**: None is selected by default. If you have selected an Office 2021 suite or Microsoft 365 Apps suite, you can choose only from a language pack option and the Office 365 Access runtime. If you've chosen an Office 2019 suite (or no Office suite at all), you also have the option to choose Skype for Business Basic 2019.

    - **Update channel**: If you have chosen a Microsoft 365 Apps suite, you can choose from the Microsoft 365 Apps channels, including Current Channel, Current Channel (Preview), Monthly Enterprise Channel, Semi-Annual Enterprise Channel, and Semi-Annual Enterprise Channel (Preview). If you have chosen an Office 2019 suite, you can only choose from the Office LTSC Perpetual Enterprise option corresponding to your selected edition of Office.

    - **Select the version**: Depending on the Office suite selection, you can choose from **Latest** or one of the existing published previous versions.

    - **App selection**: By default, Access, Excel, OneDrive Desktop, OneNote, Outlook, PowerPoint, Publisher, and Word are toggled **On**. You can select any combination of apps to deploy. Skype for Business is available if you choose one of the legacy Office suite versions. If you choose one of the Microsoft 365 Apps suites, you also have the option to enable the OneDrive (Groove) app in addition to the Skype for Business option.

    - **Language**: Select a primary language (either **Match Operating System** or select a specific language from the list). You also can select additional language packs and the corresponding proofing tools to add to the deployment.

    - **Installation**: Under **Where do you want to deploy Office from**, **Office Content Delivery Network (CDN)** is selected by default. You can also choose **Local source** and specify a source path or select **Microsoft Endpoint Configuration Manager**. The **Show installation to user** option is toggled **On** by default. The **Shut down running applications** option is toggled **Off** by default.

- **Update and upgrade**: There are multiple sub-sections available.

  Under **Where do you want to deploy Office from, Office Content Delivery Network (CDN)** is selected by default. You can also choose **Local source** and specify an update path or select **Microsoft Endpoint Configuration Manager**:

  - If you select either **Office Content Delivery Network (CDN)** or **Local source** as your update options, the **Automatically check for updates** option is selected **On** by default.

  - If you select **Microsoft Endpoint Configuration Manager**, the **Automatically check for updates** option is grayed out.

  Under **Upgrade options**, there are a number of sub-options as well:

  - The **Uninstall any MSI versions of Office, including Visio and Project** option is set to **On** by default. The child options to uninstall Visio, Project, SharePoint Designer, and InfoPath are all selected **On** by default. Changing the **Uninstall...** toggle to **Off** disables selecting any of the child options.

  - The **For uninstalled MSI versions of Office, install the same languages** option is set to **Off** by default.

  - The **Automatically upgrade to the selected architecture** option is set to **Off** by default.

- **Licensing and activation**: The licensing and activation section has three sections:

  - The **Automatically accept the EULA** option is set to **Off** by default. It is recommended to turn it on if you want a silent deployment of Office or Microsoft 365 Apps.

  - The **Product key** section is only available if you are deploying one of the volume-licensed products or suites. If you are deploying a Volume License edition, you can choose between the **Key Management Server (KMS)** or **Multiple Activation Key (MAK)** licensing options.

  - The **Product activation** section is only available if you are deploying a subscription-based suite or product. You can choose from **User based**, **Shared Computer**, or **Device based** activation. The default option is **User based** activation. Device-based licensing is only available for certain commercial and education customers and is not currently available for Government Community Cloud customers.

- **General options**: You can provide an organization name, which will be used to populate the **Company** property on Office documents. You can also enter a description of the configuration.

- **Application preferences**: The **Application preferences** section contains the preferences (such as file associations), as well as the options configured by default for each of the included applications. Configure the desired options.

6. When finished, click **Finish** to save the configuration and **Download** to save the configuration XML file to your computer.

The OCT also has built-in configurations that you can adapt for your organization on the **Standard configurations** tab (**Customization | Device Configuration | Standard configurations**), as shown in *Figure 10.5*.

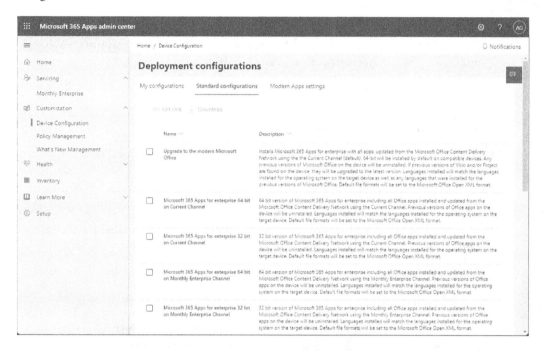

Figure 10.5 – Standard configurations

You can download the XML file for any of the standard configurations to be used with Microsoft Endpoint Manager or Configuration Manager.

> **Exam tip**
>
> The Microsoft 365 Apps admin center allows you to create up to 100 custom deployment configurations with the OCT and currently has 18 built in (labeled Standard configurations), which can be used to deploy apps to Current Channel, Monthly Enterprise Channel, Semi-Annual Enterprise Channel, **Long-Term Servicing Channel** (LTSC), and the Standard Volume License build. Each of the options is available for both 32-bit and 64-bit deployments. **Standard configurations** also includes options for Visio and Project, as well as one that only uninstalls products.

Policy management

In addition to managing the deployment options, such as languages, licensing, or application preferences, you can also use the Microsoft 365 Apps admin center to manage policies. Policies are used to control the behavior of capabilities inside the apps, such as deciding whether users can create and view loop files or allowing co-author chat within a document. Policies are enforced through the **Cloud Policy service for Microsoft 365**.

Policies can be scoped so that different groups of users in your environment can have different experiences.

To begin configuring a policy, follow these steps:

1. Navigate to the Intune admin center (`https://endpoint.microsoft.com` or `https://intune.microsoft.com`).

2. Expand **Customization** and select **Policy Management**.

3. Click **Create** to start a new policy.

4. On the **Basics** page, enter a **Name** value for the policy and, optionally, your choice of **Description**. Click **Next**.

5. On the **Scope** page, select the scope of users to whom this policy will apply. You can select **This policy configuration applies to users in the specified scope** or **The policy applies to users that access documents anonymously using Office on the web**. If you select to apply it to a specified group, you can only choose one group per policy.

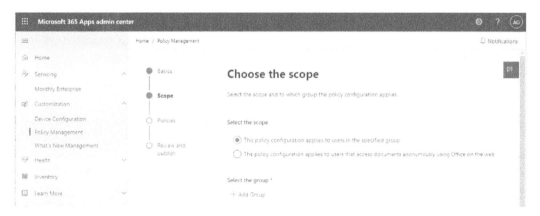

Figure 10.6 – Selecting the user scope for policy

6. Click **Next**.

7. On the **Policies** page, select an individual policy to manage.

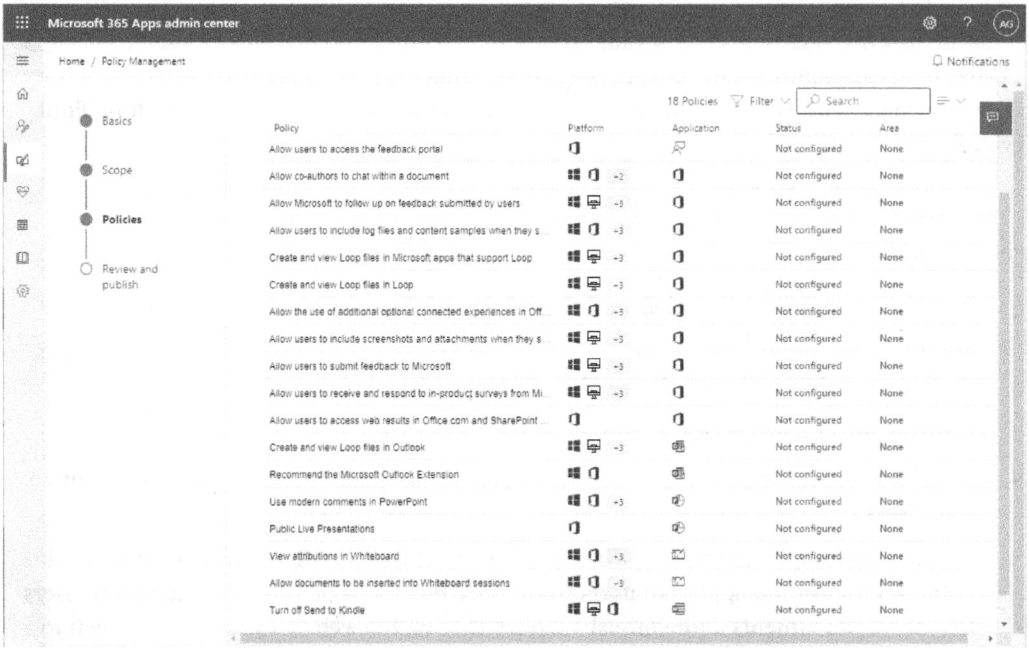

Figure 10.7 – Available cloud policy options

8. On the **Policy details** page, review the details and settings and set a configuration setting option. When you're finished, click **Apply**.

9. When you've finished editing policy items, click **Next**.

10. On the **Review and publish page**, verify the settings and click **Create**.

11. Click **Done**.

The C2R service that underpins the modern app deployment methodologies is responsible for communicating with the Cloud Policy service. As users in the scope of a policy launch Microsoft 365 apps, the C2R service will communicate with the policy service and refresh the allowed application features.

> **Further reading**
>
> For more information on the Cloud Policy service for Microsoft 365, see `https://learn.microsoft.com/en-us/deployoffice/admincenter/overview-cloud-policy`.

Microsoft Intune

For organizations new to Microsoft 365 or those without Configuration Manager, **Intune** is one of the preferred ways to deploy the Microsoft 365 Apps.

Per Microsoft's recommendations, you should select a subset of users that will be subscribed to Semi-Annual Enterprise Channel (Preview) to test new features coming out. In these next sections, we'll configure deployments for the pilot group (who will get the Semi-Annual Enterprise Channel Preview Microsoft 365 Apps build) and the Broad group (who will get the normal Semi-Annual Enterprise Channel build).

The pilot group

To deploy Microsoft 365 Apps using Microsoft Endpoint Manager, follow these steps:

1. Navigate to the Microsoft Intune admin center (`https://endpoint.microsoft.com` or `https://intune.microsoft.com`).

2. Select **Apps** from the navigation menu and then select **Windows** under the **By platform** section, as shown in *Figure 10.8*.

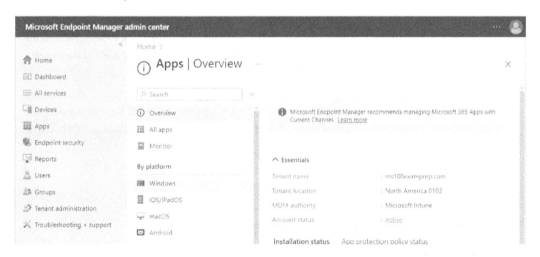

Figure 10.8 – Microsoft Endpoint Manager overview page

3. Click **Add** and then select **Windows 10 and later** under **Microsoft 365 Apps**.

Figure 10.9 – Selecting the Microsoft 365 Apps installation option

4. Click **Select** to choose the **Microsoft 365 Apps for Windows 10 and later** option.

5. On the **App suite information** page, review the default options. Update **Suite Name** to reflect that this package is for the Semi-Annual Enterprise Channel Preview build and click **Next**.

6. Under **Configuration settings format**, select **Configuration designer** to use the default Microsoft Endpoint Manager configuration tool. You can also select **Enter XML data** to use a previously saved configuration file from the OCT.

7. On the **Configure app suite** page, under the **Configure app suite** section, select which Office apps to deploy. By default, all apps are selected except Skype for Business. Depending on your organization's requirements, you may choose to only deploy certain apps to certain groups of users.

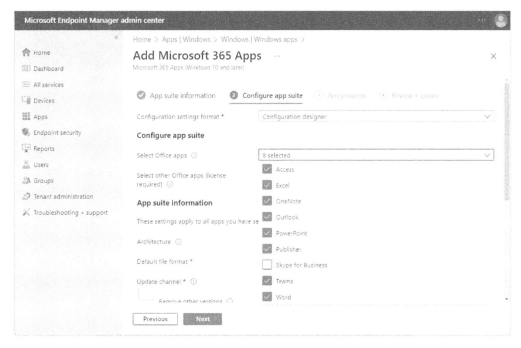

Figure 10.10 – Configuring app suite options

8. Under the **Configure app suite** section, you can use the **Select other Office apps** dropdown to choose to install either Project or Visio (each requires a separate product license).

9. Under the **App suite information** section, select an **Architecture** option (32-bit or 64-bit).

10. Select a **Default file format** option. The default for Microsoft 365 Apps is the **Office Open XML Format** option, which is what Microsoft recommends. The other available option is **Office Open Document Format**.

11. Select **Semi-Annual Enterprise Channel (Preview)** from the **Update channel** dropdown.

12. Review the remaining options:

    *   **Remove other versions** (default: **Yes**)

    *   **Version to install** (default: **Latest**)

    *   **Use shared computer activation** (default: **No**)

    *   **Accept the Microsoft Software License Terms on behalf of users** (default: **Yes**)

    *   **Install background service for Microsoft Search in Bing** (default: **Yes**)

    *   **Language** (default: **No languages selected**)

13. Click **Next**.

14. On the **Assignments** page, select an assignment method for the app. You can choose to have the deployment required for a group, all users, or all devices. You can also make it available for self-install for a group or all users on Intune-enrolled devices. Finally, you can select to uninstall the app for assigned users, devices, or groups. For this option, you should select a group that represents your pilot users.

> **Uninstall requirement**
>
> An app can only be uninstalled via Intune or Microsoft Endpoint Manager if it was deployed via Intune or Endpoint Manager.

15. Click **Next**.

16. On the **Review + create** page, click **Create**.

Depending on the distribution options chosen, the application will be either automatically deployed or available for users to install from the company portal.

The broad group

These steps mirror the pilot group settings with two exceptions:

- In *step 5*, update **Suite Name** to a value that reflects Semi-Annual Enterprise Channel.

- In *step 11*, instead of selecting **Semi-Annual Enterprise Channel (Preview)**, select **Semi-Annual Enterprise Channel**.

- In *step 14*, on the **Assignments** tab, instead of selecting a group that represents the pilot group, select a group that represents the broad group.

Once you have configured your apps and deployment, you can view the status of the deployment by navigating to **Apps | Windows | Windows Apps** and selecting the app package that you've configured. See *Figure 10.11* for an example of the app deployment dashboard.

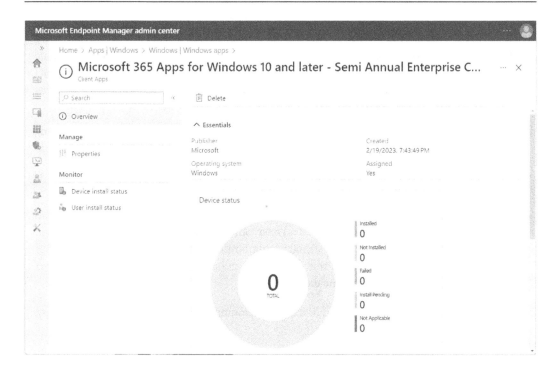

Figure 10.11 – App deployment dashboard

You can view both device and user installation statuses for an individual application package.

Microsoft Configuration Manager

For organizations that already use a supported version of Configuration Manager, Configuration Manager is not only an obvious choice, but the Microsoft-recommended one as well.

> **Exam tip**
>
> Configuration Manager includes the Office Client Management dashboard, which can be used to deploy Office and monitor updates.

Configuration Manager supports a number of deployment features, such as being able to remove previous versions of Office, the ability to deploy VBA macro settings, as well as configuring the Windows default file handler and default file locations used by the apps.

From a best practices perspective, Microsoft makes the following recommendations:

- Create two **collections**. In Configuration Manager terminology, a collection is a logical grouping of users or devices. One collection will be for your pilot group and will receive the Semi-Annual Enterprise Channel Preview build, while the other collection is the broad group that represents all others who will receive the Semi-Annual Enterprise Channel build.

- Build two **applications** (or **application packages**) per platform. For example, if you are deploying to 64-bit machines, you would build an application for Semi-Annual Enterprise Channel and one application for Semi-Annual Channel (Preview).

- Ensure you are running the current branch release of Configuration Manager.

- Enable **peer cache** on the client devices. Peer cache is a feature that allows clients to stream content (such as installation files or updates) from other devices on the local network instead of each contacting a server or other distribution point. The concept is similar to consumer technologies such as BitTorrent in that endpoints can be used as content servers for other devices trying to download the same data.

Once you've configured your Configuration Manager environment appropriately, it's time to deploy.

Creating collections

In Configuration Manager, a collection is a group used to identify users or devices that will be targeted for running tasks, such as inventories, deploying applications, or configuring client settings. A collection can contain either devices or users, but cannot contain both.

Collections can be managed by placing users or devices directly (called a **direct rule**) or dynamically (called a **query rule**) based on attributes such as the members of an organizational unit or the version of a device's operating system. Collections can also include or exclude other collections.

Further reading

Creating and managing collections is outside the scope of the MS-100 exam. The MS-100 exam only requires you to know that collections are groups of users or computers.

You can learn more about how to manage direct and query-based collections here: `https://learn.microsoft.com/en-us/mem/configmgr/core/clients/manage/collections/create-collections`.

Creating and deploying the Microsoft 365 apps

In this section, we'll briefly cover the step to create and deploy the application package.

The pilot group

As previously mentioned, the Microsoft 365 Apps software is compiled into a package known as an application in Configuration Manager. From a best practices perspective, it's important to have groups of individuals using the Semi-Annual Enterprise Channel (Preview) build of the Microsoft 365 apps to help detect any issues before they reach the broad group with the Semi-Annual Enterprise Channel build.

To configure the application, follow these steps:

1. On the Configuration Manager server, launch the Configuration Manager console.
2. Expand **Software Library | Overview** and select **Office 365 Client Management**.
3. On the **Application Settings** page, enter a name and description for the application package, as well as the location where the installation media will be stored (specified as `\\server\ share`).
4. Click **Next**.
5. On the **Office Settings** page, select **Go to the Office Customization Tool**.
6. As you did with the Intune deployment, select the appropriate settings from the customization tool, including the update channel (Semi-Annual Enterprise Channel (Preview)), languages, accepting the EULA, whether to remove the previous MSI version of Office, and any other application settings.
7. After the options have been selected, click **Submit**.
8. Click **Yes** on the **Deployment** page to deploy the package now. You can also exit the wizard and deploy the package at a later time.
9. Select the pilot collection for deployment and then click **Next**.

The broad group

These steps mirror the pilot group settings with two exceptions:

*   In *step 6*, instead of selecting **Semi-Annual Enterprise Channel (Preview)**, select **Semi-Annual Enterprise Channel**
*   In *step 9*, instead of selecting the pilot collection, select the collection that represents the broad group

Using the Office 365 Client Management dashboard

The **Office 365 Client Management dashboard**, starting with Configuration Manager version 1802, is the go-to place for viewing information about the state of your Configuration Manager-deployed Office apps.

The dashboard shows a variety of health and configuration data for your managed devices. Beginning in version 1906, it also includes a **Microsoft 365 Apps readiness dashboard**, which is used to determine the readiness state when moving from Office 365 ProPlus to Microsoft 365 Apps, as shown in *Figure 10.12*:

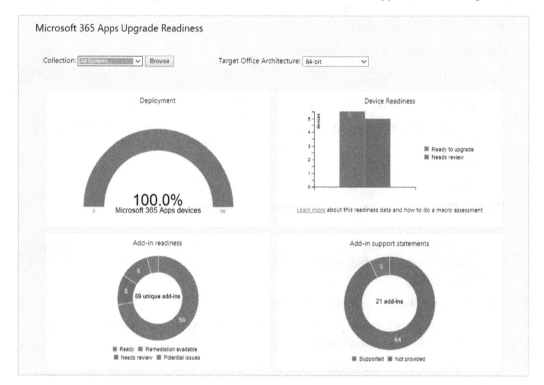

Figure 10.12 – The Microsoft 365 Apps Upgrade Readiness dashboard

The Microsoft 365 Apps readiness dashboard includes several features specifically for understanding the readiness of add-ins and macros:

- Device readiness
- Add-in readiness
- Add-in support statements
- Top add-ins by the version count
- Number of devices that have macros

- Macro readiness

- Macro advisories

Each of these support areas will help you understand which devices, macros, and add-ins need to be remediated prior to upgrading to Microsoft 365 Apps.

> **Further reading**
>
> You can learn more about the Office 365 Client Management dashboard at `https://learn.microsoft.com/en-us/mem/configmgr/sum/deploy-use/office-365-dashboard`.

Whether you deploy Microsoft 365 apps via Microsoft Endpoint Manager (formerly Intune) or Configuration Manager, Microsoft provides a number of tools to use to configure, manage, and monitor your progress.

Summary

In this chapter, you learned about the tools and strategies for deploying Microsoft 365 apps to devices. For most organizations, Microsoft recommends creating a pilot group to ensure your organization can review and test upcoming releases.

Depending on your organization's existing infrastructure, you can take several approaches to deploying Microsoft 365 apps to endpoints. Understanding the different paths to deployment is key to making sure you choose the right one for your scenario.

Next, we will learn about planning an Exchange Online deployment.

Knowledge check

In this section, we'll test your knowledge of some key elements from this chapter.

Questions

1. For most enterprise deployments, what two channels does Microsoft recommend?

    A. Semi-Annual Enterprise Channel

    B. Semi-Annual Enterprise Channel (Preview)

    C. Current Channel

    D. Current Channel (Preview)

    E. Monthly Enterprise Channel

    F. Monthly Enterprise Channel (Preview)

2. The _____ is used to configure policies for use with the Cloud Policy Service for Microsoft 365.

   A. Microsoft Endpoint Manager admin center

   B. Microsoft Intune admin center

   C. Microsoft 365 Defender admin center

   D. Microsoft 365 Apps admin center

3. Which group is used to target the majority of users in an organization's Microsoft 365 Apps deployment strategy?

   A. The pilot group

   B. The production group

   C. The broad group

   D. The enterprise group

4. Which tool can be used to build XML configuration files for specifying Microsoft 365 Apps settings?

   A. The ODT

   B. The OCT

   C. The Configuration Manager Customization tool

   D. The Configuration Manager Deployment tool

5. Which tool is used to review compatibility data for VBA code inside of Office documents?

   A. OTD

   B. The Office VBA Toolkit

   C. The Readiness Toolkit

   D. The Office Deployment Assistant

Answers

1. A: Semi-annual Enterprise Channel; B: Semi-Annual Enterprise Channel (Preview)

2. D: The Microsoft 365 Apps admin center

3. C: The broad group

4. B: The OCT

5. C: The Readiness Toolkit

11
Planning and Implementing Exchange Online Deployments

When many people think of Microsoft's services and software, they frequently gravitate toward email and collaboration. Microsoft originally entered the email arena in 1988 with Microsoft Mail; 8 years later, it revolutionized the corporate landscape with the release of Exchange Server 4.0. The rest, as they say, is history.

Over the years, Microsoft has continued to refine and develop Exchange, eventually making it available online as a service as part of the Business Productivity Online Suite—the forerunner to Office 365 and the Microsoft 365 offering. Microsoft's latest editions allow organizations to send email and host mailboxes seamlessly between cloud and on-premises environments. Exchange hybrid solutions use a combination of on-premises Exchange servers in conjunction with Exchange Online—most often, as part of a migration strategy, but sometimes in long-term coexistence scenarios as well.

In this chapter, we'll focus on the following areas of Exchange Online deployments:

- Planning for DNS records
- Planning and implementing mail routing
- Planning and implementing organizational settings
- Planning and implementing an Exchange hybrid organization

By the end of this chapter, you should be able to describe the components of an Exchange Online deployment, as well as the concepts of hybrid connectivity and mail routing.

Let's go!

Planning for DNS records

If you're reading this book in chronological order, you're already familiar with the importance of DNS records from the perspective of enabling a Microsoft 365 tenant. In *Chapter 1*, you learned how Microsoft 365 uses TXT DNS records to show proof of ownership for domains. Exchange Online is no different; in fact, every domain you add as part of the domain verification process is automatically added as an accepted domain and made available to use in Exchange Online.

In addition to the TXT records used to verify domain ownership, Exchange Online also employs several other DNS records:

Record type	Hostname	Target or value	Purpose or Description
CNAME	`autodiscover`	`autodiscover.outlook.com`	Helps messaging clients locate a mailbox
MX	`@`	`domain.mail.protection.outlook.com`	Indicates what service is responsible for accepting mail on behalf of a domain
TXT (SPF)	`@`	`include:spf.protection.outlook.com`	Helps prevent unauthorized senders from spoofing or masquerading as your domain

TXT (DKIM)	`Selector1._domainkey`
	
	`Selector2._domainkey`
		`selector1-domain._domainkey.initialdomain`
		
		`selector2-domain._domainkey.initialdomain`
			Helps prevent unauthorized senders from spoofing or masquerading as your domain

TXT (**Domain-based Message Authentication, Reporting, and Conformance (DMARC)**)	`_dmarc`	`V="DMARC1; p=reject; pct=100; rua=mailto:d@rua.domain.com; ruf=mailto:d@ruf.domain.com; fo=1"`	Instructs recipient servers on how to handle mail based on **Sender Policy Framework (SPF)** and **DomainKeys Identified Mail (DKIM)** values

Record type	Hostname	Target or value	Purpose or Description
TXT (Fed)	@	A value provided by the Exchange **Hybrid Configuration Wizard (HCW)**	Exchange 2010-based hybrid deployments require an additional DNS record to establish a relationship with the Microsoft Federation Gateway

Table 11.1 – DNS records

Let's look at what some of the records are used for in the next few sections.

MX

Most administrators, especially if they have been working with email, are familiar with **mail exchanger (MX)** records. Depending on your deployment or migration strategy, you may wish to update your MX record to point to Exchange Online (as opposed to an on-premises mail gateway or other mail service provider). Strategies for when to update the MX record can vary greatly—some organizations may wish to update it right away, while some wait until after a migration is complete. Still others maintain separate mail hygiene infrastructure and never update their records to point to Exchange Online.

As long as there is a clear path to deliver mail to mailboxes, the target address for a domain's MX record doesn't matter from an overall functional perspective.

> **Further reading**
> The foundations for mail routing records were laid in very early **Request For Comments (RFC)** documents such as 821, 897, and 992. The MX record itself was first defined in RFC 974 in 1986. You can learn more about historical and current RFCs at https://www.rfc-editor.org/.

Autodiscover

The Autodiscover record is used by Outlook email clients to locate an Exchange mailbox server. In on-premises and Exchange hybrid environments, the Autodiscover record points to an on-premises Exchange server with either the Client Access Server role (Exchange Server 2010/2013) or the Mailbox/Client Access Server role (Exchange 2016/2019). In fully deployed Exchange Online environments, the Autodiscover record points to Exchange Online.

> **Further reading**
>
> The Autodiscover protocol has a lot of nuance and configurability, which you can learn about in detail here: https://aka.ms/autodiscover.

SPF

SPF is a DNS-based technology that domain owners configure to identify servers that are allowed to send as a particular domain. SPF records are formatted as text records, specifying the IP addresses and names of servers authorized to send on a domain's behalf. SPF was first defined by RFC 4408.

> **Further reading**
>
> You can learn more about how Microsoft implements SPF records in Microsoft 365 here: https://learn.microsoft.com/en-us/microsoft-365/security/office-365-security/email-authentication-spf-configure.

DKIM

DKIM is another email verification technology. DKIM also uses a DNS. DKIM uses a form of public key cryptography to sign messages that are authorized to originate from your domain. DKIM was first introduced in RFC 4871, and later revised with RFCs 5585 and 6376.

> **Further reading**
>
> You can learn more about how Microsoft implements DKIM in Microsoft 365 here: https://learn.microsoft.com/en-us/microsoft-365/security/office-365-security/email-authentication-dkim-configure.

DMARC

DMARC works in conjunction with SPF and DKIM to authenticate mail systems and specifies how to handle messages whose validation values don't line up. DMARC provides instructions for receiving mail systems when a message fails SPF or DKIM checks. DMARC was first defined in RFC 7489.

> **Further reading**
>
> You can learn more about how Microsoft implements DMARC in Microsoft 365 here: https://learn.microsoft.com/en-us/microsoft-365/security/office-365-security/email-authentication-dmarc-configure.

As you deploy to Exchange Online and Microsoft 365 services, implementing and updating these DNS records will help ensure mail flows to your environment and that other organizations can trust the validity of mail purporting to be from your domain(s).

Planning and implementing mail routing

Mail routing is the collection of processes that happens after a message has left the sender. Actions taken along the route may include examining for malware or spam, redirecting based on message properties, adding **Carbon copy (Cc)** or **Blind carbon copy (Bcc)** recipients, adding additional mail headers, encrypting or decrypting content, or even rejecting mail.

Understanding domains

Domains (sometimes referred to as namespaces) are the configuration objects that are used to reference groups of related objects managed by a single organization. Domains are typically names of some sort and are composed of two parts:

- **Second level domain** – Typically used to refer to the managing organization. For example, in `fabrikam.com`, `fabrikam` is the second-level domain name.

- **Top-level domain** – The top-level domain is used to group types of related second-level domains. You're probably familiar with the most common top-level domains—the original seven are `.com` (commercial), `.edu` (educational institution), `.gov` (government), `.mil` (US military), `.net` (network), `.us` (intended for US citizens, residents, and organizations), and `.org` (a truncated form of organization, originally intended for second level domains that don't fit anywhere else).

In the context of Exchange (and other mail systems), domains are used to identify where groups of related mailboxes and mail-enabled groups exist. Similar to Active Directory (and Azure Active Directory), domains in the Exchange realm are used for naming and locating objects. While on-premises Active Directory can only have one domain associated with it, Exchange (both on-premises and Online) can support multiple domains. These alternate domains are sometimes called aliased domains.

Exchange has two core types of domains: **accepted** and **remote**. **Accepted domains** are the domains that your environment owns and is responsible for. **Remote domains** are configuration objects that refer to domains outside your organization. Remote domains are typically used to manage certain delivery aspects of email, such as specifying particular message formats or preventing the forwarding of out-of-office replies.

Managing accepted domains

You typically configure accepted domains for each domain name that you own and want Exchange Online to manage. You can see the accepted domains in the Exchange admin center (`https://admin.exchange.microsoft.com`) under **Mail flow** | **Accepted domains**, as shown in *Figure 11.1*:

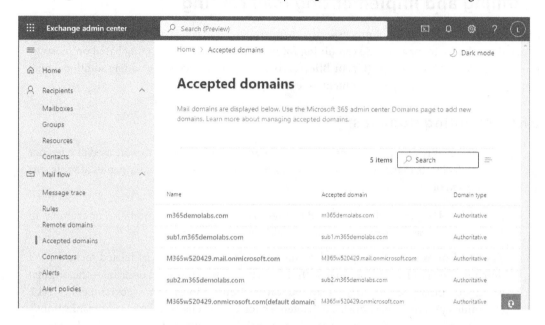

Figure 11.1 – Accepted domains page

Every domain you add as a verified domain in the Microsoft 365 admin center is automatically added to Exchange Online as an accepted domain. This integrated behavior is different from Exchange on-premises, where Active Directory domains and Exchange-accepted domains are managed independently.

Domains in Exchange Online can be one of two types:

- **Authoritative** – Exchange Online owns the domain and is the source of truth for what mail-enabled objects exist in the domain.

- **Internal Relay** – Recipients can exist either in the Exchange Online organization or in another environment (typically, a hybrid-connected Exchange Online environment). If a message recipient isn't found in Exchange Online, messages are forwarded to other mail systems to attempt delivery.

Next, let's look at managing remote domains.

Managing remote domains

By default, all external domains (represented by an asterisk) are configured with the same properties. The screenshot in *Figure 11.2* shows the default configuration for remote domains.

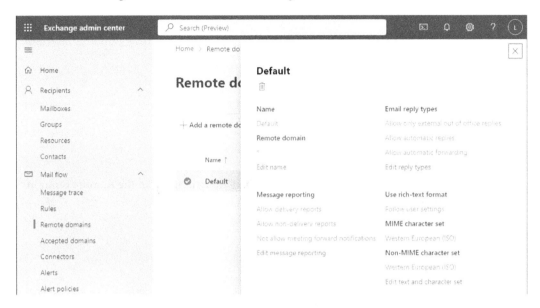

Figure 11.2 – Remote domains default configuration

You can change the properties for all remote domains globally by editing the various properties. For example, you may want to prevent all external organizations from receiving out-of-office replies.

You can also configure specific settings for individual domains. For example, you may have a partner organization with whom you work closely that uses a legacy email system that can't accept rich text or HTML-formatted messages.

In the following example, we'll create a remote domain and specify custom settings to prevent the domain from receiving rich text messages:

1. Navigate to the Exchange admin center (`https://admin.exchange.microsoft.com`). Expand **Mail flow** and select **Remote domains**.
2. Select **Add a remote domain.**

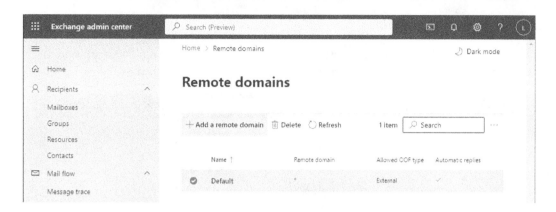

Figure 11.3 – Remote domains page

3. Enter a friendly **Name** for the domain and the DNS domain name in the **Remote domain** field. Click **Next**.

Figure 11.4 – Remote domain name configuration

4. Configure what types of automatic email replies you want to allow and click **Next**.

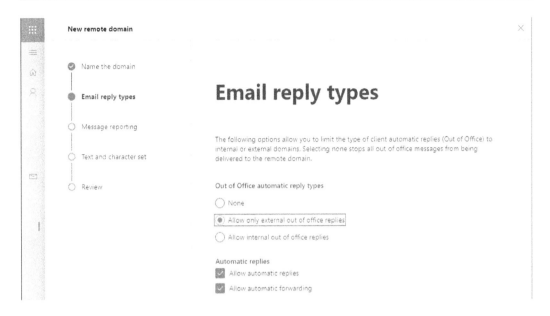

Figure 11.5 – Email reply types

5. On the **Message reporting** page, select which type of reporting and notification options you want to allow to be sent to the remote domain. Click **Next**.

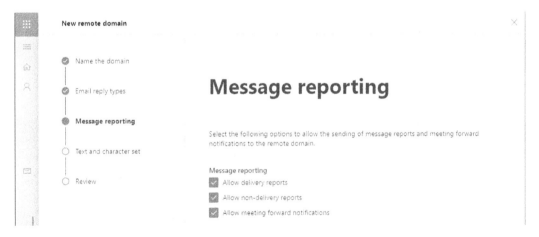

Figure 11.6 – Message reporting

6. On the **Text and character set** page, select the text formatting options. In this example, the remote domain is being configured for an environment that can't process HTML or rich text messages, so select **Never** to override the formatting that the user specifies on their mail client. Click **Next**.

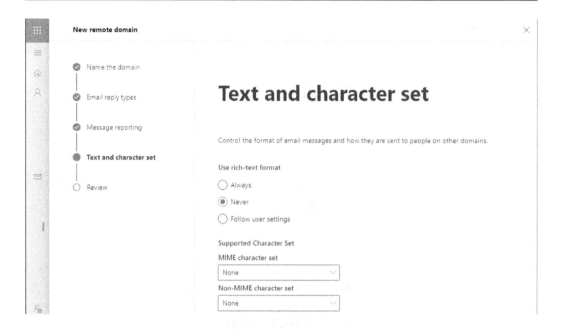

Figure 11.7 – Text and character set

7. Review the configured settings and click **Save**.

8. Click **Done** to return to the **Remote domains** page.

New messages sent to recipients in this domain will be modified or filtered to match the configured options.

Next, let's look at other ways of managing the flow and transformation of email.

Understanding mail flow rules

In addition to using remote domains to manage some aspects of the message configuration, you can use **mail flow rules** to process messages. Mail flow rules (frequently referred to as **transport rules** or **Exchange transport rules** (**ETRs**)) are essentially a type of automated workflow that performs actions on messages matching certain criteria.

Learning about mail flow rules

Before you begin configuring rules, it's important to understand how they're structured. Mail flow rules have three components:

- **Conditions** – Criteria used to select which messages will be acted upon, such as whether the message participant is inside or outside of the Microsoft 365 environment or whether the message participant's address matches a text pattern.

- **Exceptions** – Exceptions are used to specify or refine the conditions used to select which messages are in scope for a rule. For example, you may configure a condition that says *all senders in the fabrikam.com domain* but then configure an exception for *senders in the us.fabrikam.com domain* to exclude those senders from the rule.

- **Actions** – What particular actions or tasks you wish to invoke on a message. Common actions include blocking executable attachments, adding message disclaimers, or routing messages for approval.

You can have multiple mail flow rules configured in your environment. Rules are processed in order of priority, starting at 1. Any message may get processed by one or more rules; sometimes, it may be beneficial to configure Exchange Online to stop further processing rules after the conditions in one rule are matched.

> **Further reading**
>
> The complete list of mail flow conditions and exceptions (collectively called predicates) can be found at `https://learn.microsoft.com/en-us/exchange/security-and-compliance/mail-flow-rules/conditions-and-exceptions`. The complete list of mail flow actions can be found at `https://learn.microsoft.com/en-us/exchange/security-and-compliance/mail-flow-rules/mail-flow-rule-actions`. While it's not important, from the MS-100 exam perspective, to know all the parameters of every predicate or action, you should spend a few minutes reviewing the parameters so you're familiar with the types of things that transport rules can accomplish.

Configuring transport rules

Mail flow rules are configured inside the Exchange admin center (`https://admin.exchange.microsoft.com`) under **Mail flow | Rules** or through Exchange Online PowerShell.

In this example, we'll configure a mail flow rule that redirects incoming mail sent to the members of a technical support distribution group to the service ticketing mailbox:

1. Navigate to the Exchange admin center (`https://admin.exchange.microsoft.com`), expand **Mail flow**, and select **Rules**.

2. Select **Add a rule**:

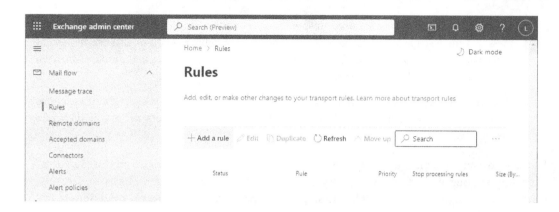

Figure 11.8 – Mail flow rules

3. From the pop-up menu, select **Create a new rule**.

4. On the **Set rule conditions** page, enter a **Name** label for the rule. Under **Apply this rule if**, select **The sender**. In the second dropdown, select **is external/internal** and then select **Outside the Organization**. Click **Save** to configure the first part of the condition.

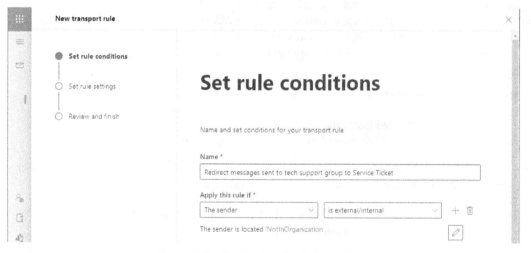

Figure 11.9 – Configuring the first condition

5. Next to the condition, click the + button to add another condition. In the first dropdown of the second condition, select **The recipient**. In the second dropdown of the second condition, select **is a member of this group** and then choose a group from the address list.

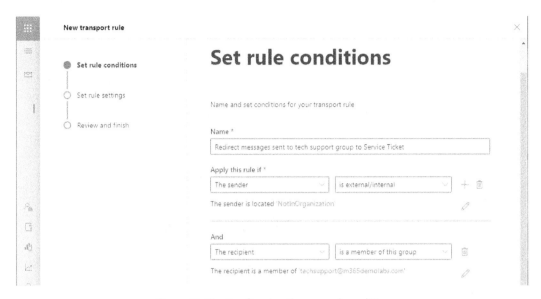

Figure 11.10 – Configuring the second condition

6. Under the **Do the following** section, expand the first dropdown and select **Redirect the message to**.

7. Expand the second dropdown under the **Do the following** section and select **these recipients**. Select a recipient from the address book and click **Save**. See *Figure 11.11*.

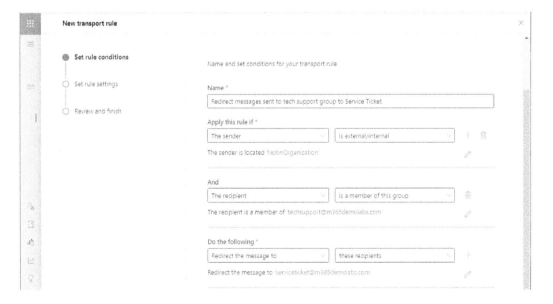

Figure 11.11 – Configuring the action

8. Click **Next**.

9. On the **Set rule settings** page, select the mode for the rule:

   - **Enforce** enables the rule, while the two test modes don't put the rule into action but instead allow you to generate notifications that tell you whether the message would have triggered the rule. To use the test modes, you need to configure a **Generate an incident report** action.

   - You can also specify a **Severity** level for the rule, which will be displayed when you run message traces.

   - You can select the timeframe for which the rule should be active.

   - Additionally, you have options to determine whether you will stop processing more rules after this one executes or defer the message and rerun it through the mail transport queue if the rule processing times out.

   - Finally, for **Condition criteria**, you can determine what parts of the message are used for matching sender criteria (**Header**, **Envelope**, or **Header and Envelope**).

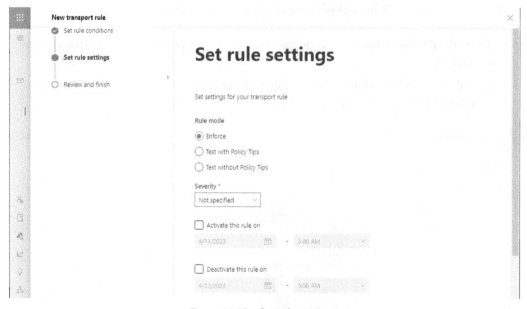

Figure 11.12 – Set rule settings

10. Click **Next**.

11. Review the rule settings and click **Finish** to save the new rule.

12. Click **Done** to return to the **Rules** page.

After you have configured a new rule, it is still in a **Disabled** state. You must update the rule by sliding the **Enable or disable rule** toggle to **Enabled**, as shown in *Figure 11.13*.

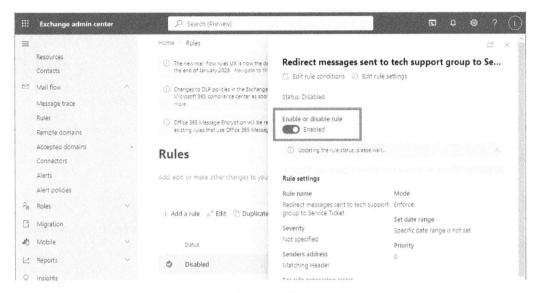

Figure 11.13 – Enabling the rule

It may take up to 30 minutes for it to become active. Once the rule is active, Microsoft recommends sending test messages to ensure that it is performing as you anticipate.

Understanding connectors

Connectors are Exchange configuration objects that define mail flow relationships between mail systems. Exchange Online features inbound connectors (used to receive mail from other organizations or systems) and outbound connectors (used to send mail to other organizations or systems).

Understanding default connectors

By default, Exchange Online has no connectors configured. Inbound mail from the internet is automatically routed to your tenant through Exchange Online Protection based on the domain names configured in your tenant. Outbound mail is relayed directly out through Exchange Online Protection to external recipients. See *Figure 11.14*.

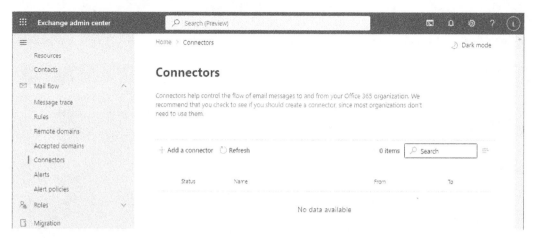

Figure 11.14 – Exchange Online connectors

You can use connectors to manage how mail is received by your organization or how it is sent to others. Common scenarios for configuring connectors may include the following:

- Your organization has non-Exchange mail systems

- You exchange sensitive information via email with known business partners and want to enforce transport-level encryption

- Your organization uses third-party mail hygiene services

- Your organization uses a standalone Exchange Online Protection subscription for message hygiene for on-premises systems and you are not going to configure an Exchange hybrid deployment

- Your organization has on-premises devices or applications that need to send mail to external recipients

If you implement Exchange hybrid in your organization, the HCW automatically creates inbound and outbound connectors in Exchange Online for secure cross-premises mail flow.

Configuring custom connectors

Once you've determined that you need a connector, you can use the Exchange admin center or PowerShell to create one.

In this example, we'll create a custom inbound connector for a fictitious organization that's using a third-party mail hygiene solution. To create the connector, follow these steps:

1. Navigate to the Exchange admin center (`https://admin.exchange.microsoft.com`). Expand **Mail flow** and select **Connectors**.

2. Click **Add a connector**.

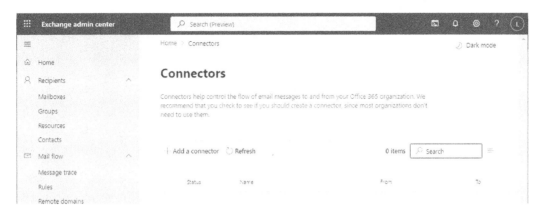

Figure 11.15 – Add a connector

3. On the **New connector** page, under **Connection from**, select **Partner organization** to create an inbound connector. Click **Next**.

Figure 11.16 – Selecting the connector directionality

4. Enter a connector **Name** and **Description** and select **Turn it on**. Click **Next**.

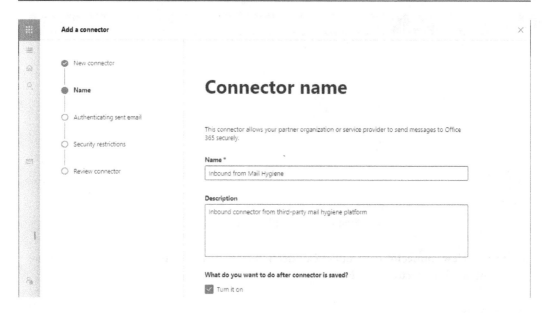

Figure 11.17 – Configuring the connector name

5.   On the **Authenticating sent email** page, select a method for determining how mail will get accepted. Select the appropriate radio button, add the necessary values, and click **Next**:

   ▪ If you're working with a trusted business partner, you can opt to match based on the domain value its server advertises when it connects to Exchange Online

   ▪ Most third-party mail hygiene solutions, like we're configuring in this example, have IP address ranges that mail will be processed through

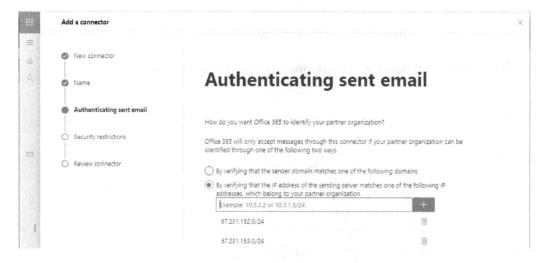

Figure 11.18 – Authenticating sent email

6. On the **Security restrictions** page, choose to enable or disable mandatory TLS. This will depend on whether your partner organization supports SMTP over SSL/TLS. Click **Next**.

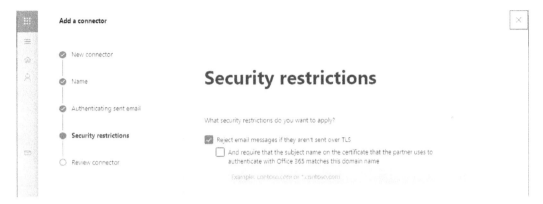

Figure 11.19 – Configuring security restrictions

7. Review the configured options and click **Create connector**.

8. Click **Done** to return to the **Connectors** page.

Custom outbound connectors follow a similar path, allowing you to configure the remote endpoint or mail host to which Exchange Online will send messages.

> **Further reading**
>
> Microsoft provides a handy guide for determining whether you need to create custom connectors here: https://learn.microsoft.com/en-us/exchange/mail-flow-best-practices/use-connectors-to-configure-mail-flow/do-i-need-to-create-a-connector.

Planning and implementing organizational settings

One of the advantages of Exchange Online is the scale of the environment and the need to not have to manage individual servers, databases, and specific policies. Instead, those can be left as default configuration objects, which are set by Microsoft.

However, there may be times when you need to manage settings to improve the experience for your users. That's where the Exchange organizational settings come into play.

The organizational settings are a set of dozens of parameters configured through PowerShell that enable you to customize the Exchange Online experience.

These settings, however, are not available by default and require you to enable them. To enable the customization of organization settings, you will need to follow these steps:

1. Launch a PowerShell session.

2. In the console interface, enter `Connect-ExchangeOnline`. When prompted, enter your administrative credentials.

3. Run the `Enable-OrganizationCustomization` command.

You can use the `Get-OrganizationConfig` and `Set-OrganizationConfig` cmdlets to retrieve and configure parameters, respectively.

Common parameters to configure include the following:

- `ActivityBasedAuthenticationTimeoutInterval` – This property is used to specify the period of inactivity before **Outlook on the Web (OotW)** or Outlook Web App is automatically logged out. The default value is `06:00:00` or 6 hours.

- `AppsForOfficeEnabled` – This parameter controls whether or not centrally managed apps can be activated to integrate with Microsoft 365 Apps.

- `AutoExpandingArchive` – This parameter is used to enable auto-expanding archives for Exchange Online mailboxes. Auto-expanding archives automatically grow a user's archive once it gets close to the storage limit. Once enabled, this option cannot be disabled.

- `BookingEnabled` – Determines whether or not **Books** is enabled in the organization.

- `DefaultGroupAccessType` – Configure the default access type for Microsoft 365 Groups. The default value is **Private**, but you can also choose **Public**.

- `DefaultMinutesToReduceShortEventsBy` – When used in conjunction with `ShortenEventScopeDefault`, you can choose to automatically create shorter meetings (for example, creating 55-minute meetings when an hour-long or shorter meeting is scheduled).

- `EnableOutlookEvents` – Used to allow Ootw to discover events in email messages and automatically create items on the calendar.

- `EwsAllowList` – Specify **Exchange Web Services (EWS)**-based applications that are allowed to use Exchange Online.

- `ShortenEventScopeDefault` – When used in conjunction with `DefaultMinutesToReduceShortEventsBy`, you can choose how to automatically shorten meetings (either `EndEarly` or `StartLate`). For example, you can configure the organization settings to automatically start meetings 5 minutes later than the scheduled time. If a user schedules a meeting from 2:00 P.M. to 3:00 P.M., the calendar app will update the meeting to run from 2:05 PM to 3:00 PM.

For example, if you wanted to configure the Exchange Online organizational settings to set meetings less than 1 hour long to start 7 minutes late, you would connect to Exchange Online PowerShell and run the following command:

```
Set-OrganizationConfig -ShortenEventScopeDefault StartLate
-DefaultMinutesToReduceShortEventsBy 7                  `
```

As with other PowerShell commands, the `Set-OrganizationConfig` command allows you to configure any of the parameters independently without impacting other organizational configuration settings.

> **Further reading**
>
> The full list of organization settings is available at `https://learn.microsoft.com/en-us/powershell/module/exchange/set-organizationconfig`.

Planning and implementing an Exchange hybrid organization

The easiest deployment of Exchange Online is simply performed by assigning Exchange Online mailbox licenses to users. The service already has all the necessary supporting infrastructure components in place—all that's missing are users' mailboxes.

That, however, is not how most organizations adopt Exchange Online. Many organizations have existing on-premises Exchange Server-based organizations. Fortunately, Microsoft provides a native mechanism to help organizations methodically onboard users to the Exchange Online environment. This process, commonly referred to as an Exchange hybrid migration, involves enabling either a new or existing Exchange server with configuration objects to allow data to flow between the on-premises and cloud environments. This hybrid functionality allows for cross-premises free/busy calendar lookups, distribution list membership, mail routing, and even mailbox migration.

Exchange hybrid deployments can range in complexity, depending on the on-premises versions of Exchange in use and what the goals of the deployment are—such as long-term coexistence, quick mailbox migrations, or a more methodical mailbox migration process.

Enabling a hybrid configuration involves selecting Exchange servers that will be used to participate in hybrid mail flow, as endpoints for mailbox migrations, or with both functions. Servers that will be used as hybrid mail flow will be configured to use new Send and Receive Connectors, while those selected for hybrid client access have the **Mailbox Replication Service** (**MRS**) proxy service configured.

> **Note**
>
> It's important to note that hybrid is not actually an Exchange role. While many people refer to the servers that have been assigned roles in a hybrid topology as **hybrid servers**, they're still technically just client access, mailbox, and transport servers.

Understanding the prerequisites

An Exchange hybrid configuration can be deployed to any on-premises organization with at least one server running Exchange Server 2010 **Service Pack 3 (SP3)**. An Exchange hybrid configuration is deployed by running the Exchange HCW, entering your credentials, and selecting the appropriate servers, certificates, and other settings as part of the process.

The following table identifies the versions of Exchange Server supported for various hybrid deployment topologies:

On-premises organization	Exchange 2019 hybrid	Exchange 2016 hybrid	Exchange 2013 hybrid	Exchange 2010 hybrid
Exchange 2019	Supported	Not Supported	Not Supported	Not Supported
Exchange 2016	Supported	Supported	Not Supported	Not Supported
Exchange 2013	Supported	Supported	Supported	Not Supported
Exchange 2010	Not Supported	Supported	Supported	Supported

Table 11.2 – Support Exchange Server topologies

Microsoft generally recommends using the latest Exchange versions that your environment will support and that all servers are running the latest **Cumulative Update (CU)** or **Update Rollup (RU)** available. Microsoft supports N-1 updates for all versions of Exchange hybrid.

In addition to the supported Exchange versions, a hybrid deployment has the following requirements:

- Azure Active Directory synchronization

- Domains verified in Microsoft 365 for any custom domains in the on-premises environment that you wish to use with Exchange Online

- Autodiscover records pointed to an on-premises Client Access Server endpoint (Exchange Server 2010/2013) or Exchange Mailbox Server (Exchange Server 2016/2019)

- Third-party trusted certificate configured with the EWS and Autodiscover external domain names as part of the **Subject Alternative Name (SAN)** name field

- EdgeSync (for organizations that wish to include Exchange Edge Transport servers as part of the Exchange hybrid configuration)

- Appropriate inbound and outbound networking (inbound on port 443, outbound on port 80, and inbound and outbound on port 25 between Exchange server(s) and Exchange Online Protection gateway address ranges)

- You can run the Exchange HCW on any server, as long as you can reach the servers that will be configured as part of the process

---

Modern Hybrid Topology

Some organizations may be unable to configure a full hybrid experience due to network or security constraints. For these scenarios, Microsoft offers a hybrid topology called Modern Hybrid Topology, which is based on a customized Azure AD App Proxy configuration. Since it is based on the Azure AD App Proxy platform, Modern Hybrid does not require inbound HTTPS access to the Exchange Server on-premises environment, which is a selling point for many environments with restrictive security configurations.

There are some trade-offs, however, as it does not offer the full experience (such as cross-premises mailbox searching, cross-premises MailTips, cross-premises message tracking, or full integration of Microsoft Teams with Exchange on-premises mailboxes). Modern Hybrid still requires port 25 bidirectional communication between on-premises and Exchange Online protection.

Running IdFix

As you learned in *Chapter 4*, IdFix is a tool that can be used to help validate your on-premises Active Directory organization's user, group, and contact objects prior to synchronization. While IdFix can't detect and resolve all issues, it can help you fix the most common ones.

Since full Exchange hybrid capabilities (such as mailbox migration) rely on directory synchronization, you should already have run this tool prior to preparing to work with Exchange hybrid.

For detailed examples and usage of IdFix, please refer back to *Chapter 4*.

Configuring networking

Generally speaking, an Exchange hybrid deployment needs to meet the following networking requirements:

- Allow users to be able to connect inbound on port 443 (HTTPS) to the on-premises Autodiscover endpoint

- Allow the Exchange Online service to be able to connect inbound via port 443 (HTTPS) for free/busy lookups and, if configured, hybrid public folder lookups, multi-mailbox search, mailbox migrations, and message tracking

- Allow the Exchange Online Protection service to be able to connect inbound on port 25 for hybrid mail routing

- Allow the Exchange Server environment to be able to connect outbound to Exchange Online Protection on port 25 for hybrid mail routing

- Allow the Exchange Server environment to be able to connect outbound on the certificate trust list on port 80 for certificate validation

From a best practices perspective, you should not configure intermediate inspection of packets between Exchange Online and Exchange Server environments. Packet disassembly, inspection, and reassembly can interfere with secure SMTP transport and mailbox migration services.

Some organizations may wish to limit inbound networking traffic (specifically for SMTP traffic) to the Microsoft data center IP ranges. Microsoft maintains an up-to-date list of data center ranges at `https://aka.ms/o365endpoints`.

Running the HCW

The Exchange HCW is a downloadable tool that is used to establish a new Exchange hybrid deployment or update an existing Exchange hybrid deployment.

Use the following steps to run the HCW:

1. On a server (such as the server that will be used to enable the hybrid configuration or a server that will participate in the hybrid topology), open a browser and navigate to `https://aka.ms/HybridWizard`.

2. When prompted to open **Microsoft.Online.CSE.Hybrid.Client.application**, click **Open**.

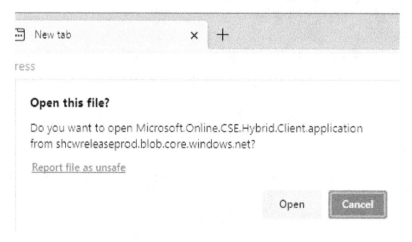

Figure 11.20 – Downloading and opening the HCW

3. Click **Install** to download and install the Microsoft Office 365 HCW.

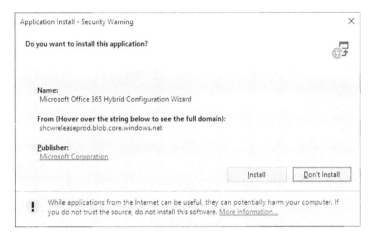

Figure 11.21 – Installing the Microsoft Office 365 HCW

4. Click **next** to begin the configuration.

Figure 11.22 – Office 365 HCW

5. Select an on-premises Exchange server for the HCW to use as the configuration endpoint (this doesn't have to be a server that will be configured as part of the hybrid topology). You can let the HCW detect a server or choose one. Additionally, select which sovereign cloud your Microsoft 365 subscription is in. Click **Next**.

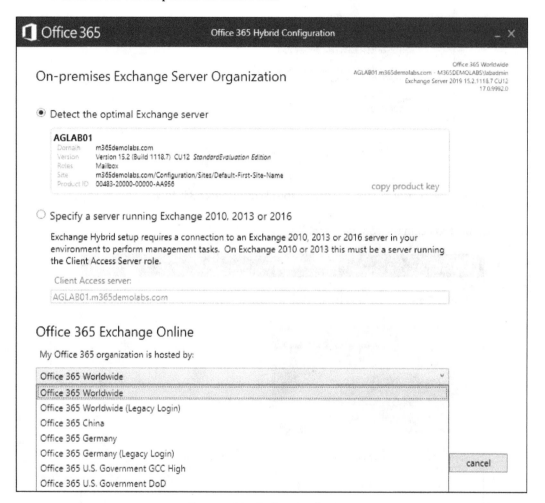

Figure 11.23 – Exchange selections

6. Configure the credentials for both the on-premises Exchange organization and the Exchange Online organization and click **Next**.

7. On the **Gathering Configuration Information** page, wait while the HCW connects to the Exchange environments and retrieves the existing configurations. Click **next** when ready.

Figure 11.24 – Gathering Configuration Information page

8. Select either **Minimal Hybrid Configuration** or **Full Hybrid Configuration**. The core factors impacting this decision are how many users exist in the on-premises organization and how long a hybrid coexistence will last. If you're just quickly migrating a mailbox to Exchange Online in a single event and have no need for long-term coexistence, you can select **Minimal Hybrid Configuration**. Otherwise, select **Full Hybrid Configuration**. Click **next**.

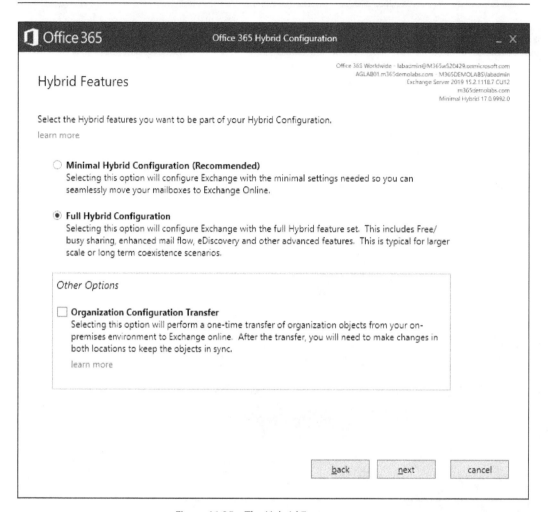

Figure 11.25 – The Hybrid Features page

9.   On the **Hybrid Topology** page, choose either **Use Exchange Classic Hybrid Topology** or **Use Exchange Modern Hybrid Topology** and click **next**.

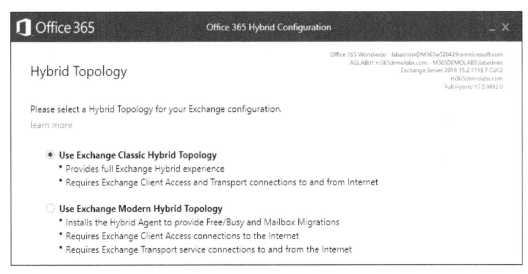

Figure 11.26 – Hybrid Topology page

10. On the **On-premises Account for Migration** page, enter a credential that will be used to create a migration endpoint. Click **Next**.

11. On the **Hybrid Configuration** page, select which options to configure. The default option, **Configure my Client Access and Mailbox servers for secure mail transport (typical)**, applies to organizations that either do not have Edge Transport servers or do not wish to use Edge Transport servers as part of the hybrid topology. Click **Next**.

- **Centralized mail transport** (**CMT**) is another feature that most organizations will not require. Typically, **Enable centralized mail transport** is used when organizations have deployed specialized third-party content filtering or **data loss prevention** (**DLP**) scanning solutions.

Figure 11.27 – Hybrid Configuration page

12. On the **Receive Connector Configuration** page, select which servers will be configured for mail transport with Exchange Online. The selected servers will be configured with a receive connector. Click **Next**.

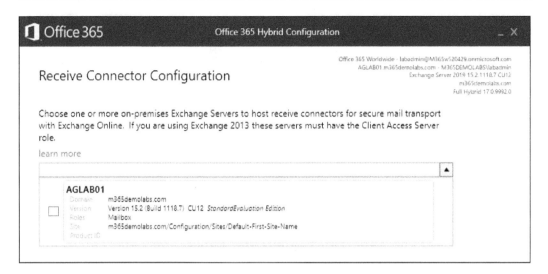

Figure 11.28 – Receive Connector Configuration

13. Select which servers will be responsible for sending mail to Exchange Online. Click **Next**.

Figure 11.29 – Send Connector Configuration

14. On the **Transport Certificate** page, select which SSL/TLS certificate will be bound to the SMTP service and used to communicate with Exchange Online. This certificate must be installed on all servers being used for hybrid transport. Click **Next**.

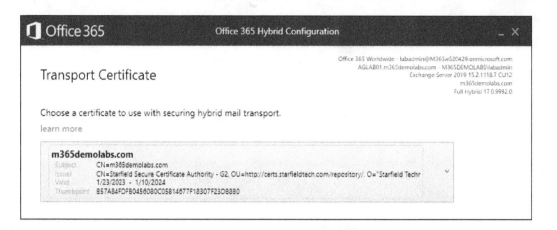

Figure 11.30 – Transport Certificate page

15. On the **Organization FQDN** page, enter the name that will be presented to Exchange Online protection when relaying to Exchange Online from your on-premises mail system. This name must exist in either the **Subject** field or the SAN name field of the certificate. Click **Next**.

16. On the **Ready for Update** page, click **Update** to enable the configuration.

17. Review the changes being made.

Figure 11.31 – Enabling the hybrid configuration

After the configuration has been put in place, depending on the options you've selected, you should be able to perform free/busy lookups from on-premises to cloud mailboxes (and vice versa) and send mail successfully between cloud and on-premises mailboxes.

If you configured a hybrid topology that includes mail routing, you should see inbound and outbound connectors in Exchange Online as well on the **Connectors** page, as shown in *Figure 11.32*:

Figure 11.32 – New inbound and outbound connectors after the HCW

> **Further reading**
> Enabling a hybrid configuration is really the first step in preparing for a hybrid migration to Exchange Online. You can find step-by-step guidance for creating migration batches and moving users here: `https://learn.microsoft.com/en-us/exchange/hybrid-deployment/move-mailboxes`.

Summary

In this chapter, you learned about the features of Exchange Online, including DNS, domains, transport rules, connectors, and organization settings. You also learned about the various hybrid configuration options available for connecting Exchange Server on-premises with Exchange Online.

In the next chapter, we'll begin working with SharePoint Online, OneDrive for Business, and Microsoft Teams.

Knowledge check

In this section, we'll test your knowledge of some key elements from this chapter.

Questions

1. SPF is an acronym for what service, feature, capability, or configuration?

    A. SenderID Protection Filtering

    B. Sender Policy Framework

    C. Secured Policy Framework

    D. Secured Policy Filtering

2. In order to configure secure hybrid communications between an Exchange Server environment and Exchange Online, you must use which of the following?

    A. A self-signed SSL/TLS certificate

    B. A reverse proxy

    C. Azure AD App Proxy

    D. A third-party SSL/TLS certificate

3. You can perform additional processing on messages using which of the following?

    A. Exchange transport rules

    B. Exchange transform rules

    C. Azure AD Connect transform rules

    D. Connectors

4. The _____ record is used for instructing systems where to deliver mail.

    A. SPF

    B. DKIM

    C. DMARC

    D. MX

5. The _____ is used to configure an Exchange Hybrid Deployment.

   A. Hybrid Configuration App

   B. Hybrid Enablement Wizard

   C. Hybrid Configuration Wizard

   D. Hybrid Enablement App

Answers

1. B: Sender Policy Framework

2. D: A third-party SSL/TLS certificate

3. A: Exchange transport rules

4. D: MX

5. C: Hybrid Configuration Wizard

12

Planning and Implementing Microsoft SharePoint Online, OneDrive, and Microsoft Teams

SharePoint Online underpins many Microsoft 365 features by providing foundational storage, search, indexing, and content metadata management. SharePoint Online is the glue that connects many services together, including OneDrive for Business and Microsoft Teams.

In this final chapter, we'll focus on the following areas for SharePoint Online, OneDrive for Business, and Teams:

- Understanding SharePoint site types, collections, and lists
- Planning a migration strategy for SharePoint Online and OneDrive for Business
- Identifying hybrid requirements for SharePoint Online
- Managing access configurations for SharePoint Online and Microsoft Teams
- Managing SharePoint Online tenant and site settings
- Mapping Phone System features to requirements
- Planning and implementing organizational settings
- Planning, implementing, and managing guest and external access

By the end of this chapter, you should be able to describe and manage the core components and settings related to SharePoint Online and OneDrive, as well as articulate the features of Microsoft Teams Phone.

Let's go!

Understanding SharePoint site types, collections, and lists

SharePoint Online is a web content, document collaboration, and application platform that is organized into a hierarchical system of **site collections**, **sites**, and **libraries**. It has many of the same features as SharePoint Server, but some features are hidden, abstracted, or not available. SharePoint Online removes many underlying management tasks, leaving the content management to the customer, while Microsoft handles tasks such as scheduling and updating. This allows users to manage content, plugins, and integration with on-premises environments.

SharePoint Online has two core architecture types – **classic** and **modern**. While classic architecture is still available for use, Microsoft encourages organizations to migrate to modern architecture, which supports new web parts and responsive page designs specifically for mobile applications.

In classic SharePoint architecture, site collections were used to organize content based on business boundaries, which could cause issues such as broken internal links when sites needed to be migrated to new site collections. The modern site architecture uses Microsoft 365 group-connected site collections, each with its own membership and permissions control, as well as classic SharePoint groups:

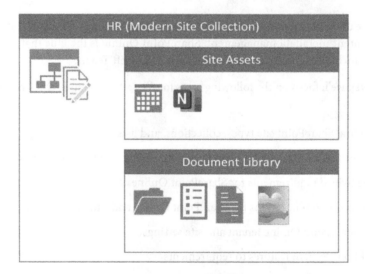

Figure 12.1 – A modern SharePoint site

Sites can be associated with a **hub** that allows easy reorganization. This allows for more dynamic organization of the sites and helps organizations more easily reflect business changes in their technology infrastructure, while maintaining links to documents and files as well as permissions and sharing settings (see *Figure 12.2*):

Figure 12.2 – Modern sites organized into a hub

Modern sites can be built with two core templates – **Communications** and **Team**:

- **Team**: The default template, the Team site template, is used for collaboration. Typical use case scenarios include projects, products, business units, or external partner and customer work. Microsoft 365 services such as Planner and Teams also use the Team site template when provisioning resources. Team sites use Microsoft 365 Groups for permissions management.

- **Communications**: A site built with the Communications template is frequently geared toward showcasing content and one-way communication. A Communications site typically has two distinct personas that interact with it – content creators or authors and readers. Communications sites might be used for product marketing material, storing HR forms, or other announcements. Communications sites use SharePoint groups to manage security.

Regardless of what SharePoint site template you use to create sites, most site artifacts are stored in logical containers called **libraries**. Libraries can contain documents, images, spreadsheets, or other files. SharePoint also has the concept of **lists**. Lists are similar to spreadsheets in how they present data. Data is stored in **rows** and **columns**, with rows being an entry item that is made up of associated columns. Columns are configured with a **type** (a form of data validation) that controls what type of data or formatting is allowed.

Next, we'll shift gears to plan SharePoint deployments.

Planning a migration strategy for SharePoint Online and OneDrive for Business

Organizations who wish to migrate content to SharePoint Online can do so through a number of different mechanisms – whether it's by simply copying and pasting content between windows or through an orchestrated migration strategy.

After an organization has decided what's in scope to migrate, it can begin strategizing the best way to complete the tasks.

A migration effort, whether it's for SharePoint or OneDrive for Business, follows a similar design pattern:

- Inventorying data sources
- Selecting the migration tools
- Planning the network requirements
- Preparing the environment
- Migrating data

We'll look at each of these areas in brief.

Inventorying data sources

The inventory process helps you determine what data is in scope to migrate. You'll need to gather data from a lot of different sources – whether it's software inventory tools you already have or interviewing business owners to find out where their data is stored. Source data repositories might include the following:

- Shares on network-attached storage systems or file servers
- Files located on cloud services such as Google or Box
- SharePoint Server document libraries and lists
- SharePoint workflows
- Intranet websites

For each of these data sources, you'll need to determine where it will fit in your Microsoft 365 strategy – whether the data needs to be migrated to SharePoint, OneDrive, or Teams. The types of data sources, as well as the mapped destinations, will inform what migration tools you use.

Selecting migration tools

You may need to use one or more content migration tools, depending on your content sources. *Table 12.1* shows the currently supported content sources and which migration tools are needed:

Data source	Migration tool
Box	SharePoint Migration Manager
Cross-tenant OneDrive for Business (excludes consumer, Government Community Cloud (FedRAMP moderate), Government Community Cloud High, and **Department of Defense (DoD)**)	PowerShell
Dropbox	SharePoint Migration Manager

Data source	Migration tool
Egnyte	SharePoint Migration Manager
File shares	SharePoint Migration Manager or the SharePoint Migration Tool
Google Workspace	SharePoint Migration Manager
MySites	The SharePoint Migration Tool
SharePoint Server sites	The SharePoint Migration Tool
SharePoint Server workflows	The SharePoint Migration Tool
Stream (Classic)	SharePoint Migration Manager

Table 12.1 – The migration tool matrix

Both the **SharePoint Migration Manager** (MM) and **SharePoint Migration Tool** (SPMT) require one or more servers (or workstations) on which to run the tools when migrating from on-premises content sources.

MM has a concept of agents – computers that are used to transfer data between on-premises servers and the target Microsoft 365 workloads.

Exam tip

For the MS-100 exam, Microsoft only focuses on the **SPMT and MM**. While there are several high-quality third-party migration tools, they are not in scope for the exam.

Both MM and the SPMT require either SharePoint Administrator or Global Administrator roles in the destination Microsoft 365 tenant.

Planning network requirements

One important aspect of successfully executing a migration means ensuring that your network is capable and your configuration allows for the appropriate communication. Network-based migrations require sustained peak loads. Network planning activities should involve the following areas:

- **Proxy devices**: Microsoft recommends bypassing proxy-type devices, services, or applications when communicating with Microsoft 365 and SharePoint Online for the duration of the migration.

- **Intrusion detection, intrusion prevention, or other security traffic monitoring systems**: Many network security apparatuses designed to detect data exfiltration will flag migration traffic. It's important to exclude the source servers and Microsoft 365 tenant destinations from these systems during the duration of the migration.

- **Stateful packet filtering firewalls**: All communications between Microsoft 365 and the on-premises environment are SSL/TLS-encrypted. Microsoft recommends excluding migration activity from inspection.

The following table details the endpoints that MM and the SPMT need to communicate with for a migration to be successful:

Endpoint	Description
`https://secure.aadcdn.microsoftonline-p.com`	Authentication services
`https://login.microsoftonline.com`	Authentication services
`https://api.office.com`	Microsoft 365 APIs
`https://graph.windows.net`	Microsoft 365 APIs
`https://spmtreleasescus.blob.core.windows.net`	SPMT media source
`https://*.queue.core.windows.net`	Azure migration API
`https://*.blob.core.windows.net`	Azure migration API
`https://*.pipe.aria.microsoft.com`	Telemetry
`https://*.sharepoint.com`	SharePoint Online service endpoint
`https://login.microsoftonline.us`	Authentication Services for the US government
`https://*.sharepoint.us`	SharePoint Online service endpoint for the U.S. government
`https://graph.microsoft.com`	Microsoft 365 APIs for Worldwide and GCC moderate
`https://graph.microsoft.us`	Microsoft 365 APIs for GCC High
`https://dod-graph.microsoft.us`	Microsoft 365 APIs for the DoD
`https://*.queue.core.usgovcloudapi.net`	Azure migration API for the U.S. Government
`https://*.blob.core.usgovcloudapi.net`	Azure migration API for the U.S. Government
`https://spoprod-a.akamaihd.net`	User interface content
`https://static2.sharepointonline.com`	User interface content

Table 12.2 – SharePoint Online endpoints

Next, we'll look at how to prepare content for migration.

Preparing the environment

Content scanning only affects migrating from on-premises file services such as network-attached storage, Windows-based file shares, or on-premises SharePoint Server content (content that will be migrated using the **SharePoint Migration Assessment Tool** (**SMAT**)). Content scanning is performed using the SMAT.

As part of the migration process, you'll need to ensure that identities with access to on-premises resources have access to cloud resources and that the content you plan to migrate meets the prerequisite checks.

Mapping identities

The SMAT has a component called the **SharePoint Migration Identity Mapping Tool** (**SMIT**). The SMIT can be run to build a mapping file that identifies users and groups that are synchronized to **Azure Active Directory** (**AD**), and it can be used to highlight on-premises users that do not have a corresponding cloud account. *Figure 12.3* depicts the output of the SMIT.

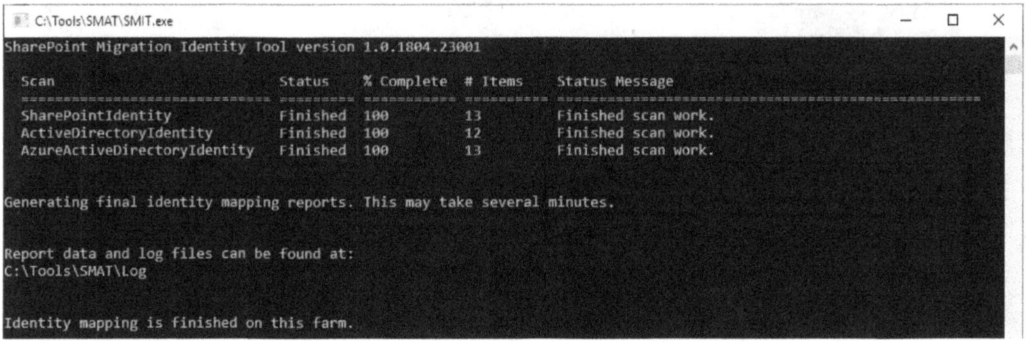

Figure 12.3 – The SMIT

The primary output of the SMIT is `FullIdentityReport.csv`, which contains one row per identity granted access to a resource. The **TypeOfMatch** column contains data that shows whether a corresponding cloud identity was found (**Match**, **PartialMatch**, or **NoMatch**).

Scanning content

Depending on the tools used to perform migrations, you may encounter scanning at different times. When using the SPMT, the content scanning process utilizes the SMAT and can be used to scan file shares and SharePoint Server farms. The SMAT should be installed on a server in a SharePoint farm.

SMAT is a console application. When executing a scan, the console will return information about the sites that have been processed, as shown in *Figure 12.4*:

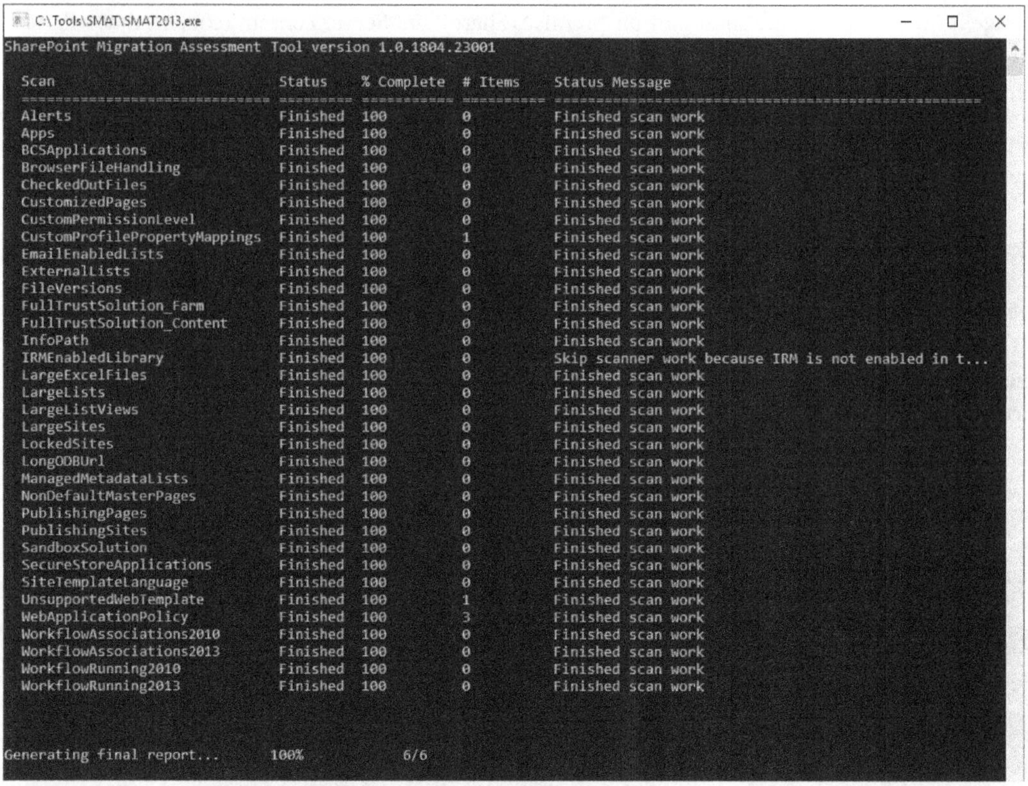

Figure 12.4 – SMAT

SMAT can be customized using the `SiteSkipList.csv` file, which allows you to list the sites you don't want to scan, and `ScanDef.json`, which allows you to configure which types of scanned tasks to enable or disable.

MM also performs scanning, although it does it as part of the migration process itself.

Further reading

You can learn more about the SMAT at `https://aka.ms/SMAT`.

Resolving issues detected during scanning

You may encounter files or other content that cannot be migrated to SharePoint Online using SMAT. These items will be listed in a variety of output files, including the following:

- `SMAT.log`: This file contains the information, error, and warning messages that SMAT generates. Error conditions are migration-blocking issues that should be resolved to migrate content successfully.

- `UnsupportedWebTemplate-Detail.csv`: If your organization uses website templates that are not supported by SharePoint Online, sites with those templates will be listed in this file. SPMT will allow you to map them to new supported templates.

- `SMAT_Errors.log`: This file contains a subset of the items listed in `SMAT.log` that contains only the error items.

A successful migration will require resolving items that appear in the SMAT_Errors.log file. Next, we'll look at managing content that can't be migrated.

Planning for content that cannot be migrated

There may be some content that SMAT has identified that cannot be migrated. For that content, you will need to determine an acceptable outcome, such as the following:

- Using a new application, feature, or service in SharePoint Online
- Updating the source application, feature, or content to something that is compatible with SharePoint Online
- Deprecating or decommissioning the application, feature, or content
- Excluding the application, feature, or content from migration and leaving it in place
- Investigating third-party migration alternatives

After you have made decisions about what will be migrated, it's time to move data.

Migrating data

Depending on the type of content you're migrating, you'll need to choose between SharePoint MM and the SPMT.

SharePoint MM

Running a migration from MM is the best way to migrate content from other cloud services as well as on-premises file shares. While the dialog boxes and credential prompts may differ slightly between environments, the general process is the same. The only difference is when running MM against on-premises file servers, as this requires the deployment of agents before adding content.

SharePoint MM is launched from within the SharePoint admin center. To start using it, navigate to the SharePoint admin center, select **Migration**, and then choose the content source, as shown in the following screenshot:

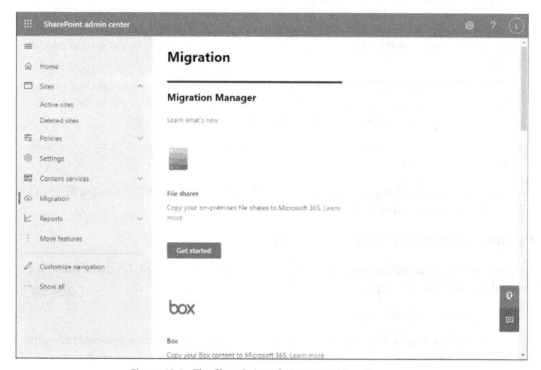

Figure 12.5 – The SharePoint admin center Migration page

Once you've identified your content source, you can follow the wizard-driven interface to configure the migration details.

In the following example, you can see how MM works by connecting to a cloud data source such as Dropbox:

1.   Navigate to the SharePoint admin center.

2.   Expand **Migration** and then select **Get started** under **Dropbox**:

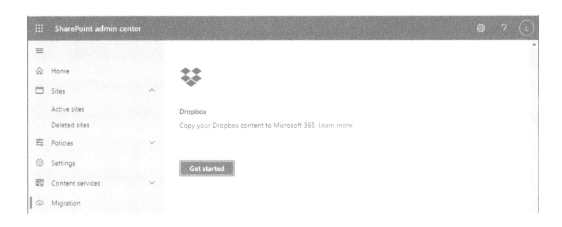

Figure 12.6 – The Migration home page

3. On the **Migrate your Dropbox content to Microsoft 365** page, select **Connect to Dropbox**:

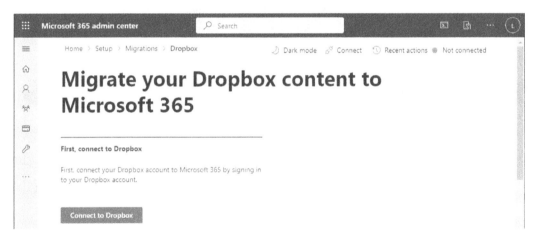

Figure 12.7 – The Migrate your Dropbox content to Microsoft 365 page

4. On the **Connect to Dropbox** flyout, select **Sign in to Dropbox**:

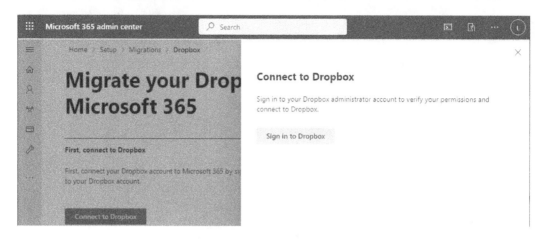

Figure 12.8 – The Connect to Dropbox flyout

5.   Provide credentials if necessary.

6.   On the Dropbox authorization page, review the list of permissions being granted and click **Allow**.

7.   Click **Finish** to close the flyout.

8.   Scroll to the bottom of the page and select **Add source path**:

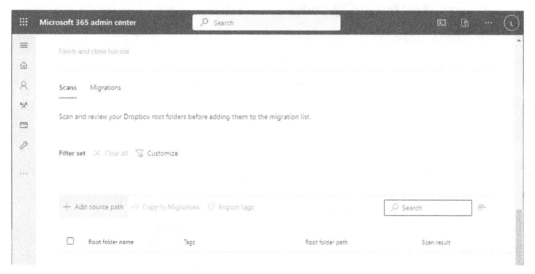

Figure 12.9 – Adding a source path to the Dropbox migration

9. Select an option to locate files. If you are migrating as an administrator with access to member and team folders, you can select **Look for new member and team folders in Dropbox**. Otherwise, you can supply a single source path or upload a CSV file containing the paths to folders to include in the migration. Click **Add**:

Figure 12.10 – Adding source paths to a migration

10. Wait while MM enumerates folders in the source and scans them. This can take some time, depending on the number of files in the content source. *Figure 12.11* shows MM running the inventory process:

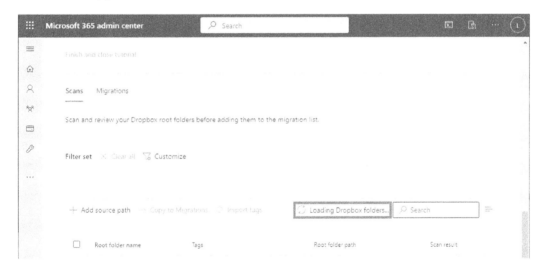

Figure 12.11 – Enumerating the content source

11. After MM has enumerated all the files and folders, select the files and folders to scan and click **Scan**. Scanning will identify potential problems to resolve before migrating data. If warnings or errors appear, you can view them on this page. After resolving errors in the content source, you can select the file or folder again and click **Scan**:

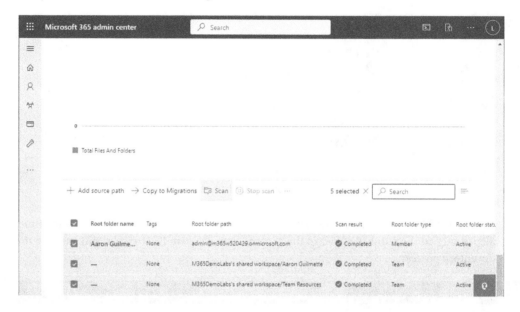

Figure 12.12 – Selecting files and folders to scan

12. Select which files or folders to migrate and then click **Copy to Migrations**:

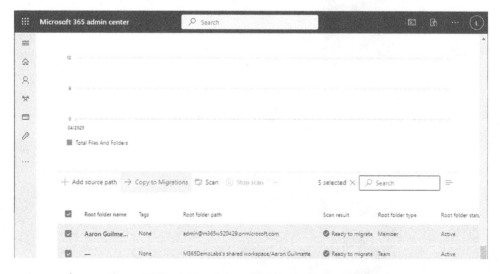

Figure 12.13 – Adding files and folders to a migration batch

13. On the flyout, click **Copy to Migrations**.

14. Scroll up in the window and select the **Migrations** tab:

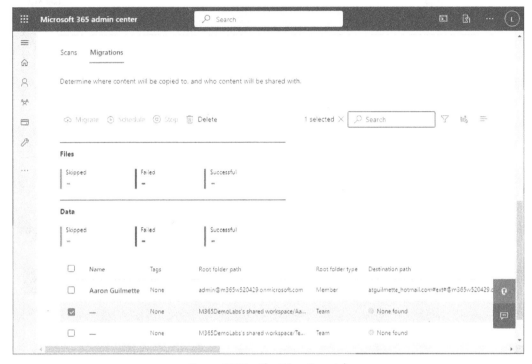

Figure 12.14 – The Migrations tab

15. For items that have no destination path set, review each one by clicking on the object. In the flyout, you can select **Edit** to set the destination:

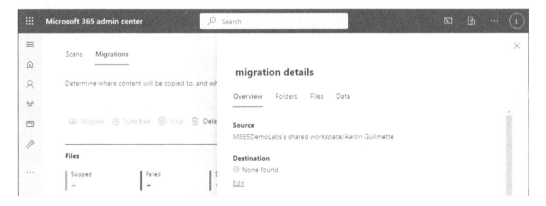

Figure 12.15 – The migration details flyout

16. Select a destination, as shown in *Figure 12.16*:

Figure 12.16 – The Select destination path flyout

17. It's important to note that you can only migrate to existing targets. The flyout does not allow you to provision new target users, sites, or teams (see *Figure 12.17*).

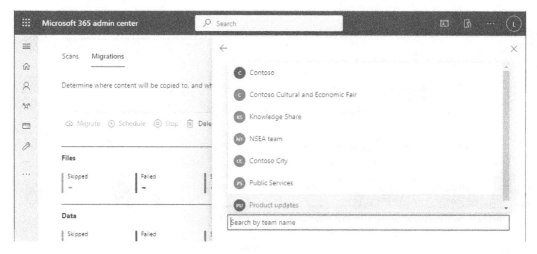

Figure 12.17 – Selecting a destination from available teams

If you select **Teams**, you can choose a destination team, and then choose an existing channel or create a new one. If you select SharePoint, you can select an existing document library on a site or create a new one. If you select a OneDrive site, you can choose an existing folder or create a new one. *Figure 12.8* depicts a SharePoint site configured as a destination path.

Figure 12.18 – Selecting a destination path on a SharePoint site

18. Click **Save path** once you have made a selection. Repeat for the remaining objects.

19. Select the folders to include in the migration. Click **Migrate** to start the migration immediately, or click **Schedule** to set a future date for migration activities to begin:

Figure 12.19 – Configuring a migration

20. Click **Migrate** on the **Migrate folder content** flyout (or **Schedule** on the **Schedule migration tasks** flyout, if you want to set a future date for the migration).

21. Review the dashboard for status updates, as shown in *Figure 12.20*:

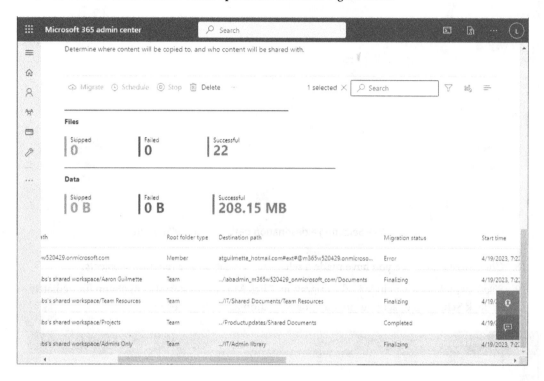

Figure 12.20 – Reviewing the status

22. You can also view an individual task's migration status by selecting its line item and then viewing the **Overview**, **Folders**, **Files**, and **Data** tabs:

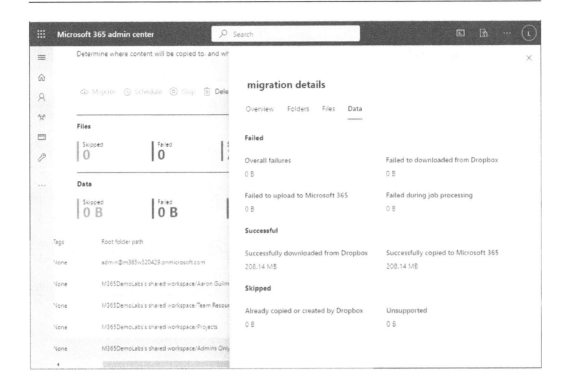

Figure 12.21 – Reviewing migration data

Once a migration has finished, it's recommended to do a spot check to ensure that things were migrated as you anticipated them. You can continue adding content data paths from the same or different content sources. If you need to log in to a different account for a content source, you can select **Disconnect** to close your authentication session.

SPMT

Like MM, you can launch the SPMT from the SharePoint admin center, as shown in the following screenshot:

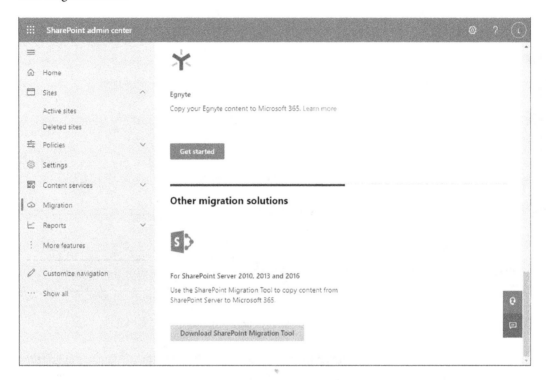

Figure 12.22 – SPMT

You'll be prompted to save the download and then can launch it.

The SPMT can be used to migrate SharePoint server sites, workflows, and libraries along with Windows file shares. The process is very similar for each—simply specifying a top-level folder or site to include as part of a migration.

To use SharePoint MM, follow these steps:

1. Navigate to the SharePoint admin center.

2. Expand **Migration** and then select **Download SharePoint Migration Tool** under **Other migration solutions**.

3. Launch the downloaded application.

4. When prompted, enter credentials for an account with SharePoint Administrator or Global Administrator credentials.

5. In the SPMT window, click **Start a new migration**.

6. On the **Copy content from** page, select the content source, as shown in the following screenshot:

Figure 12.23 – The Copy content from page

7. Once you have selected the type of content, select the appropriate options. If you select **SharePoint Server**, you'll be prompted to choose from **Site migration**, **List or document library migration**, and **Workflow migration** options, along with the URL for the site, list, library, or workflow. If you choose **File share**, you'll be prompted to enter a local or network drive path. If you choose **JSON or CSV file for bulk migration**, you'll be prompted to input the path to a JSON or CSV file:

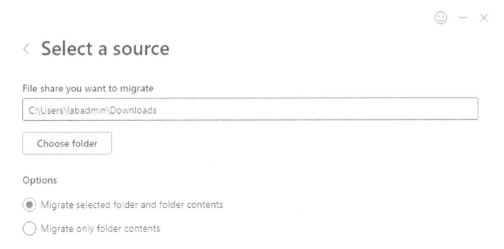

Figure 12.24 – Selecting a source for file share migration

8. Click **Next**.

9. On the **Copy content to** page, select a destination:

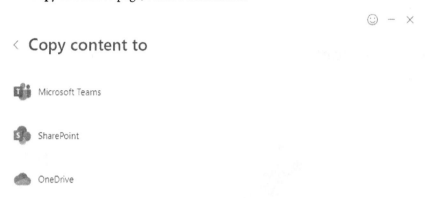

Figure 12.25 – The Copy content to page

10. On the **Select a destination** page, enter the destination. If the target site or team does not exist, the SPMT will create it for you. Click **Next**.

11. On the **Review migration** page, enter a name for the migration and review the settings. You can click **Add another migration** and choose additional sources – whether they are a file share, SharePoint Server, or workflow sources. When finished, click **Next**:

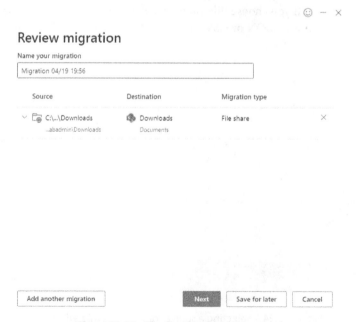

Figure 12.26 – The Review migration page

12. On the **Choose your settings** page, select which options you want the SPMT to perform. The **View all settings** button exposes additional settings, such as being able to specify a particular user mapping file, date ranges for migrating files, hidden files, options to replace invalid characters in filenames, an automatic rerun of the application, and a custom Azure storage location:

Figure 12.27 – Choosing the migration settings

13. Click **Migrate** to begin the migration process.

Post-migration, it's recommended to check the destination libraries, teams, sites, or workflows to ensure that they've been migrated successfully and update any configurations or permissions as necessary.

Next, we'll dive into SharePoint hybrid features and requirements.

Identifying hybrid requirements for SharePoint Online

A SharePoint hybrid deployment does not perform the same functions as an Exchange hybrid deployment with regard to migrating data. With SharePoint hybrid, you establish a certain level of coexistence, integration, and redirection between on-premises SharePoint Server farms and SharePoint Online.

SharePoint hybrid features

With a SharePoint hybrid deployment, you configure the extension of infrastructure into the cloud. This can be achieved through the four core components of SharePoint Online hybrid:

- **Hybrid OneDrive for Business**: Hybrid OneDrive for Business allows you to redirect data consumption and sharing from on-premises SharePoint OneDrive to OneDrive for Business in Microsoft 365. This component enables users to continue using on-premises SharePoint sites and services while also utilizing the cloud-based OneDrive for Business for personal files. Content migration from My Sites to OneDrive for Business is not a hybrid feature and must be performed with a tool such as the SPMT.

- **Hybrid search**: SharePoint hybrid offers two hybrid search topologies, each of which can index and return both on-premises and cloud content in a single search interface. **Cloud hybrid search** is the simplest to deploy and involves an on-premises crawler that stores its search index data in SharePoint Online. **Hybrid federated search** maintains two separate indices (one in SharePoint Online and one in a SharePoint Server farm) – suitable for organizations that have requirements prohibiting them from storing data remotely.

- **Hybrid taxonomy**: The hybrid taxonomy feature allows you to maintain a single SharePoint taxonomy across cloud and on-premises farms. With hybrid taxonomy, you manage the metadata and taxonomy in SharePoint Online and synchronize it down to your on-premises environments.

- **Hybrid Auditing**: A preview feature for SharePoint 2016 that has now been deprecated, Hybrid Auditing enabled administrators to have visibility of on-premises workload usage. It was removed after SharePoint Server 2016.

Combined, these components allow users to take advantage of both SharePoint Online and SharePoint Server features.

In addition to this deeper hybrid integration, SharePoint also supports other enhancements:

- Updating the Microsoft 365 app launcher to help users navigate to on-premises content

- Using SharePoint Online in conjunction with SharePoint Server to enable hybrid business-to-business extranet scenarios

Now that you have an understanding of the features that SharePoint hybrid brings to an organization, we'll look at the requirements to get started.

SharePoint hybrid requirements

All SharePoint hybrid features have the same base requirements:

- You must have a supported version of SharePoint Server (2013, 2016, or 2019), where services are running locally on a farm and not federated.

- The **SharePoint Security Token Service** must have a certificate enabled and in use. By default, the hybrid configuration tool (known as the **Hybrid Picker**) uses the built-in certificate, but you can also use a third-party trusted certificate.

- Server farms with SharePoint Server 2013 are required to have SharePoint Service Pack 1 or later installed; otherwise, site redirection features will not be available.

- The SharePoint Subscription Settings service application must be configured.

- AD must be configured to synchronize with the User Profile service application.

- The App Management service application must be deployed and configured.

- My Sites must be configured for OneDrive for Business redirection.

- The Managed Metadata service application must be deployed and configured.

- You must have identity synchronization between on-premises AD and Microsoft Azure AD.

A SharePoint Server farm can run any number of servers, with service applications deployed on any of the servers in the farm. Single-server farms are supported.

Next, we'll look at some of the access controls for SharePoint Online and Microsoft Teams.

Managing access configuration for SharePoint Online and Microsoft Teams

Since Microsoft Teams uses SharePoint Online and Azure guest identities, it stands to reason that the controls affecting those items have a direct impact on Microsoft Teams.

Learning your way around

The user interfaces for SharePoint and Teams make it easy to traverse both environments and find the appropriate content in either interface.

For example, when browsing a SharePoint site, you can see that it's connected to a Microsoft Teams team by the presence of the Teams icon next to the site name:

Figure 12.28 – A Teams-enabled SharePoint site

Conversely, you can access the corresponding SharePoint site for a Teams channel by selecting the **Open in SharePoint** option, as shown in *Figure 12.29*:

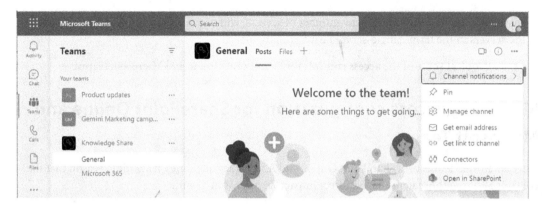

Figure 12.29 – Accessing SharePoint from Teams

In either scenario, it's easy to move between the tools.

Managing Teams and SharePoint settings

Since Teams and SharePoint have shared components, it's important to understand where things are managed. Teams-specific features are managed either in the **Teams admin center** (**TAC**) or the Teams app itself, while SharePoint-specific features are managed either in the SharePoint admin center or the settings of a particular site.

The following table shows common features and where to administer them:

Setting or feature	Team site	Channel site
Site permissions	Teams-enabled SharePoint site permissions should be managed through the connected Microsoft 365 Group and its membership settings.	Channel site permissions are inherited from the channel and can't be managed inside the SharePoint interface.
Site sharing settings	Team and SharePoint site owners can manage the sharing settings for files, folders, and the site, either through the site's sharing settings or from the SharePoint admin center.	Site sharing settings are inherited.

Setting or feature	Team site	Channel site
Guest access expiration	Guest access expiration for content is set in the SharePoint admin center.	Guest expiration settings are inherited from the tenant's default settings.
Sensitivity labels	Sensitivity labels can be applied in Teams or the SharePoint parent site.	The sensitivity of channel sites is inherited from the parent site.
Site quota	Quotas are managed in the SharePoint admin center.	Quotas are managed in the SharePoint admin center.
Default link sharing type	The default link sharing type is managed in the SharePoint admin center.	The default link sharing type is managed in the SharePoint admin center.
Hub association	Hub site topologies are maintained in SharePoint.	Channel sites (including private and shared) follow the parent's hub association.

Table 12.3 – SharePoint and Teams settings locations

Next, we'll specifically explore broad settings that apply to Teams and SharePoint.

Planning and implementing organizational settings

There are several areas where Microsoft Teams and SharePoint Online overlap from a configuration perspective. It's important to understand the impact that SharePoint Online settings can have on Teams usage and vice versa.

Managing SharePoint Online tenant and site settings

SharePoint Online tenant settings are configured in the SharePoint admin center. There are three main areas where settings are configured, as highlighted in *Figure 12.30*:

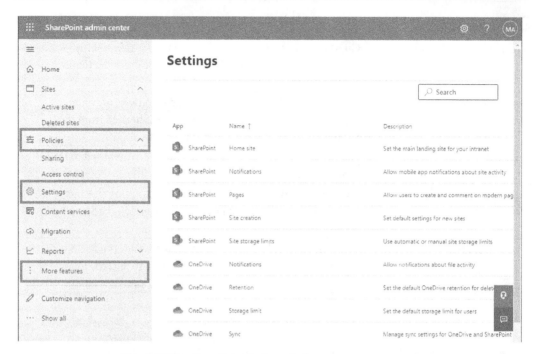

Figure 12.30 – SharePoint Online admin center settings areas

The three core settings areas are the following:

- **Policies**
- **Settings**
- **More features**

Let's quickly look at the settings located under each.

Policies

The policies area is used to manage tenant-wide controls, with regard to broad sharing controls and security or other access controls.

Sharing

The **Sharing** controls page has a myriad of settings, and it can be used to set both the permissiveness of SharePoint sharing controls (whether you can invite new guests to share content) as well as finer-grained controls (such as who can do the inviting).

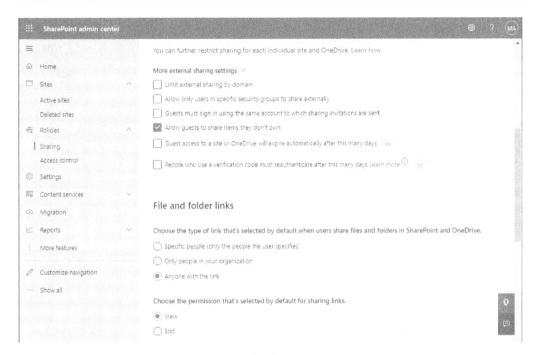

Figure 12.31 – Sharing policy controls

The sharing controls available are the following:

- **External sharing sliders**: This area features separate sliders for SharePoint and OneDrive, specifying what sharing recipients are allowed. You can choose from (ranging from most permissive to most restrictive) **Anyone**, **New and existing guests**, **Existing guests**, and **Only people in your organization**. As previously noted, the SharePoint and OneDrive sliders can be moved independently, but the OneDrive slider cannot be more permissive than the SharePoint slider.

- **Limit external sharing by domain**: This setting allows you to control what domains sharing requests can be sent to, as either a list of allowed domains or a list of blocked domains.

- **Allow only users in specific security groups to share externally**: This setting allows you to create one or more security groups that contain individuals that can share externally. Users outside of those groups will be unable to initiate sharing requests to external users, even if the SharePoint slider is set to **Anyone**.

- **Guests must sign in using the same account to which sharing invitations are sent**: This setting prevents external recipients from forwarding sharing invitations to another address. When signing in, the guest will be prompted to enter the email address that was originally allowed and then receive a code via email to complete authentication.

- **Allow guests to share items they don't own**: Guests can initiate sharing invitations for items they are not the owners of.

- **Guest access to a site or OneDrive will expire automatically after this many days**: This setting allows you to choose an expiry date for links to shared sites, preventing stale access grants.

- **People who use a verification code must reauthenticate after this many days**: This setting forces guests to reauthenticate periodically.

In addition to the sharing restrictions, there are controls that manage the life cycle and capabilities for file and folder links:

- **Choose the type of link that's selected by default when users share files and folders in SharePoint and OneDrive**: This selection has three options, including **Specific people**, **Only people in your organization**, and **Anyone with the link**. This doesn't prevent the user from changing the audience scope. This setting works in conjunction with the SharePoint or OneDrive permissiveness control – for example, if the SharePoint and OneDrive permissiveness sliders are set to **New and existing guests**, the **Anyone** with a link option is unavailable.

- **Choose the permission that's selected by default for sharing links**: This option allows you to specify the default selection to share links. The default can be either **View** or **Edit**. The person sharing can choose either permission – this just controls the default setting.

- **Choose expiration and permissions options for Anyone links**: You can select **These links must expire within this many days** to specify how long **Anyone** (previously referred to as **Anonymous**) links can live. You can also specify the permissions that can be granted for **Anyone** links. For **Files**, you can choose **View and Edit** or **View**, and for **Folders**, you can select **View, edit, and upload** or **View**.

Finally, there are some miscellaneous settings that round out the sharing controls:

- **Show owners the names of people who viewed their files in OneDrive**: This option allows you to see the names of people who have accessed and viewed a file by looking at the file card (the popup displayed when hovering over a file in OneDrive)

- **Let site owners choose to display the names of people who viewed files or pages in SharePoint**: Related to the previous setting, this also allows SharePoint site owners to make this information available on SharePoint sites

- **Use short links for sharing files and folders**: Configure SharePoint to use an abbreviated short link instead of the full path to a file in a sharing email request

Next, we'll look at the network and device access control settings.

Access control

The **Access control** page is used to restrict device and network access using the following settings:

- **Unmanaged devices**: The available settings are **Allow full access from desktop apps, mobile apps, and the web**, **Allow limited, web-only access**, and **Block access**. These are organization-wide settings.

- **Idle session sign-out**: This selection only affects users on unmanaged devices who don't select **Keep me signed in**. You can choose to sign users out automatically after a given period of time.

- **Network location**: You can configure ranges of IP addresses allowed to access SharePoint content. This affects all users (internal and guests) and all connected applications. Applications that support network boundaries are Teams, Yammer, and Exchange. If these boundaries are enabled, non-location-aware apps (such as Power Automate, Power Apps, OneNote, etc.) will be blocked from accessing SharePoint content, even if they operate and access from within a defined network boundary.

- **Apps that don't use modern authentication**: You can allow or block applications that don't support modern authentication.

- **Restrict OneDrive access**: You can limit who can access OneDrive for Business content based on security group membership. You can specify up to 10 security groups. Users not in these groups will lose access to their OneDrive content (though the content itself will continue to exist).

These are broad, tenant-wide controls. Microsoft recommends using Conditional Access policies and Microsoft Defender for Cloud Apps in their place.

Settings

The **Settings** page manages additional tenant-wide settings for SharePoint and OneDrive:

- **Home site** (SharePoint): This is used to set the main landing page for your site.

- **Notifications** (SharePoint): This is used to enable or disable notifications sent to the SharePoint mobile app.

- **Pages** (SharePoint): This enables or disables features to allow users to create new modern pages and allow commenting on modern pages.

- **Site creation** (SharePoint): This setting has four main options:

  - **Users can create SharePoint sites** is used to control whether users can create sites from SharePoint, OneDrive, or scripting/REST interfaces. This has no impact on whether users can create Teams or Microsoft 365 Group-connected sites.

  - **Show the options to create a site in SharePoint and create a shared library from OneDrive** is used to show or hide the site and library options in the SharePoint and OneDrive for Business web interfaces.

- The **Create team sites under** setting is used to select the managed path where SharePoint team sites will be provisioned.

- You can use **Default time zone** to specify the default time zone for SharePoint sites.

- **Site storage limits** (SharePoint): This setting is used to manage quotas for your sites. You can choose **Automatic** to allow sites to grow as necessary, or **Manual**, which allows you to specify the maximum storage that a particular site can consume from your tenant's total storage allocation (up to 25 TB per site collection).

- **Notifications** (OneDrive): This allows you to choose whether to allow notifications to be sent to users about file sharing or `@mention` activity.

- **Retention** (OneDrive): This setting controls how long a OneDrive for Business site stays active after a user has been de-provisioned and the license removed. While the setting name is **Retention**, it is not a compliance feature used to protect data – it only determines whether the site stays provisioned.

- **Storage limit** (OneDrive): This allows you to manage the default storage limit for OneDrive accounts.

- **Sync** (OneDrive): This allows you to manage service-side synchronization settings for the OneDrive for Business client. Options include the following:

  - The **Show the Sync button on the OneDrive website** option allows you to display or hide the **Sync** button.

  - The **Allow syncing only on computers joined to specific domains** option allows you to list domain GUIDs, representing domains that machines wishing to use the OneDrive client must reside in.

  - With the **Block upload of specific file types** option, you can limit the file extensions that a OneDrive for Business sync client will process. Users can still upload the files manually through the browser, however, as the block feature only affects the OneDrive synchronization engine.

Next, we'll explore the configuration options available under **More features**.

More features

The **More features** page allows you to configure additional groups of settings. Many of these features or settings are service applications for SharePoint Server. The available options include the following:

- **Term store**: The **term store** is a service application that allows you to define a metadata taxonomy to classify content in SharePoint.

- **User profile**: The **User Profile** service application controls the OneDrive for Business site provisioning process. You can do things such as set default secondary administrators or even control which users have access to provision sites.

- **Search**: This manages how the Search service application works across the tenant, including things such as **Search schema**, **Search dictionaries**, **Result sources** (which are useful for hybrid search capabilities), and **Query rules**.

- **Apps**: These manage integration with the SharePoint store.

- **BCS**: This manages the configuration of **Business Connectivity Services** (**BCS**) to data sources outside of SharePoint Online.

- **Secure store**: The Secure store service application is used to manage authentication for BCS.

- **Records management**: This is the interface to manage the legacy SharePoint records management site. Microsoft recommends using in-place records management instead of this feature.

- **InfoPath**: This manages the integration of InfoPath forms with SharePoint Online. Microsoft recommends shifting to Forms and Power Apps in place of InfoPath.

- **Hybrid Picker**: This launches the hybrid configuration tool.

Finally, there is a section of settings that don't fit anywhere else – mostly related to legacy SharePoint features that haven't been fully integrated or deprecated. These additional settings are referred to as **Classic settings**.

> **Further reading**
>
> For more information on the classic settings, see `https://learn.microsoft.com/en-us/sharepoint/get-started-new-admin-center`.

Microsoft Teams tenant settings

There are several Teams management settings available in the TAC that affect tenant-wide features. For reference, the TAC is located at `https://admin.teams.microsoft.com`.

Teams settings are used to configure notifications, various collaboration integrations, some device management features, some communications security features, and connectivity to third-party file services tenant-wide.

The **Teams settings** page is shown in *Figure 12.32*:

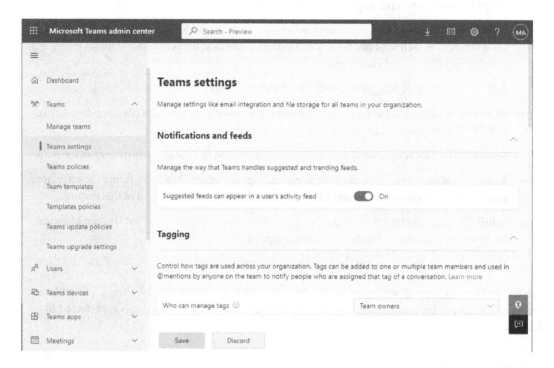

Figure 12.32 – Teams settings

The Teams settings menu has eight management sections:

- **Notifications and feeds**: This area features a single toggle – **Suggested feeds can appear in a user's activity feed**. This setting controls whether Teams will highlight or display feeds from users who have content that may be of interest to the logged-in user.

- **Tagging**: This area features five settings that are used to control the use of tags when used in `@mentions` or teams:

  - **Who can manage tags**: By default, this is set to **Team owners**. Other available options include **Team owners and members** and **Not enabled**.

- **Team owners can change who can manage tags**: This toggle controls whether team owners can change who manages tags within a team.

- **Suggested tags**: Using this setting, you can add additional text tags that can be suggested for all teams. You can have up to 25 tags, each with 25 characters.

- **Custom tags**: This toggle controls whether users can add their own tags or only use the suggested tags.

- **Shifts app can apply tags**: For organizations that use the Shifts app, this setting controls whether Shifts can set tags.

- **Email integration**: Email integration manages how Teams interacts with email:

  - **Users can send emails to a channel email address**: Each channel has its own individual address. Enabling this option allows users to send messages to the channel's email address, which will appear in the **Posts** tab. Mail-enabled channels are not available in GCC or DoD tenants.

  - **Accept channel email from these SMTP domains**: If you allow users to send mail to channels, you can also manage which domains can send to channels.

- **Files**: The files area allows you to toggle whether users can connect their Teams client to five popular cloud service file integrations – **Citrix files**, **DropBox**, **Box**, **Google Drive**, and **Egnyte**.

- **Organization**: The single toggle in this area, **Show Organization tab for users**, allows you to see the organization chart setting on a user's card.

- **Devices**: While most devices are managed under **Teams devices**, there are three settings here that control Surface Hub features:

  - **Require a secondary form of authentication to access meeting content**: This setting only applies to Skype for Business users who join a meeting with a Surface Hub. The available options are **No access**, **Partial access**, and **Full access**.

  - **Set content PIN**: This setting also only applies to Skype for Business users that join a meeting with a Surface Hub. The available options are **Required for outside scheduled meeting**, **Not required**, and **Always required**.

  - **Surface Hub accounts can send emails**: This enables Surface Hub devices to send emails.

- **Search by name**: This setting area has one control – **Scope directory search using an Exchange address book policy**. You can manage how and whether users are located in a search by using Exchange **Address Book Policies (ABPs)**.

- **Safety and communications**: This setting area also only has one toggle – **Role-based chat permissions**. This option determines who can initiate chats and is typically only used in educational settings.

Planning, implementing, and managing guest and external access

Both Microsoft Teams and SharePoint Online have settings that govern external access and guest accounts. Managing a Microsoft 365 tenant requires ensuring that both sets of controls are configured optimally to support your organization's needs.

SharePoint guest access

Internal site access in SharePoint is easily managed through group membership, while external access is managed using additional sharing controls. The decision of whether to allow external access is important in the context of managing security.

External access can be controlled at the organization (tenant) or site level, and by default, it is enabled organization-wide. Blocking sharing at the site collection level will prevent anyone, including site owners, from sharing content with users outside the Microsoft 365 tenant, while blocking sharing at the tenant level will prevent users administering any site collection from being shared.

When a user sends an invitation to access data, and when the recipient is external to the organization, SharePoint creates an **Azure Business-to-Business** (**B2B**) guest account in the home organization's Azure AD. The external recipient will receive a sharing invitation email containing a link to complete their Azure account signup or provisioning. If you remember from *Chapter 5*, this process of accepting the invitation is also known as **invitation redemption**.

At the tenant level, settings can be configured with four levels of permissiveness that impact both SharePoint and OneDrive, as shown in *Table 12.4*:

Permission	Description
Anyone: Users can share files and folders using links that don't require sign-in.	Also known as Anonymous links, this setting allows users to create a link that anyone can open without authentication.
New and existing guests: Guests must sign in or provide a verification code.	With this option, external recipients receive an invitation email that they will use to complete the redemption process. Sharing recipients can be new users who have never received a sharing invitation or those who already have a guest identity.
Existing guests: Only users already in your organization's directory.	Users can only send to recipients that already have a guest identity in the home organization's Azure AD. No new external guests can be added through the sharing interface.
Only people in your organization: No external sharing is allowed.	This is the most restrictive option, prohibiting all external sharing.

Table 12.4 – Sharing permissions

The permissions are displayed as two sliders in the SharePoint admin center, as shown in *Figure 12.33*:

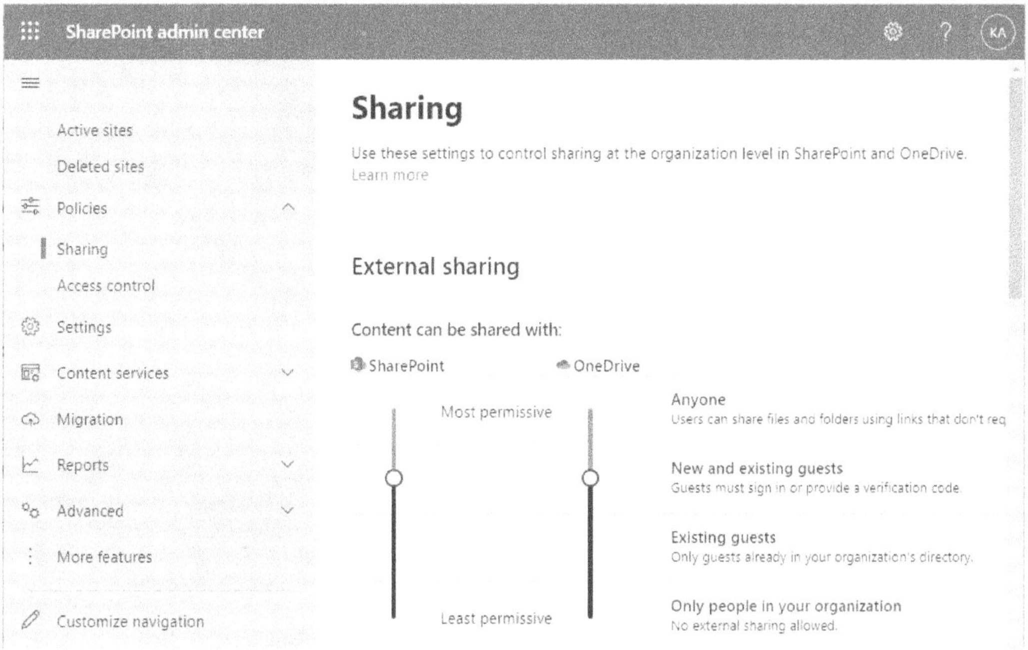

Figure 12.33 – The SharePoint admin center sharing controls

It's important to note that while the SharePoint and OneDrive for Business sliders can be managed independently, the OneDrive slider *cannot* be more permissive than the SharePoint slider.

Teams guest access

Teams also has guest and external access settings. Let's look at each of those settings areas.

Guest access

Guest access controls how people outside your organization interact with teams and channels. Using the settings on the **Guest access** page, you can control the features guests can use:

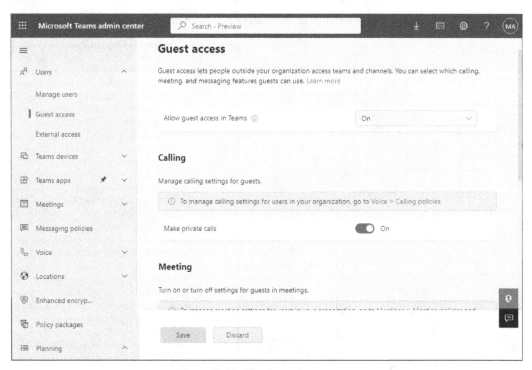

Figure 12.34 – The Guest access page

The **Guest access** page can be accessed through the TAC under **Users | Guest access**. In addition to a general **Allow guest access in Teams** toggle, there are three feature areas that can be used to manage how guests use various parts of Teams:

- **Calling**: Under the **Calling** area, there is a single toggle, **Make private calls**, that controls whether guests have the ability to make PC-to-PC calls.

- **Meeting**: The Meeting area features three settings to manage how guests can use meetings:

  - **IP video**: This toggle controls whether guests can turn on their cameras in meetings.

  - **Screen sharing mode**: This toggle controls what level of sharing guests can use. The options are **Entire screen**, **single application**, or **Not enabled**.

  - **Meet Now**: The **Meet Now** toggle determines whether guests can start ad hoc meetings.

- **Messaging**: The options in this area control how guests can participate in 1xN chats as well as channel conversations:

  - **Edit sent messages**: Controls whether guests are able to edit messages after sending them.

  - **Delete sent messages**: Controls whether guests can delete messages after sending them.

- **Delete chat**: Controls whether guests can delete 1:x conversations.

- **Chat**: Determines whether guests can participate in a chat.

- **Giphy in conversations**: Controls whether guests can have access to Giphy in conversations.

- **Giphy content rating**: If this is enabled, this dropdown lets you select the content rating to allow or disallow GIFs. The available values are **Allow all content**, **Strict**, and **Moderate**.

- **Memes in conversations**: This setting controls the use of memes in conversations.

- **Stickers in conversations**: This setting manages the use of stickers in conversations.

- **Immersive reader for messages**: This setting enables guests to toggle the immersive reader.

External access

The **External access** page focuses on how your organization's users are able to interact with external users:

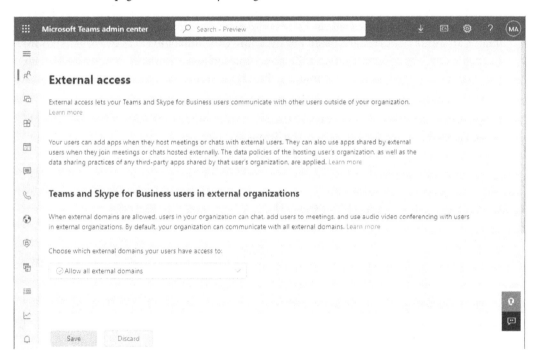

Figure 12.35 – The External access page

There are three configuration areas on the **External access** page:

- **Teams and Skype for Business users in external organizations**: This controls which domains your organization can communicate with and has four settings: **Allow all external domains**, **Allow only specific external domains**, **Block only specific external domains**, and **Block all external domains**. You can only select one of the options from the drop-down list. If you choose either **Allow only specific external domains** or **Block only specific external domains**, you can specify a list of domains that your organization either can or cannot communicate with via chat or join meetings. This setting controls both inbound and outbound chat messages and meetings. As a caveat, users from blocked domains can join meetings if they join anonymously (this is also dependent on whether the host organization allows anonymous participant access in the Teams meeting policy).

- **Teams accounts not managed by an organization**: This setting controls whether you allow your organization's users to communicate with Teams consumer products or Teams Free (unmanaged) through **People in my organization can communicate with Teams users whose accounts aren't managed by an organization**. There is also a sub-option available, **External users with Teams accounts not managed by an organization can contact users in my organization**, to enable one-way communication initiation – internal users can start conversations with external, unmanaged users, but unmanaged users cannot initiate conversations with your organization's users.

- **Skype users**: The **Allow users in my organization to communicate with Skype users** toggle is used to enable or disable access between Teams and Skype users.

Next, we'll examine the Phone System features available in Teams.

Mapping Phone System features to requirements

Microsoft Teams Phone System provides a broad array of features that can be used to meet the requirements of most organizations. You can use the following table to map Teams Phone System features and capabilities to both business and licensing requirements:

Phone System feature	Business requirement	Licensing requirement
Calls to the Public Switched Telephone Network (PSTN)	Make and receive normal phone calls to the PSTN.	A Teams Phone System license and then either Calling Plans, Operator Connect, or Direct Routing enabled
Auto attendants	Provide an **Interactive Voice Response (IVR)** system, allowing callers to navigate to the appropriate recipient.	Teams Phone System, a Teams Resource Account license, and a service number

Phone System feature	Business requirement	Licensing requirement
Call queues	Provide an internal waiting area for callers while operators or call recipients are busy.	Teams Phone System, a Teams Resource Account license, and an optional service number
Voicemail	Provide voicemail to users.	Teams Phone System
Music on hold	Provide hold music, either custom or administrator-provided.	Teams Phone System
Common area phones	Allow for standalone phones not assigned to users.	Teams Phone System, a Teams Resource account, and a Teams Shared Devices license
Caller ID and call blocking	Provide a mechanism to block inbound unwanted numbers and set various caller ID display options.	Teams Phone System
Busy on busy	Provide options for how to handle inbound calls when the recipient is busy.	Teams Phone System
Shared line appearance	Allow users to make calls on behalf of another.	Teams Phone System and then either Calling Plans, Operator Connect, or Direct Routing enabled
Make and receive video calls	Make and receive PC-to-PC video calls.	A Microsoft Teams license
Call park, hold, transfer, and pickup	Provide a mechanism to allow users to place calls on hold or park, and then pick them up at the same device or another.	Microsoft Teams and Microsoft Teams Phone System
Integrate with on-premises phone systems	Provide a mechanism to integrate with existing on-premises phone systems.	Microsoft Teams Phone System, session border controllers, and either carrier-provided calling features or Operator Connect
Cloud-only phone system	Use a phone system without any on-premises integration or requirements.	Microsoft Teams Phone System and Calling Plans
Provider-managed integration	Use an existing phone system.	Microsoft Teams Phone System and Operator Connect

Table 12.4 – Microsoft Teams Phone System requirements mapping

Each organization will have unique business requirements that drive the use of specific features.

Further reading

For a full breakdown of Microsoft Teams licensing options, see `https://learn.microsoft.com/en-us/microsoftteams/teams-add-on-licensing/microsoft-teams-add-on-licensing`.

Summary

In this chapter, you learned about managing the security, sharing, and external access features of SharePoint Online, OneDrive for Business, and Microsoft Teams. In addition, you also learned about Microsoft 365's native migration tools (SharePoint MM and SPMT) for moving content to SharePoint Online, OneDrive for Business, and Teams, depending on the content source.

Finally, you learned about the core Microsoft Teams Phone System features and how they map to business requirements and licensing.

Knowledge check

In this section, we'll test your knowledge of some key elements from this chapter.

Questions

1. What feature, service, or application is responsible for integrating SharePoint server with SharePoint Online?

    A. SharePoint Hybrid Picker

    B. SharePoint MM

    C. The SPMT

    D. SharePoint external access controls

2. You are planning to migrate from Dropbox to SharePoint Online. What feature, tool, service, or app should you plan to use?

    A. The SPMT

    B. The SMAT

    C. SharePoint MM

    D. SharePoint Hybrid Picker

3. When configuring SharePoint tenant-wide sharing controls, which statement is accurate?

    A. The SharePoint sharing settings can be more permissive than the OneDrive for Business sharing settings.

    B. The SharePoint sharing settings can be less permissive than the OneDrive for Business sharing settings.

    C. The SharePoint sharing settings must be the same as the OneDrive for Business sharing settings.

    D. There are no tenant-wide sharing controls.

4. BCS is an acronym for what?

    A. Built-In Container Services

    B. Business Communications Services

    C. Business Connectivity Services

    D. Bitwise Communication Syntax

5. When planning a Teams Phone System, which feature is used to describe a holding area for inbound callers waiting to talk to an agent?

    A. Auto attendant

    B. Call queue

    C. Call waiting

    D. Call parking

Answers

1. A. SharePoint Hybrid Picker

2. C. SharePoint MM

3. A: The SharePoint sharing settings can be more permissive than the OneDrive for Business sharing settings.

4. C: Business Connectivity Services

5. A: Auto attendant

Part 5: Preparation

In this final part, you'll be presented with two full-length practice exams. Each exam features 60 multiple-choice questions based on the material presented in this book. Along with an answer key at the end of each exam, you'll also find explanations and links to the supporting Microsoft documentation.

This part has the following chapters:

- *Chapter 13, Practice Exam 1*
- *Chapter 14, Practice Exam 2*

13
Practice Exam 1

The MS-100 exam will have 40-60 questions. The exam is timed at 120 minutes.

Questions

1. You are preparing to integrate a SharePoint Server farm with Microsoft 365 and SharePoint Online. You want to configure Search in such a way that there is a single index stored in Microsoft 365 that can return results for both on-premises and Microsoft 365 content. Which option should you choose?

   A. Cloud hybrid search

   B. Hybrid federated search

   C. Remote results source

   D. Local results source

2. You manage Exchange Online for your organization. One of your organization's business partners uses a legacy email system that is unable to correctly process rich text or HTML-formatted messages. Which option will allow you to manage the formatting for messages sent to the business partner's organization?

   A. An accepted domain

   B. An authoritative domain

   C. A relay domain

   D. A remote domain

3. You are preparing to deploy a Microsoft Teams Phone System solution. You want a totally cloud-based solution with no on-premises integration. Which option is the easiest to deploy?

    A. Calling plans

    B. Operator Connect

    C. Media bypass

    D. Direct routing

4. You need to create administrative units for your organization. Where should you perform this task?

    A. The Microsoft 365 admin center

    B. The Privileged Identity Management blade

    C. Azure AD Connect

    D. On-premises Active Directory

5. You are the Microsoft 365 administrator for a new organization that has no existing on-premises infrastructure. You need to select a cloud identity solution that will be easy to manage and require no additional investment in servers or networking equipment. Which solution should you choose?

    A. Azure AD Connect cloud sync

    B. Azure AD Connect

    C. Cloud identity

    D. **Active Directory Federation Services (AD FS)**

6. You need to provision a guest user identity for a Google Workspace user so that they can access an application hosted in your Microsoft 365 tenant. Where should you provision the identity?

    A. The Google Workspace Admin console

    B. On-premises Active Directory Users and Computers

    C. Azure AD

    D. Exchange Server on-premises

7. You are configuring message security for your Exchange Online organization. You want to direct external recipients to reject emails that fail to pass DKIM and SPF checks. What should you configure?

    A. SenderID

    B. Domain-based Message Authentication, Reporting, and Conformance

    C.   Exchange Online Protection

    D.   Exchange transport rules

8. You need to configure just-in-time access to allow users to request elevation for administrative purposes. What feature should you configure?

    A.   Privileged identity management

    B.   Role-based access control

    C.   Resource-based access control

    D.   Administrative units

9. The service desk manager for your organization is looking for ideas to enable users to reset their own passwords without placing a call to the service desk. What Microsoft 365 feature could be a potential solution?

    A.   Self-service Password Manager

    B.   Self-service Password Update Manager

    C.   Self-service Password Reset

    D.   Self-service Password Reset Manager

10. If your organization does not have its own domain, it cannot use Microsoft 365.

    A.   True

    B.   False

11. The IT director for Contoso has instructed you to ensure that a small group of IT staff receive Office 365 updates before the rest of the users. What option should you configure?

    A.   Set the **Release preference** to **Standard release for everyone**

    B.   Set the **Release preference** to **Targeted release for everyone**

    C.   Set the **Release preference** to **Targeted release for select users**

    D.   Set the **Release preference** to **Insider**.

12. After adding a domain to Microsoft 365, you want to ensure it is automatically selected when creating new cloud-based users or groups. What should you do?

    A.   Set the domain to be the default domain

    B.   Set the domain to be the initial domain

    C.   Set the domain to be the managed domain

    D.   None of the above

13. Privileged Identity Management alerts can be used to detect what potential risks?

    A. Users are logging in from unmanaged devices

    B. Users are logging in from mobile devices

    C. Roles are being activated too frequently

    D. Users have not reset their password in more than 180 days

14. The **Chief Security Officer** (**CSO**) for your organization has recently shifted her view on non-expiring passwords and would like to implement them in Microsoft 365. Where can you update the password policy?

    A. The Microsoft 365 admin center | **Org settings** | **Security & privacy**

    B. The Microsoft 365 admin center | **Org settings** | **Services**

    C. The Microsoft Azure portal | **Azure Active Directory** | **Properties**

    D. The Microsoft Azure portal | **Azure Active Directory** | **Security**

15. The most common licensing model for Microsoft 365 Apps is which of the following?

    A. Per-user

    B. Per-device

    C. Per-tenant

    D. Per-organization

16. Microsoft 365 Apps use what deployment technology?

    A. Click-to-Activate

    B. Click-to-Deploy

    C. Click-to-Run

    D. Click-to-Install

17. Which tool is used to identify and review potential issues with macros and add-ins as they relate to a Microsoft 365 Apps deployment?

    A. Microsoft 365 Telemetry Dashboard

    B. Microsoft 365 Apps Deployment Assistant

    C. Configuration Policy Dashboard

    D. The Readiness Toolkit

18. Click-to-Run is integrated with which Microsoft 365 Apps service?

    A. Cloud Policy service for Microsoft 365 Apps

    B. Microsoft 365 Apps admin center

    C. Microsoft Endpoint Manager

    D. Office Customization Tool

19. In order to maintain full access to the Microsoft 365 apps, apps must be able to verify a user's license every _____ days.

    A. 90

    B. 60

    C. 45

    D. 30

20. You have configured Azure AD Connect for your environment. You want to collect additional performance and monitoring data for your AD FS farm. What should you do?

    A. Deploy the Azure AD Connect Health for AD FS agent

    B. Deploy the Azure AD Connect Health for DS agent

    C. Deploy the Azure AD Connect Health for Sync agent

    D. Enable Health Reporting in the Azure AD portal.

21. The Adoption Score covers which two insight areas?

    A. Engagement experiences

    B. People experiences

    C. Technology experiences

    D. Remote work experiences

22. The IT director for your organization has been asked to provide high-level details about the overall status of your Microsoft 365 tenant. Where can you direct them to this information?

    A. Log Analytics

    B. The Health dashboard

    C. Provisioning logs

    D. The Office 365 Reporting API

23. The CSO for your organization wants to review the Azure AD Provisioning logs. What data are they looking for?

    A. Azure AD Connect user provisioning details

    B. Enterprise application provisioning activities

    C. Microsoft Defender for Identity integration activities

    D. Microsoft 365 Groups that were provisioned via Graph

24. Your organization's human resources department is investigating ways to improve work-life balance and employee well-being. They are interested in learning about research-based behavioral insights. What tool, feature, or service should you recommend?

    A. Microsoft Viva Personal insights

    B. Microsoft Viva Organization trends

    C. Microsoft Viva Advanced insights

    D. Microsoft 365 Adoption Score People experiences

    E. Microsoft 365 Adoption Score Technology experiences

25. When installing Azure AD Connect, the account used should have which of the following group memberships or role assignments?

    A. Hybrid Identity Administrator

    B. User Administrator

    C. Security Reader

    D. Exchange Hybrid Administrator

26. The CSO for your organization is interested in reviewing how third-party integrated applications access user account data. Where should you direct them?

    A. Enterprise application audit logs

    B. Access reviews

    C. Azure AD provisioning logs

    D. Azure AD sign-in logs

27. You need to configure domain-based filtering for Azure AD Connect. Where should you perform this?

    A. The Azure AD portal

    B. The Microsoft 365 admin center

C. The Synchronization Rules Editor

D. The Azure AD Connect configuration wizard

28. Your organization has recently subscribed to a well-known third-party SaaS application. You need to configure Microsoft 365 to communicate with the application and make it available for users in your organization. What should you do?

A. Configure Azure App Proxy

B. Add the enterprise application from the Azure app gallery

C. Configure Microsoft 365 Defender to allow the application

D. Create an application in Microsoft Endpoint Manager

29. You have been asked to create a Conditional Access policy that manages access to data and limited experiences inside SharePoint Online. Which feature can you use?

A. **Session controls | Use app enforced restrictions**

B. **Session controls | Persistent browser session**

C. **Session controls | Continuous access evaluation**

D. **Session controls | Require token protection for sign-in sessions**

30. Your organization has developed a simple web-based application that uses **Integrated Windows Authentication** (**IWA**) to grant access. The application is not accessible via the internet. The application owner has asked you to you assist them in making it available to users through the Microsoft 365 My Apps page. What should you do?

A. Configure an application registration

B. Instruct the application owner to deploy a third-party tunneling app

C. Deploy Azure App Proxy

D. Ask the network team to create a custom VPN profile

31. You have recently configured a new enterprise application and assigned it to a group. However, after assigning it to `AppGroup1`, some users who were previously able to access the application can no longer access it, although they can still access other enterprise applications. From the list provided, what are the two most likely causes?

A. The user is not part of `AppGroup1`

B. The user is a member of `Group2`, which was made a member of `AppGroup1`

C. The user has an unsupported browser

D. Kerberos-constrained delegation has not been configured

32. As part of an end user experience support program, your organization is implementing **Self-Service Password Reset (SSPR)** for cloud-only accounts. What should you configure?

    A. Azure AD Connect Password writeback

    B. The Active Directory Delegation of Control wizard

    C. Azure Active Directory | **Password reset**

    D. Azure Active Directory | **Password policy**

33. You have been asked to review application permissions. Where can view this data?

    A. Azure AD Enterprise Applications

    B. The Microsoft 365 Purview compliance portal

    C. Microsoft Graph

    D. The Microsoft 365 Reporting API

34. You have been asked to configure Azure AD Application Proxy. What software needs to be installed?

    A. Azure AD Connect

    B. Azure AD App Proxy Connector

    C. Azure AD Hybrid Proxy Connector

    D. Azure AD Remote App Connector

35. Which two of the following can be configured as part of a Conditional Access policy?

    A. Locations

    B. Device risk

    C. Sign-in risk

    D. Limits

36. Configuring password hash synchronization requires which of the following two rights in Active Directory?

    A. Replicating Directory Changes

    B. Replicating Directory Passwords

    C. Replicating Directory Scopes

    D. Replicating Directory Changes All

37. In simple terms, what is a transformation or a transform?

    A. A synchronization rule component used to modify or map attributes

    B. A manual process run to convert an object

    C. A process to convert one object type into another

    D. When objects are migrated between connector spaces

38. What feature, function, attribute, or component is used to uniquely identify an object throughout its lifetime in regards to Active Directory and Azure AD?

    A. `anchor`

    B. `sourceAnchor`

    C. `msGuid`

    D. `ExchangeGuid`

39. You are planning to deploy directory synchronization for your distributed organization. You do not have connectivity to all Active Directory forests from one location. You do not need to deploy advanced custom synchronization rules. Which product would be the best choice?

    A. Azure AD Connect

    B. Azure AD Connect cloud sync

    C. DirSync

    D. Microsoft Identity Manager

40. You are configuring least-privilege access for your Microsoft 365 tenant. You have decided to use security groups as part of the strategy. Which property must you ensure is configured during the security group creation to allow roles to be assigned to it?

    A. `IsAssignableToRole:$True`

    B. `IsAssignableToRole:$False`

    C. `IsEligibleForRole:$True`

    D. `IsEligibleForRole:$False`

41. What type of account or service principal does the Azure AD Connect cloud sync provisioning agent setup configure?

    A. **Managed Service Account (MSA)**

    B. **Group Managed Service Account (gMSA)**

    C. **Kerberos Service Principal Name (KSPN)**

    D. **Global Managed Service Account (gMSA)**

42. Which object types are supported for Azure AD Connect Cloud sync password hash synchronization?

    A. User

    B. InetOrgPerson

    C. Contact

    D. Group

43. You have configured Azure AD Connect sync. After the sync cycle completes, you notice that some objects do not appear in the Azure portal. What tool can you use to troubleshoot?

    A. The Azure AD Connect troubleshooting tool

    B. Azure AD Connect Health Sync

    C. Azure AD Connect Health for DS

    D. Azure AD Connect Health for AD FS

44. You need to quickly add 500 cloud users to your tenant. Which two methods would be most effective?

    A. Adding bulk users through the Microsoft 365 admin center

    B. Adding bulk users through the Azure AD portal

    C. Adding bulk users to on-premises AD

    D. Adding bulk users through Microsoft Azure AD PowerShell

45. After creating a group in Azure AD, you are notified that it needs to have Azure role memberships added to it. You did not originally configure the group to be eligible for Azure role assignment. What should you do?

    A. Edit the group and slide the **Azure AD Role** toggle to **On**

    B. Use `Set-AzureADMSGroup`

    C. Delete and recreate the group

    D. Create a new group with the Azure role and nest this group inside it

46. Your organization has built a new application that is hosted in your Microsoft 365 tenant. You want to be able to grant users in one of your organization's partner tenants permission to automatically request access to the new application, as well as a supporting SharePoint site. What two things should you configure?

    A. Connected organization

    B. Access review

    C.   Access package

    D.   Identity package

47. You need to identify guest users who have not yet completed the redemption process. What should you look for in the Azure AD portal?

    A.   The invitation state set to `PendingAcceptance`

    B.   `UserPrincipalName` containing `#EXT#`

    C.   An unread invitation email

    D.   `LastLogonDate` set to `2147483647`

48. Your organization is adding new support staff to the service desk. What principle should you plan to implement so that new support staff can manage only user accounts and not modify settings service-wide?

    A.   The Exchange Administrator role

    B.   Least-privilege access

    C.   Access reviews

    D.   Access controls

49. You are selecting a password-less authentication mechanism for your organization. Your organization does not have the budget for new hardware devices for all users. All of the organization's users already have either Android or iOS phones. What password-less solution meets the business requirement of not needing additional hardware investment?

    A.   Windows Hello for Business

    B.   FIDO2 security keys

    C.   YubiKey

    D.   The Microsoft Authenticator app

50. As part of your operational security, you want to configure Azure AD account lockout settings to match your on-premises settings. What feature should you configure?

    A.   Banned passwords

    B.   Smart lockout

    C.   Azure AD Password protection for Active Directory

    D.   Self-Service Password Reset

51. You need to instruct another administrator on how to enable FIDO2 security keys as an authentication method for your Microsoft 365 tenant. Where should you direct them?

    A. Microsoft 365 admin center | Org settings

    B. The Azure AD portal | Security | Authentication methods

    C. The Azure AD portal | Password reset | Authentication methods

    D. Group Policy

52. You are administering your organization's Exchange Online system. You have been asked to configure attachment blocking for messages originating outside of the organization. What should you configure?

    A. An Exchange transport rule

    B. Microsoft Defender for Cloud Apps

    C. Microsoft Information Protection

    D. A **Data Loss Prevention (DLP)** policy

53. A user is reporting an inability to log in to Microsoft 365 services. Where should you begin your investigation?

    A. Azure AD sign-in logs

    B. Azure AD Sentinel

    C. Conditional Access audit reports

    D. Microsoft 365 audit logs

54. In an Exchange hybrid deployment, the on-premises server configured as a hybrid endpoint must be able to communicate outbound on port 80 for what purpose?

    A. Azure AD App Proxy

    B. SMTP

    C. The Certificate Trust List

    D. Exchange Web Services

55. The _____ life cycle represents an identity as it moves throughout an organization.

    A. Identity

    B. Privileged identity

    C. Access

    D. Security

56. You are planning to configure an access package. As part of this access package, you wish to initiate a custom workflow to provision an identity in a line-of-business application and add an entry to a database, recording the activities taken. What should you configure?

    A. Workflow Manager

    B. A Power Automate flow

    C. A custom extension

    D. Entitlement

57. The _____ DNS record helps email clients such as Outlook locate a user's mailbox.

    A. MX

    B. SRV

    C. SPF

    D. Autodiscover

58. You are configuring an Exchange hybrid deployment. You need to choose a method that doesn't require inbound HTTPS access to your servers. Which should you choose?

    A. Minimal Hybrid

    B. Full Hybrid

    C. Classic Hybrid

    D. Modern Hybrid

59. You are planning to migrate file shares, SharePoint workflows, and SharePoint Server sites to Microsoft 365. You need to choose a tool that will be able to successfully migrate all content sources. Which should you choose?

    A. SharePoint Migration Manager

    B. The SharePoint Migration Tool

    C. Azure Resource Manager

    D. AzCopy

60. As part of a security review, the **Chief Information Security Officer (CISO)** has requested that you restrict access to SharePoint Online sites to your organization's IP address ranges. What is the best way to configure this?

    A. SharePoint admin center | **Network locations**

    B. Conditional Access policies

    C. A VPN

    D. Azure AD App Proxy

Answers

1. A. Cloud hybrid search.

    Cloud hybrid search is the only option that uses a single index to provide results for both on-premises and cloud content: `https://learn.microsoft.com/en-us/sharepoint/hybrid/hybrid-search-in-sharepoint`.

2. D: A remote domain.

    Remote domains allow you to manage message content and some features for external domains. For example, with remote domains, you can force plain-text message delivery or prevent out-of-office replies from being sent: `https://learn.microsoft.com/en-us/exchange/mail-flow-best-practices/remote-domains/remote-domains`.

3. A: Calling plans.

    Calling plans are a cloud-native Teams Phone System feature and requires no on-premises infrastructure to be deployed: `https://learn.microsoft.com/en-us/microsoftteams/calling-plans-for-office-365`.

4. A: The Microsoft 365 admin center.

    Of the options listed, you can create administrative units in the Microsoft 365 admin center: `https://learn.microsoft.com/en-us/microsoft-365/admin/add-users/admin-roles-page?view=o365-worldwide`.

5. C: Cloud identity.

    Cloud identity is the only solution that does not require additional server or network infrastructure: `https://learn.microsoft.com/en-us/azure/cloud-adoption-framework/decision-guides/identity/`.

6. C: Azure AD.

    Provisioning a guest user account is performed through the Azure AD portal by using the **New user | Invite external user** workflow: `https://learn.microsoft.com/en-us/azure/active-directory/external-identities/b2b-quickstart-add-guest-users-portal`.

7. B: Domain-Based Message Authentication, Reporting, and Conformance.

    Domain-Based Message Authentication, Reporting, and Conformance (DMARC) instructs messaging systems on how to process mail that purports to originate from your organization, including how to handle messages that fail SPF and DKIM checks: `https://learn.microsoft.com/en-us/microsoft-365/security/office-365-security/email-authentication-dmarc-configure`.

8. A: Privileged identity management.

    Privileged identity management is used to allow users to request elevated rights to perform administrative duties: `https://learn.microsoft.com/en-us/azure/active-directory/privileged-identity-management/pim-configure`.

9. C: Self-Service Password Reset.

    Self-service Password Reset can be configured to allow users to reset their own passwords using personal security information: `https://learn.microsoft.com/en-us/microsoft-365/admin/add-users/let-users-reset-passwords`.

10. B: False.

    Any organization can use Microsoft 365. By default, every tenant is provisioned with a managed domain (`tenant.onmicrosoft.com`). Organizations can use their own previously purchased domains with Microsoft 365 or purchase new domains through the Microsoft 365 admin center: `https://learn.microsoft.com/en-us/microsoft-365/admin/setup/add-domain`.

11. C: Set the release preference to **Targeted release for select users**.

    From the Microsoft 365 admin center, you can set the release preference to **Targeted release for select users** and choose users who should receive Microsoft 365 updates before everyone else: `https://learn.microsoft.com/en-us/microsoft-365/admin/manage/release-options-in-office-365`.

12. A: Set the domain as the default domain.

    By setting the domain as the default domain, it will be automatically selected when creating new cloud-based users or groups. As an administrator, you can still change the domain during the creation process (or afterward).

13. C: Roles are being activated too frequently.

    Of the listed options, the only one that triggers an alert is how often roles are being activated. Repeatedly reactivating a role may be a sign that an account has been compromised: `https://learn.microsoft.com/en-us/azure/active-directory/privileged-identity-management/pim-how-to-configure-security-alerts`.

14. A: The Microsoft 365 admin center | **Org settings** | **Security & privacy**.

The password expiration policy settings are managed through the Microsoft 365 admin center. Expand **Settings**, select **Org settings**, and then select **Password expiration policy** on the **Security & privacy** tab: `https://learn.microsoft.com/en-US/microsoft-365/admin/misc/password-policy-recommendations`.

15. A: Per-user.

Microsoft 365 Apps are licensed per user in most scenarios. There are some commercial and education scenarios where per-device licensing may be obtained: `https://learn.microsoft.com/en-us/deployoffice/overview-licensing-activation-microsoft-365-apps`.

16. C: Click-to-Run.

Microsoft 365 Apps uses a new deployment and servicing technology called Click-to-Run. It is different from the previous MSI (Windows Installer) deployment method: `https://learn.microsoft.com/en-us/deployoffice/about-microsoft-365-apps#whats-different-about-microsoft-365-apps`.

17. D: The Readiness Toolkit.

The Readiness Toolkit is a data-gathering and analysis tool that allows you to review Office documents, macros, and add-ins deployed on a machine to evaluate compatibility: `https://learn.microsoft.com/en-us/deployoffice/readiness-toolkit-application-compatibility-microsoft-365-apps`.

18. A. The Cloud Policy service for Microsoft 365 Apps.

Click-to-Run is responsible for communicating with the Cloud Policy service for Microsoft 365 Apps to update the policies applied to end user devices: `https://learn.microsoft.com/en-us/deployoffice/admincenter/overview-cloud-policy`.

19. D: 30.

Microsoft 365 Apps require access to the internet to validate a user's license every 30 days. Without verification, the applications will fall back to a reduced functionality mode, which only allows viewing and printing: `https://learn.microsoft.com/en-us/deployoffice/overview-licensing-activation-microsoft-365-apps#activating-microsoft-365-apps`.

20. A: Deploy the Azure AD Connect Health for the AD FS agent.

The Azure AD Connect Health for AD FS agent allows you to gather health, performance, and operational information for your AD FS farm: `https://learn.microsoft.com/en-us/azure/active-directory/hybrid/how-to-connect-health-adfs`.

21. B: People experiences, and C: Technology experiences.

    The Microsoft 365 Adoption Score is used to deliver data insights regarding people experiences in the areas of collaboration, mobility, teamwork, and meetings. The Adoption Score can also be used to provide insights about technology experiences as it pertains to device health and network communications: https://learn.microsoft.com/en-us/microsoft-365/admin/adoption/adoption-score.

22. B: The Health dashboard.

    The Health dashboard is used to keep an eye on the status of apps and services inside your Microsoft 365 tenant, including service issues, app updates, and usage information: https://learn.microsoft.com/en-us/microsoft-365/admin/manage/health-dashboard-overview.

23. B: Enterprise application provisioning activities.

    Azure AD provisioning logs capture data about integrated provisioning activities that happen through third-party applications: https://learn.microsoft.com/en-us/azure/active-directory/reports-monitoring/concept-provisioning-logs.

24. C: Microsoft Viva Advanced insights.

    Advanced insights is a research-based tool that provides insights into your organization's work patterns, including hybrid work, work-life balance, and employee well-being. Personal insights is an end user tool that individuals can use to review their own work habits: https://learn.microsoft.com/en-us/viva/insights/advanced/introduction-to-advanced-insights.

25. A: Hybrid Identity Administrator.

    Of the roles and groups listed, only the Hybrid Identity Administrator role has the necessary permissions to configure Azure AD Connect: https://learn.microsoft.com/en-us/azure/active-directory/hybrid/how-to-connect-install-custom.

26. A: Enterprise application audit logs.

    Azure AD audit logs provide a comprehensive view of the activities performed in Azure AD. You can view the audit logs as they pertain to enterprise applications by selecting **Enterprise applications** and then choosing **Audit Logs**. You can also filter an enterprise application's activity: https://learn.microsoft.com/en-us/azure/active-directory/reports-monitoring/concept-audit-logs.

27. D: The Azure AD Connect configuration wizard.

    You should perform domain- and organizational unit-based filtering through the Azure AD Connect configuration wizard: https://learn.microsoft.com/en-us/azure/active-directory/hybrid/how-to-connect-install-custom#domain-and-ou-filtering.

28. B: Add the enterprise application from the Azure app gallery.

   The Azure app gallery contains preconfigured templates for thousands of SaaS-based applications. You can add the app from the gallery to enable your organization's users to access the application: `https://learn.microsoft.com/en-us/azure/active-directory/manage-apps/overview-application-gallery`.

29. A: **Session controls | Use app-enforced restrictions**.

   You can use app-enforced restrictions to manage access and limited experiences within certain cloud applications, such as SharePoint Online: `https://learn.microsoft.com/en-us/azure/active-directory/conditional-access/concept-conditional-access-session`.

30. C: Deploy Azure App Proxy.

   Azure App Proxy can be used to publish web-based applications that use IWA to access Microsoft 365: `https://learn.microsoft.com/en-us/azure/active-directory/app-proxy/application-proxy`.

31. A: The user is not part of `AppGroup1`, and B: The user is a member of `Group2`, which was made a member of `AppGroup1`.

   The most likely scenarios are that the users who are unable to access the application are either not members of the group or are members of a nested group that was given access. Nested groups are not supported by enterprise application assignments: `https://learn.microsoft.com/en-us/azure/active-directory/manage-apps/assign-user-or-group-access-portal`.

32. C: Azure Active Directory | **Password reset**.

   SSPR is configured in the Azure portal under Azure Active Directory | **Password reset**. The The Azure AD Connect password writeback feature is used to manage updating on-premises passwords after a successful Self-Service Password Reset operation in Azure AD: `https://learn.microsoft.com/en-us/azure/active-directory/authentication/tutorial-enable-sspr`.

33. A: Azure AD Enterprise Applications.

   You can review permissions and consent information through Azure AD Enterprise applications: `https://learn.microsoft.com/en-us/azure/active-directory/manage-apps/manage-application-permissions`.

34. B: Azure AD App Proxy Connector.

   In order to configure App Proxy, you must deploy at least one Azure AD Application Proxy connector: `https://learn.microsoft.com/en-us/azure/active-directory/app-proxy/application-proxy-connectors`.

35. A: Locations, and C: Sign-in risk.

    Locations and sign-in risk are both selections that can be configured as part of a Conditional Access policy: `https://learn.microsoft.com/en-us/azure/active-directory/conditional-access/concept-conditional-access-policies`.

36. A: Replicating Directory Changes, and D: Replicating Directory Changes All.

    Password hash synchronization requires the local Azure AD Connect service account to have Replicating Directory Changes and Replicating Directory Changes All rights. These rights are necessary to read the password data from a domain controller: `https://learn.microsoft.com/en-us/azure/active-directory/hybrid/how-to-connect-configure-ad-ds-connector-account`.

37. A: A synchronization rule component used to modify or map attributes.

    A transform or transformation is part of an Azure AD Connect synchronization rule responsible for modifying or mapping attribute values between objects in connected systems. A transform rule can pass an attribute through unmodified or perform calculations to modify the values of an attribute: `https://learn.microsoft.com/en-us/azure/active-directory/hybrid/how-to-connect-fix-default-rules`.

38. B: sourceAnchor.

    sourceAnchor is the attribute used to identify an object as it moves through AD, Azure AD Connect connector spaces, and Azure AD: `https://learn.microsoft.com/en-us/azure/active-directory/hybrid/plan-connect-design-concepts`.

39. B: Azure AD Connect Cloud sync.

    Azure AD Connect supports topologies that are disconnected or do not have network connectivity between organizations: `https://learn.microsoft.com/en-us/azure/active-directory/cloud-sync/what-is-cloud-sync`.

40. A: IsAssignableToRole:$True.

    In order to be eligible for role assignments, a security group must be created with the `IsAssignableToRole` property set to $True. It cannot be changed afterward: `https://learn.microsoft.com/en-us/azure/active-directory/roles/groups-create-eligible`.

41. B: **Group Managed Service Account (gMSA)**.

    Azure AD Connect Cloud sync setup configures a gMSA. A KSPN is not a real account type, and neither is a gMSA: `https://learn.microsoft.com/en-us/azure/active-directory/cloud-sync/how-to-prerequisites`.

42. A: User.

Only `User` objects are supported for password hash synchronization with Azure AD Connect Cloud sync. `InetOrgPerson` objects are specifically identified as out of scope: `https://learn.microsoft.com/en-us/azure/active-directory/cloud-sync/how-to-prerequisites?tabs=public-cloud`.

43. A: The Azure AD Connect troubleshooting tool.

The Azure AD Connect troubleshooting tool can be used to troubleshoot object synchronization errors: `https://learn.microsoft.com/en-us/azure/active-directory/hybrid/tshoot-connect-objectsync`.

44. B: Adding bulk users through the Azure AD portal, and D: Adding bulk users through Microsoft Azure AD PowerShell.

From a "most effective" standpoint, only adding users through the Azure AD portal or Microsoft Azure AD PowerShell is the correct solution. You can add bulk users through the Microsoft 365 admin center, but you are limited to 249 users per batch. To add 500 users, you would have to go through the bulk user process three times. Adding users through on-premises AD would result in on-premises users that would be synchronized to Azure AD, making them not cloud-only users: `https://learn.microsoft.com/en-us/microsoft-365/enterprise/add-several-users-at-the-same-time`.

45. C: Delete and recreate the group.

The option to make an Azure AD group eligible for Azure AD role assignments must be selected when the group is provisioned. It cannot be changed afterward: `https://learn.microsoft.com/en-us/azure/active-directory/roles/groups-create-eligible`.

46. A: Connected organization, and C: Access package.

Connected organizations are organizations (including Microsoft 365 and Azure AD) with which you maintain a close relationship. Access packages can be used to grant permissions to SharePoint sites and applications: `https://learn.microsoft.com/en-us/azure/active-directory/governance/entitlement-management-organization`.

47. A. The invitation state set to **PendingAcceptance**.

The only way to identify users that have not completed the redemption process from the list of options is to check the invitation state. If it is set to **PendingAcceptance**, the user has not yet accepted and redeemed their invitation. The user principal name attribute for all external guests contains #EXT#, regardless of whether they have accepted the invitation or not: `https://learn.microsoft.com/en-us/azure/active-directory/external-identities/user-properties`.

48. B: Least-privilege access.

    Least-privilege access ensures that individuals use the fewest rights necessary to perform a function. For example, while the Global Administrator role grants the ability to create users, the User Administrator role is a better choice for a least-privilege model, since it has few administrative capabilities: `https://learn.microsoft.com/en-us/azure/active-directory/privileged-identity-management/pim-configure`.

49. D: The Microsoft Authenticator app.

    Given that users already have supported mobile devices, the Microsoft Authenticator app is the lowest-cost option to adopt passwordless authentication: `https://learn.microsoft.com/en-us/azure/active-directory/authentication/howto-authentication-passwordless-deployment`.

50. B: Smart lockout.

    Smart lockout can be configured with a lockout duration and lockout threshold to match your on-premises password policy. Azure AD Password Protection for AD allows the Azure AD custom-banned password list to be checked during on-premises password reset operations: `https://learn.microsoft.com/en-us/azure/active-directory/authentication/howto-password-smart-lockout`.

51. B: The Azure AD portal | **Security** | **Authentication methods**.

    FIDO2 security keys are enabled via the authentication policy under the **Security** | **Authentication methods** area: `https://learn.microsoft.com/en-us/azure/active-directory/authentication/howto-authentication-passwordless-security-key`.

52. A: An Exchange transport rule.

    You can configure attachment blocking in several ways. Of the options listed, the only correct choice is an Exchange transport rule: `https://learn.microsoft.com/en-us/exchange/security-and-compliance/mail-flow-rules/common-attachment-blocking-scenarios`.

53. A: Azure AD sign-in logs.

    Azure AD sign-in logs can be used to help resolve authentication issues: `https://learn.microsoft.com/en-us/azure/active-directory/reports-monitoring/concept-sign-ins`.

54. C: The **Certificate Trust List**.

    In order to validate that communications certificates are still valid, servers must be able to periodically check the Certificate Trust List for any certificate revocations: `https://learn.microsoft.com/en-us/exchange/hybrid-deployment-prerequisites`.

55. A: Identity.

The identity life cycle manages and automates the digital life cycle process: `https://learn.microsoft.com/en-us/azure/active-directory/governance/what-is-identity-lifecycle-management`.

56. C: A custom extension.

Azure Logic Apps can be used as part of a custom extension to automate processes outside of an entitlement management workflow: `https://learn.microsoft.com/en-us/azure/active-directory/governance/entitlement-management-logic-apps-integration`.

57. D: Autodiscover

Autodiscover DNS records are used by email clients to find a user's mailbox server and configure the email client's settings: `https://aka.ms/autodiscover`.

58. D: Modern Hybrid.

The Modern Hybrid topology is based on the Azure AD Application Proxy product and does not require inbound HTTPS access: `https://learn.microsoft.com/en-us/exchange/hybrid-deployment/hybrid-agent`.

59. B: The SharePoint Migration Tool.

Of the options listed, the SharePoint Migration Tool is the only one that can migrate file shares, workflows, and SharePoint sites to Microsoft 365 sites and Power Automate: `https://learn.microsoft.com/en-us/sharepointmigration/spmt-workflow-overview` and `https://learn.microsoft.com/en-us/sharepointmigration/introducing-the-sharepoint-migration-tool`.

60. B: Conditional Access policies.

While you can use the network locations configuration in the SharePoint admin center, not all services or apps that store content in SharePoint Online are network location-aware. The best choice is to use Conditional Access policies: `https://learn.microsoft.com/en-us/sharepoint/control-access-based-on-network-location`.

14

Practice Exam 2

The MS-100 exam will have 40-60 questions. The exam is timed at 120 minutes.

Questions

1. You are preparing to integrate a SharePoint Server farm with Microsoft 365 and SharePoint Online. You have data in your on-premises farm that you do not want to be indexed in Microsoft 365, but you still want to be able to provide users with a single search interface. Which option should you choose?

   A. A cloud hybrid search

   B. A hybrid federated search

   C. A remote results source

   D. A local results source

2. You manage Exchange Online for your organization. As part of the hybrid configuration process, you need to ensure what port is open for SMTP traffic between your Exchange hybrid transport servers and Exchange Online?

   A. 25

   B. 53

   C. 389

   D. 445

3. You are configuring a Teams Phone System. While planning, several business units indicated that they wanted to be able to use **interactive voice response (IVR)** features to be able to help callers navigate to the right call agent. Which feature should you plan to configure?

   A. Calling Plans

   B. An auto attendant

    C.   A call queue

    D.   Call parking

4.   You need to configure dynamic administrative units. Where should you perform this task?

    A.   The Microsoft 365 admin center

    B.   The Azure AD portal

    C.   Active Directory Users and Computers

    D.   Azure AD Connect

5.   You are providing consulting services to a large organization that is going to adopt Microsoft 365. They have an existing on-premises identity solution and want to continue to use it. They have a security requirement that all authentications are processed on-premises. What hybrid identity solution meets this requirement?

    A.   Azure AD Connect with password hash synchronization

    B.   Cloud identity

    C.   Azure AD Connect with Active Directory Federation Services

    D.   Azure Active Directory Domain Services

6.   When planning for connectivity to Microsoft 365 Apps, which Microsoft resource should you consult?

    A.   Microsoft 365 Worldwide endpoints (`https://aka.ms/o365endpoints`)

    B.   Microsoft 365 Network Telemetry Dashboard

    C.   Microsoft 365 Network latency tool

    D.   A Microsoft 365 Content Delivery Network

7.   You are managing the messaging configuration for your organization. Currently, you have multiple email systems on-premises, including an Exchange organization configured in a hybrid deployment and a non-Exchange system. You have added the domain managed by the on-premises messaging system to Exchange Online as an accepted domain. Recipients in the non-Exchange system are not represented by objects in the Exchange Online global address list.

You need to ensure that messages sent to recipients that are not in Exchange Online can reach their destination. What should you do?

    A.   Configure the domain for the non-Exchange system as an Internal Relay domain

    B.   Configure the domain for the non-Exchange system as an External Relay domain

    C.   Configure the domain for the non-Exchange system as an Authoritative domain

    D.   Configure the domain for the non-Exchange system as a Remote domain

8. You need to configure Privileged Identity Management so that users' access requests expire after a period of time. What type of duration should you configure?

   A. Permanent

   B. Eligible

   C. Active

   D. Time-bound

9. The _____ is an application that collects data about Office documents and add-ins.

   A. Office Data Engine

   B. Microsoft 365 Apps Telemetry Dashboard

   C. Office Telemetry Dashboard

   D. Microsoft 365 Apps Deployment Toolkit

10. You are deploying Microsoft 365 for a new organization. You want to ensure that users can log in to Microsoft 365 services using the same password as they use on-premises. The business decision has been made to ensure that in the event of an on-premises failure, users need to continue to be able to log on to Microsoft 365 services. Which authentication solution should you choose?

    A. Azure AD Connect with password hash synchronization

    B. Azure AD Connect with Active Directory Federation Services

    C. Azure AD Connect Health

    D. Azure AD Connect with pass-through authentication

11. You have deployed the Azure AD Connect cloud sync provisioning agent on a server. After waiting an hour, you check the Azure portal and discover that no users have been synchronized. What should you do?

    A. Rerun the provisioning agent installation

    B. Reset the password for the provisioning agent **group Managed Service Account (gMSA)**

    C. Create and enable a new cloud sync configuration in the Azure portal

    D. Reset the attribute mappings to default in the Azure portal

12. Identify three deployment methods for Microsoft 365 Apps:

    A. Self-install from cloud

    B. Deploy from local source with a **content delivery network (CDN)**

    C. Deploy from local source using Configuration Manager

    D. Deploy from local source using Microsoft Intune

    E. Deploy from cloud using Microsoft Intune (Endpoint Manager)

13. The Microsoft 365 Apps admin center has prebuilt configurations under which area?

    A. My configurations

    B. Standard configurations

    C. Modern configurations

    D. My apps

    E. Standard apps

    F. Modern apps

14. The _____ is responsible for enforcing policy settings on user devices.

    A. The Microsoft 365 Apps admin center

    B. Cloud Policy service for Microsoft 365

    C. Configuration Manager Management Agent

    D. Microsoft 365 Endpoint Manager

15. You have been instructed to publish both a new application for a group of business users and an internal company website to the Microsoft 365 App launcher. Which three things should you do?

    A. Configure an enterprise application

    B. Configure a custom App launcher tile

    C. Configure Active Directory Federation Services

    D. Configure password hash synchronization

    E. Enable delegated permissions

    F. Assign the enterprise application to the group of business users

    G. Create an access package

16. Your manager has indicated that the organization wants to delay delivering the Viva Briefing email until the service desk has been trained to answer Viva questions. How would you disable the Viva Briefing email until the organization is prepared?

    A. From **Briefing email from Microsoft Viva** in the Microsoft 365 admin center

    B. From the Viva Connections admin center

    C. Instruct managers to disable the briefing email for all of their employees

    D. Create a transport rule to block the Viva briefing email from being delivered

17. The **Chief Security Officer (CSO)** for your organization wants to prevent users from being able to allow external apps to interact with Microsoft 365 data. What option would you need to configure?

    A. **User owned apps and services**

    B. **User consent to apps**

    C. **Search & intelligence usage analytics**

    D. **Microsoft Graph Data Connect**

18. _____ is a feature that allows Microsoft to manage your organization's DNS settings for you at your domain's registrar.

    A. Domain Update

    B. Domain Reflect

    C. Domain Access

    D. Domain Connect

19. You need to verify your custom domain ownership before using it with Microsoft 365.

    A. True

    B. False

20. A member of your team has set up a new enterprise application and is troubleshooting why the application isn't able to create users in your Microsoft 365 tenant. Where should you suggest they look first?

    A. Enterprise application provisioning logs

    B. Microsoft Sentinel

    C. Microsoft Graph reporting

    D. Azure AD provisioning logs

21. Your manager wants to view suggestions to create no-meeting days. Where should they look?

    A. Microsoft Viva Insights Teamwork habits

    B. Microsoft Viva Connections

    C. Microsoft Bookings

    D. Microsoft Outlook Free/Busy scheduler

22. The **Chief Information Officer (CIO)** has asked for a high-level incident response plan for a Microsoft 365 outage lasting less than one business day. What activity should you include as part of the plan?

    A. Migrating applications back on-premises

    B. Identifying a workaround or backup solution if the outage lasts longer than anticipated

    C. Preparing purchase orders for on-premises server equipment

    D. Building a fallout shelter

23. You need to understand how device health may be affecting individuals using Microsoft 365 services. What is one potential place to look?

    A. Adoption Score engagement experiences

    B. Adoption Score technology experiences

    C. The Readiness Toolkit

    D. Adoption Manager technology experiences

24. The CSO wants to easily review authentication activity, including whether users were prompted for **multi-factor authentication (MFA)**. Where could you direct them?

    A. Microsoft 365 Graph Reporting

    B. Azure AD sign-in logs

    C. Azure AD provisioning logs

    D. Report Center

25. Your organization has several custom SAML-based applications deployed on-premises. As part of an identity and access management project, you have the following requirements:

    - Applications must be configured to authenticate against Azure AD

    - Applications must be easily accessible from Microsoft 365

    • What solution should you choose?

    A. Configure Azure AD Application Proxy

    B. Create an application registration

    C. Configure an access package

    D. Configure Conditional Access

26. You need to configure attribute-based object filtering for Azure AD Connect. Where can you perform this?

    A. The Azure AD portal

    B. The Microsoft 365 admin center

    C. The Synchronization Rules Editor

    D. The Azure AD Connect configuration wizard

27. Your organization has developed a simple web-based application and currently has it deployed to an on-premises server, but the application is currently not accessible over the internet. The application owner has asked you to assist them in making it available to users through the Microsoft 365 **My Apps** page. What should you do?

    A. Configure an application registration

    B. Deploy Azure App Proxy

    C. Instruct the application owner to add SAML support

    D. Create a VPN

28. You have recently configured a new enterprise application and need to restrict access to a subset of users. What is the best way to do this?

    A. A certificate-based Conditional Access rule

    B. Group-based licensing

    C. Assigning the application to a group

    D. Configuring a VPN

29. You need to configure a control to allow users to remain signed in after they close the browser window. What feature should you configure?

    A. Conditional Access persistent browser session control

    B. Conditional Access continuous access evaluation

    C. Conditional Access token protection

    D. Conditional Access workload identities

30. You have been asked whether Azure AD supports SAML-based applications. What is SAML?

    A. Secure Application Multi-Language

    B. Server Application Modular Linkage

    C. Security Assertion Markup Language

    D. Session Authentication Model Layer

31. As part of your organizational security program, you have been asked to review OAuth applications. From the list provided, where can you view this data?

    A. The Microsoft 365 Defender portal

    B. Microsoft Graph

    C. Microsoft Sentinel

    D. Microsoft Log Analytics

32. You are planning a password-less deployment. You need to choose a solution that is integrated with the platform. Each user has their own device. Which solution best meets the requirement?

    A. The Microsoft Authenticator app

    B. FIDO2 security keys

    C. Windows Hello for Business

    D. Certificate-based authentication

33. To install and configure Azure AD Connect, you must have an account that is a member of at least one of the following roles. Which two roles can be used to install and configure Azure AD Connect?

    A. Global Administrator

    B. Identity Administrator

    C. Security Administrator

    D. Hybrid Identity Administrator

34. You need to ensure that on-premises users can use Azure AD **self-service password reset** (**SSPR**) to reset their Azure AD and on-premises passwords. What two licenses, services, configurations, or features are required?

    A. Azure AD Premium P1

    B. Azure AD Connect Premium

    C. Azure AD Connect password writeback

    D. Azure AD on-premises password filter

35. _____ are the data points that Azure AD uses to help inform security decisions.

    A. Applications

    B. Conditions

    C. Signals

    D. Risk indicators

36. Azure AD Connect can be configured to communicate through a proxy by modifying which file?

    A. `web.config`

    B. `machine.config`

    C. `adsync.management.config`

    D. `aadconnect.install.config`

37. Identify the activity that happens during an Azure AD Connect export.

    A. Object updates are sent to the connected directory

    B. Objects are exported to the Azure AD Connect database

    C. Objects are previewed in the metaverse

    D. Object changes are synchronized

38. What can you configure to provide continuity of service for Azure AD Connect?

    A. A disaster recovery server

    B. A failover server

    C. A redundant server

    D. A staging server

39. You are deploying Azure AD Connect. Your organization has 125,000 users, 75,000 workstations, and 13,000 groups. Which database technology should you use for the Azure AD Connect deployment?

    A. SQL Server Express

    B. SQL Server

    C. Windows Internal Database

    D. Access

40. You are advising another administrator on configuring Azure AD role assignments for Azure AD administrative units. Which two places can role assignments be configured for administrative units?

    A. The Azure AD portal

    B. Microsoft 365 Defender

    C. The Microsoft 365 admin center

    D. The Microsoft Purview compliance portal

41. You are instructing another administrator on how to quickly add a group of 50 cloud users to Microsoft 365. Since they are a new administrator, you want to ensure that the process is easy to follow. Which tool would be the most appropriate?

    A. The Azure AD portal

    B. Azure AD Connect

    C. The Microsoft 365 admin center

    D. Microsoft Graph PowerShell

42. When deploying the Azure AD Connect Cloud sync provisioning agent, which two roles can be used for configuration? Each answer represents a complete solution:

    A. Server Administrator

    B. Hybrid Identity Administrator

    C. User Provisioning Administrator

    D. Global Administrator

43. When configuring a scoping filter for Azure AD Connect Cloud sync, what is the maximum number of security groups that can be configured?

    A. 59

    B. 63

    C. 64

    D. 127

44. You are trying to configure group-based filtering for Azure AD Connect. After launching the setup, you are unable to configure group-based filtering. What is the likely cause?

    A. Azure AD Connect doesn't support group-based filtering

    B. You can only configure Azure AD Connect group-based filtering from the Azure portal

    C. Azure AD Connect was deployed through an express installation

    D. Azure AD Connect group-based filtering is configured in the Synchronization Service

45. You are instructing a new administrator on how to create a mail-enabled cloud security group. What two administrative interfaces could they use?

    A. The Microsoft 365 admin center | **Teams & groups** | **Active teams & groups**

    B. The Exchange admin center | **Groups**

    C. The Azure AD portal

    D. Active Directory Users and Computers

46. You currently manage a connected organization configuration. Users in the connected organization need to request access to a custom enterprise application as well as a SharePoint site and a SharePoint Online license. What feature should you configure?

    A. An access review

    B. An access package

    C. An entitlement package

    D. A Conditional Access policy

47. You are troubleshooting an authentication issue. You have configured a Conditional Access policy to prompt for MFA. During your investigation of the sign-in logs, you have determined that the policy is not triggering MFA. What is a possible cause?

    A. Per-user MFA

    B. Conditional Access

    C. Smart lockout

    D. Azure AD Password Protection

48. You need to create new synchronized users for your organization. Which interface should you use to complete this task?

    A. The Azure AD portal

    B. The Microsoft 365 admin center

    C. The Azure AD Connect Synchronization Service

    D. Active Directory Users and Computers

49. Your organization is migrating to Azure AD. Azure AD does not have organizational units to manage the delegation of administration. What feature should you implement instead?

    A.   Azure AD organizational units

    B.   Administrative units

    C.   Role-based access control

    D.   Resource-based access control

50. You have received an alert that an account is stale. What does this mean?

    A.   The account has not changed its password in more than 180 days

    B.   The account has not logged in within the configured time period

    C.   The account was left out on the counter

    D.   The account has not been synchronized from the on-premises environment

51. You are selecting a password-less authentication mechanism for your organization's manufacturing division. Many of the users access resources through shared computers. What sign-in and authentication mechanism best meets this need?

    A.   Windows Hello for Business

    B.   FIDO2 security keys

    C.   The Microsoft Authenticator app

    D.   Active Directory Federation Services

52. You manage Microsoft 365 for your organization. As an employee well-being initiative, the human resources department has asked you to set a default configuration for meetings so that they end 5 minutes earlier. What should you do?

    A.   Run `Set-OrganizationConfig` to set the shortened meeting parameters

    B.   Send out a company-wide email instructing users how to schedule meetings

    C.   Run `Set-CalendarConfiguration` on all mailboxes

    D.   Run `Set-Mailbox` to update all resource mailboxes

53. The CSO for your organization wants to ensure that on-premises passwords are checked against the Azure AD custom banned password list. What should you implement?

    A.   Smart lockout

    B.   Active Directory Federation Services

    C.   Password Protection for Windows Server Active Directory

    D.   Active Directory fine-grained password policies

54. Exchange Online uses SSL/TLS to secure which two traffic types?

    A. DNS

    B. SMTP

    C. HTTPS

    D. UDP

55. The _____ life cycle manages how identities have permissions granted or revoked throughout their lifetime:

    A. Identity

    B. Privileged identity

    C. Access

    D. Security

56. The access package manager role can only add resources inside the catalog:

    A. True

    B. False

57. In an Exchange hybrid configuration, the Autodiscover record typically points to what?

    A. Exchange Online

    B. On-premises Exchange Server with the Edge Transport role

    C. On-premises Exchange Server with Client Access server or Mailbox and Client Access server roles

    D. Exchange Online Protection

58. You are configuring an Exchange hybrid deployment. Your organization currently uses a highly-customized **data loss prevention** (**DLP**) solution that looks for engineering drawings. You need to ensure that after you migrate to Exchange Online, all outbound mail will still be scanned by the DLP engine. What should you do?

    A. Enable Exchange Online DLP integration

    B. Configure centralized mail transport

    C. Enable Microsoft Purview DLP

    D. Use MailTips

59. You are planning to migrate your organization to Microsoft Teams. Your organization is currently using a mixture of Google Workspace and Box for collaboration storage providers. What tool should you plan to use?

    A. SharePoint Migration Manager

    B. The SharePoint Migration Assessment Tool

    C. The SharePoint Identity Mapping Tool

    D. The SharePoint Migration Tool

60. You are working with the marketing department to develop a new SharePoint site that will be used to showcase new products to your internal users. Which SharePoint site template is most appropriate?

    A. An enterprise search

    B. A communication site

    C. A team site

    D. A project site

Answers

1. B: Hybrid federated search.

    Federated search allows you to maintain separate indices for SharePoint Online and SharePoint Server content, but provides an interface for cloud users to be able to query both search indices and return results in the same browser: `https://learn.microsoft.com/en-us/sharepoint/hybrid/hybrid-search-in-sharepoint`.

2. A: 25.

    Exchange Online requires port 25 to be open between Exchange Online Protection and the on-premises Exchange hybrid transport endpoints: `https://learn.microsoft.com/en-us/exchange/hybrid-deployment-prerequisites`.

3. B: An auto attendant.

    An auto attendant provides **IVR** features, allowing users to navigate options: `https://learn.microsoft.com/en-us/microsoftteams/plan-auto-attendant-call-queue`.

4. A: The Azure AD portal.

    Of the options listed, dynamic administrative units can only be configured in the Azure AD portal: `https://learn.microsoft.com/en-us/azure/active-directory/roles/admin-units-members-dynamic`.

5. C: Azure AD Connect with Active Directory Federation Services.

   Of the provided options, Azure AD Connect with Active Directory Federation Services is the only solution that processes authentications using the on-premises environment: `https://learn.microsoft.com/en-us/azure/active-directory/hybrid/plan-hybrid-identity-design-considerations-lifecycle-adoption-strategy` and `https://learn.microsoft.com/en-us/azure/active-directory/hybrid/choose-ad-authn`.

6. A: Microsoft 365 Worldwide endpoints (`https://aka.ms/o365endpoints`).

   The Microsoft 365 Worldwide endpoints page contains the most up-to-date information regarding the required network communications configuration for all apps, including Microsoft 365 Apps: `https://learn.microsoft.com/en-us/deployoffice/assess-microsoft-365-apps#step-3---assess-network-capability`.

7. A: Configure the domain for the non-Exchange system as an Internal Relay domain.

   To successfully route mail to a remote messaging system whose domain is configured in Exchange Online, set the domain mode to Internal Relay: `https://learn.microsoft.com/en-us/exchange/mail-flow-best-practices/manage-accepted-domains/manage-accepted-domains`.

8. D: Time-bound.

   Of the options listed, only time-bound relates to access rights with a start and end date: `https://learn.microsoft.com/en-us/azure/active-directory/privileged-identity-management/pim-configure#what-does-it-do`.

9. C: The Office Telemetry Dashboard.

   The Office Telemetry Dashboard collects data about apps and add-ins. Its primary function is to assist in planning and compatibility testing: `https://learn.microsoft.com/en-us/deployoffice/compat/deploy-telemetry-dashboard`.

10. A. Azure AD Connect with password hash synchronization.

    Of the provided options, only Azure AD Connect with password synchronization meets the business requirement. Azure AD Connect Health is a monitoring service, while Azure AD Connect with Active Directory Federation Services and Azure AD Connect with pass-through authentication both require access to on-premises domain controllers: `https://learn.microsoft.com/en-us/azure/active-directory/hybrid/how-to-connect-password-hash-synchronization`.

11. C: Create and enable a new Cloud sync configuration in the Azure portal.

    After deploying the provisioning service, the next step is to go to the Azure portal to set up and enable a new configuration. Without this step, objects will not get synchronized: `https://learn.microsoft.com/en-us/azure/active-directory/cloud-sync/how-to-configure`.

12. A: Self-install from cloud, C: Deploy from local source using Configuration Manager, and E: Deploy from cloud using Microsoft Intune (Endpoint Manager).

   There are a number of ways to deploy Microsoft 365 Apps, including self-installation from the cloud through the Microsoft 365 portal, using Configuration Manager, or using Microsoft Intune (Endpoint Manager): `https://learn.microsoft.com/en-us/deployoffice/deployment-guide-microsoft-365-apps`.

13. B: Standard configurations.

   The Microsoft 365 Apps admin center has nearly 20 pre-built deployment configuration templates located under the **Standard configurations** tab on the **Device Configuration** page: `https://techcommunity.microsoft.com/t5/deployment-networking/standard-deployment-configurations-for-office-deployment-now/td-p/904165`.

14. B: The Cloud Policy service for Microsoft 365.

   The Cloud Policy service for Microsoft 365 can be used to manage and enforce policy settings for groups of users as well as anonymous users accessing the web versions of Microsoft 365 apps: `https://learn.microsoft.com/en-us/deployoffice/admincenter/overview-cloud-policy`.

15. A: Configure an enterprise application, B: Configure a custom app launcher tile, and F: Assign the enterprise application to the group of business users.

   Configuring an enterprise application will publish the application automatically to the App launcher. You will need to also assign the application to a specific group of users to limit it to the appropriate business users. You can create a custom App launcher tile to publish a URL to the App launcher: `https://learn.microsoft.com/en-us/azure/active-directory/manage-apps/add-application-portal`, `https://learn.microsoft.com/en-us/azure/active-directory/manage-apps/add-application-portal-assign-users`, and `https://learn.microsoft.com/en-us/microsoft-365/admin/manage/customize-the-app-launcher`.

16. A: **Briefing email from Microsoft Viva**.

   You can disable the Microsoft Viva briefing email for the tenant through the Microsoft 365 admin center. You can also specify users that want to opt out from the email individually via PowerShell: `https://learn.microsoft.com/en-us/viva/insights/personal/briefing/be-faqs`.

17. B: **User consent to apps**.

   Through the Microsoft 365 admin center, you can enable or disable the ability for users to consent to OAuth applications. This will prevent users from being able to connect third-party applications to Microsoft 365 without administrator intervention: `https://learn.microsoft.com/en-us/microsoft-365/admin/misc/user-consent`.

18. D: Domain Connect.

    Domain Connect is an integration that allows Microsoft to update DNS records at certain registrars and hosts: `https://learn.microsoft.com/en-us/microsoft-365/admin/setup/add-domain`.

19. A: True.

    Before you can begin assigning users or groups to your custom domain, you need to verify it. Ownership verification can be done through Domain Connect or by manually configuring specific DNS entries that Microsoft 365 can check: `https://learn.microsoft.com/en-us/microsoft-365/admin/setup/add-domain`.

20. D: Azure AD provisioning logs.

    The Azure AD provisioning logs capture data about integrated provisioning activities that happen through third-party applications: `https://learn.microsoft.com/en-us/azure/active-directory/reports-monitoring/concept-provisioning-logs`.

21. A: Microsoft Viva Insights Teamwork habits.

    The shared no-meeting day plan inside Microsoft Viva Insights Teamwork habits can be used to create a time that everyone in the plan can agree on, allowing them to focus on work without interruptions: `https://learn.microsoft.com/en-us/viva/insights/org-team-insights/teamwork-habits`.

22. B: Identifying a workaround or backup solution if the outage lasts longer than anticipated.

    Business continuity planning includes identifying workaround or backup solutions should your environment be inaccessible for long periods of time. Business continuity planning should be undertaken for all aspects of an organization, not just the Microsoft 365 infrastructure: `https://learn.microsoft.com/en-us/office365/servicedescriptions/office-365-platform-service-description/service-health-and-continuity` and `https://learn.microsoft.com/en-us/compliance/assurance/assurance-ebcm-plan-rehearsal-and-user-training`.

23. B: Adoption Score technology experiences.

    This Microsoft 365 Adoption Score is used to deliver data insights regarding people experiences in the areas of collaboration, mobility, teamwork, and meetings. The Adoption Score can also be used to provide insights about technology experiences as they relate to a device's health and network communications: `https://learn.microsoft.com/en-us/microsoft-365/admin/adoption/adoption-score`.

24. B: Azure AD sign-in logs.

    Azure AD sign-in logs provide access to sign-in and authentication data, including what application interface was used to log in, the login location, whether the sign-in was successful, and whether MFA was requested: `https://learn.microsoft.com/en-us/azure/active-directory/reports-monitoring/concept-sign-ins`.

25. B: Create an application registration.

    You can create a custom application registration in Azure AD. This will allow you to authenticate users via SAML to the application and enable an application icon or tile in My Apps, enabling users to easily access the application from the Microsoft 365 interface: `https://learn.microsoft.com/en-us/power-apps/developer/data-platform/walkthrough-register-app-azure-active-directory`.

26. C: The Synchronization Rules Editor.

    To perform attribute-based object filtering, you should create a synchronization rule with a scoping filter and a transformation rule that sets `cloudFiltered` to `True`: `https://learn.microsoft.com/en-us/azure/active-directory/hybrid/how-to-connect-sync-configure-filtering`.

27. B: Deploy Azure App Proxy.

    Azure App Proxy can be used to publish web-based applications to Microsoft 365: `https://learn.microsoft.com/en-us/azure/active-directory/app-proxy/application-proxy`.

28. C: Assign the application to a group.

    The best way to restrict access to the application is by assigning the enterprise application to a group: `https://learn.microsoft.com/en-us/azure/active-directory/manage-apps/assign-user-or-group-access-portal`.

29. A: Conditional Access persistent browser session control.

    A persistent browser session allows users to remain signed in to Microsoft 365 services after closing and reopening the browser window: `https://learn.microsoft.com/en-us/azure/active-directory/conditional-access/concept-conditional-access-session#persistent-browser-session`.

30. C: Security Assertion Markup Language.

    Azure AD supports **Security Assertion Markup Language** (**SAML**), one of the open standards used to exchange identity authentication and authorization information: `https://learn.microsoft.com/en-us/azure/active-directory/fundamentals/auth-saml`.

31. A: The Microsoft 365 Defender portal.

    You can use Microsoft 365 Defender to investigate OAuth applications, including risky OAuth applications: `https://learn.microsoft.com/en-us/defender-cloud-apps/investigate-risky-oauth`.

32. C: Windows Hello for Business.

    Windows Hello for Business is the only platform-integrated solution from the choices presented: `https://learn.microsoft.com/en-us/azure/active-directory/authentication/howto-authentication-passwordless-deployment`.

33. A: Global Administrator, and D: Hybrid Identity Administrator.

    In order to install and configure Azure AD Connect, the identity used must be either a Global Administrator or a Hybrid Identity Administrator: `https://learn.microsoft.com/en-us/azure/active-directory/hybrid/reference-connect-accounts-permissions#azure-ad-connect-installation` and `https://learn.microsoft.com/en-us/azure/active-directory/hybrid/how-to-connect-install-custom`.

34. A: Azure AD Premium P1, and C: Azure AD Connect password writeback.

    Azure AD SSPR requires the Azure AD Premium P1 license (or Azure AD Premium P2) to allow on-premises writeback. It also requires you to enable password writeback in Azure AD Connect setup: `https://learn.microsoft.com/en-us/azure/active-directory/authentication/tutorial-enable-sspr`.

35. C: Signals.

    Signals are the data points that Azure AD services and features, such as Conditional Access, use to help inform decisions: `https://learn.microsoft.com/en-us/azure/active-directory/conditional-access/overview`.

36. B: `machine.config`.

    You can configure Azure AD Connect to work through a proxy by modifying the computer's .NET Framework `machine.config` file to specify the proxy server settings: `https://learn.microsoft.com/en-us/azure/active-directory/hybrid/tshoot-connect-connectivity`.

37. A. Object updates are sent to the connected directory.

    When an export process is run on an Azure AD connector, the staged changes are written to the connected directory or connected system: `https://learn.microsoft.com/en-us/azure/active-directory/hybrid/how-to-connect-sync-configure-filtering`.

38. D: A staging server.

    The supported configuration to deploy redundancy with Azure AD Connect is a staging server. A staging server should be configured with the same features, options, settings, and customizations as the primary server: `https://learn.microsoft.com/en-us/azure/active-directory/hybrid/how-to-connect-sync-staging-server`.

39. B: SQL Server.

    Since the database is over 100,000 objects, you should use a full edition of SQL Server. SQL Server Express has a 10 GB database limit: `https://learn.microsoft.com/en-us/azure/active-directory/hybrid/how-to-connect-install-prerequisites` and `https://learn.microsoft.com/en-us/azure/active-directory/hybrid/tshoot-connect-recover-from-localdb-10gb-limit`.

40. A: The Azure AD portal, and C: The Microsoft 365 admin center.

You can configure administrative units and role group assignments in both the Azure AD portal and the Microsoft 365 admin center. You cannot configure role assignments in the other two portals: `https://learn.microsoft.com/en-us/azure/active-directory/roles/groups-assign-role` and `https://learn.microsoft.com/en-us/microsoft-365/admin/add-users/admin-roles-page?view=o365-worldwide`.

41. C: The Microsoft 365 admin center.

Since they are a new administrator, the easiest interface to instruct them with is the Microsoft 365 admin center. It provides a menu-driven bulk import process: `https://learn.microsoft.com/en-us/microsoft-365/enterprise/add-several-users-at-the-same-time`.

42. B: Hybrid Identity Administrator, and D: Global Administrator.

Only the Hybrid Identity Administrator and Global Administrator roles may be used to configure Azure AD Connect Cloud sync. The User Provisioning Administrator role is not a real role and the Server Administrator role is present in on-premises Active Directory: `https://learn.microsoft.com/en-us/azure/active-directory/cloud-sync/how-to-prerequisites`.

43. A. 59.

Azure AD Connect Cloud sync supports a maximum of 59 security groups that can be used as scoping filters: `https://learn.microsoft.com/en-us/azure/active-directory/cloud-sync/how-to-prerequisites?tabs=public-cloud`.

44. C: Azure AD Connect was deployed through an express installation.

The group-based filtering option for Azure AD Connect is only available during a custom installation of Azure AD Connect. It cannot be enabled after an express installation: `https://learn.microsoft.com/en-us/azure/active-directory/hybrid/how-to-connect-install-custom`.

45. A: The Microsoft 365 admin center | **Teams & groups** | **Active teams & groups**, and B: The Exchange admin center | **Groups**.

From the listed options, only the Microsoft 365 admin center and Exchange admin center will meet the business requirement. You can create security groups in the Azure AD portal, but they are not mail-enabled: `https://learn.microsoft.com/en-us/exchange/recipients-in-exchange-online/manage-mail-enabled-security-groups`.

46. B: An access package.

You can use an access package to grant access to SharePoint sites, group and team membership, and applications. Through group membership and group-based licensing, you can also grant licenses through access packages: `https://learn.microsoft.com/en-us/azure/active-directory/governance/entitlement-management-group-licenses`.

47. A: Per-user MFA, and C: Security defaults.

    Per-user MFA can conflict with a Conditional Access policy to prompt MFA: `https://learn.microsoft.com/en-us/azure/active-directory/reports-monitoring/recommendation-turn-off-per-user-mfa`.

48. D: Active Directory Users and Computers.

    On-premises users are created through the Active Directory Users and Computers snap-in (or the newer Active Directory Administrative Center). The Azure AD Connect synchronization service is responsible for managing the actual directory synchronization process, while the Azure AD portal and Microsoft 365 admin center are used to create cloud users: `https://learn.microsoft.com/en-us/windows-server/identity/ad-ds/manage/ad-ds-simplified-administration`.

49. B: Administrative units.

    Administrative units are collections of users, devices, and groups that can be grouped together to allow delegated control and management: `https://learn.microsoft.com/en-us/azure/active-directory/roles/administrative-units`.

50. B: The account has not logged in within the configured time period.

    The stale account alert is due to a privileged role that has not logged in during the configured time period (between 1 and 365 days). Accounts that no longer need access should be removed from the list: `https://learn.microsoft.com/en-us/azure/active-directory/privileged-identity-management/pim-how-to-configure-security-alerts`.

51. B: FIDO2 security keys.

    FIDO2 security keys are a suitable solution for multiuser scenarios, including device sign-in and authentication to Microsoft 365 services: `https://learn.microsoft.com/en-us/azure/active-directory/authentication/concept-authentication-passwordless`.

52. A: Run `Set-OrganizationConfig` to set the shortened meeting parameters.

    You can use the following command to update the meeting settings: `Set-OrganizationConfig -DefaultMinutesToReduceShortEventsBy 5 -ShortenEventScopeDefault EndEarly`: `https://learn.microsoft.com/en-us/powershell/module/exchange/set-organizationconfig`.

53. C: Password Protection for Windows Server Active Directory.

    Password Protection for Windows Server Active Directory allows on-premises domain controllers to check password change requests against the Azure AD password custom banned password list: `https://learn.microsoft.com/en-us/azure/active-directory/authentication/howto-password-ban-bad-on-premises-deploy`.

54. B: SMTP, and C: HTTPS.

    Exchange requires SSL/TLS certificates for a variety of interactions, including free/busy lookups (HTTPS), mailbox migrations (HTTPS), and mail transport (SMTP): `https://learn.microsoft.com/en-us/exchange/hybrid-deployment-prerequisites`.

55. C: Access.

    The access life cycle is used to manage the granting and removing of permissions and access controls throughout the life cycle of an identity: `https://learn.microsoft.com/en-us/azure/active-directory/governance/identity-governance-overview#access-lifecycle`.

56. A: True.

    The access package manager role for a catalog can be delegated to users, and then those package managers can create packages containing resources in the catalog: `https://learn.microsoft.com/en-us/azure/active-directory/governance/entitlement-management-delegate-managers`.

57. C: On-premises Exchange Server with Client Access Server or Mailbox and Client Access Server roles.

    In a hybrid configuration, Autodiscover is usually configured to point to the on-premises Exchange environment. Valid targets are servers with the Client Access Server role (Exchange 2010/2013) or the combined Mailbox/Client Access Server role (Exchange 2016/2019). Autodiscover allows referrals from on-premises environments to the cloud, but not the other way around: `https://aka.ms/autodiscover`.

58. B: Configure centralized mail transport.

    Centralized mail transport is an Exchange hybrid configuration option that routes mail through the Exchange Online on-premises environment: `https://learn.microsoft.com/en-us/exchange/transport-options`.

59. A: SharePoint Migration Manager.

    Of the options listed, only SharePoint Migration Manager is capable of migrating from Box and Google Workspace: `https://learn.microsoft.com/en-us/sharepointmigration/mm-box-overview` and `https://learn.microsoft.com/en-us/sharepointmigration/mm-google-overview`.

60. B: A communication site.

    SharePoint communication site templates are the best choice to showcase content. They're designed to be consumption sites where users can read and digest information: `https://support.microsoft.com/en-us/office/create-a-communication-site-in-sharepoint-7fb44b20-a72f-4d2c-9173-fc8f59ba50eb`.

Index

www.packtpub.com

Subscribe to our online digital library for full access to over 7,000 books and videos, as well as industry leading tools to help you plan your personal development and advance your career. For more information, please visit our website.

Why subscribe?

- Spend less time learning and more time coding with practical eBooks and Videos from over 4,000 industry professionals

- Improve your learning with Skill Plans built especially for you

- Get a free eBook or video every month

- Fully searchable for easy access to vital information

- Copy and paste, print, and bookmark content

Did you know that Packt offers eBook versions of every book published, with PDF and ePub files available? You can upgrade to the eBook version at packtpub.com and as a print book customer, you are entitled to a discount on the eBook copy. Get in touch with us at customercare@packtpub.com for more details.

At www.packtpub.com, you can also read a collection of free technical articles, sign up for a range of free newsletters, and receive exclusive discounts and offers on Packt books and eBooks.

Other Books You May Enjoy

If you enjoyed this book, you may be interested in these other books by Packt:

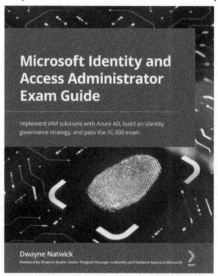

Microsoft Identity and Access Administrator Exam Guide

Dwayne Natwick

ISBN: 978-1-80181-804-9

- Understand core exam objectives to pass the SC-300 exam
- Implement an identity management solution with MS Azure AD
- Manage identity with multi-factor authentication (MFA), conditional access, and identity protection
- Design, implement, and monitor the integration of enterprise apps for Single Sign-On (SSO)
- Add apps to your identity and access solution with app registration
- Design and implement identity governance for your identity solution

Microsoft 365 Certified Fundamentals MS-900 Exam Guide

Aaron Guilmette, Yura Lee

ISBN: 978-1-83763-679-2

- Gain insight into the exam objectives and knowledge required before taking the MS-900 exam
- Discover and implement best practices for licensing options available in Microsoft 365
- Understand the different Microsoft 365 Defender Services
- Get prepared for the most common types of threats against an environment
- Identify and unblock most common cloud adoption showstoppers
- Articulate key productivity, collaboration, security, and compliance selling points of M365
- Explore licensing and payment models available for M365

Packt is searching for authors like you

If you're interested in becoming an author for Packt, please visit `authors.packtpub.com` and apply today. We have worked with thousands of developers and tech professionals, just like you, to help them share their insight with the global tech community. You can make a general application, apply for a specific hot topic that we are recruiting an author for, or submit your own idea.

Share Your Thoughts

Now you've finished *Microsoft 365 Identity and Services Exam Guide MS-100*, we'd love to hear your thoughts! Scan the QR code below to go straight to the Amazon review page for this book and share your feedback or leave a review on the site that you purchased it from.

`https://packt.link/r/1838987940`

Your review is important to us and the tech community and will help us make sure we're delivering excellent quality content.

Download a free PDF copy of this book

Thanks for purchasing this book!

Do you like to read on the go but are unable to carry your print books everywhere? Is your eBook purchase not compatible with the device of your choice?

Don't worry, now with every Packt book you get a DRM-free PDF version of that book at no cost.

Read anywhere, any place, on any device. Search, copy, and paste code from your favorite technical books directly into your application.

The perks don't stop there, you can get exclusive access to discounts, newsletters, and great free content in your inbox daily

Follow these simple steps to get the benefits:

1. Scan the QR code or visit the link below

https://packt.link/free-ebook/9781838987947

2. Submit your proof of purchase
3. That's it! We'll send your free PDF and other benefits to your email directly

www.ingramcontent.com/pod-product-compliance
Lightning Source LLC
Chambersburg PA
CBHW081458050326
40690CB00015B/2838